Saml. Willoughby Duffield
Phila 1853

THE

FIRST BOOK OF ETYMOLOGY,

DESIGNED

TO PROMOTE PRECISION IN THE USE,

AND

FACILITATE THE ACQUISITION OF A KNOWLEDGE

OF THE

ENGLISH LANGUAGE.

For Beginners.

BY JAMES LYND,

PROFESSOR OF BELLES LETTRES IN DELAWARE COLLEGE.

REVISED EDITION.

PHILADELPHIA:
E. C. & J. BIDDLE, 6 SOUTH FIFTH ST.
1853.

TO TEACHERS.

"The First Book of Etymology," by James Lynd, A. M., was published by the subscribers in the year 1847, and is now extensively in use in the Public and Private Schools of our country. Among the former class the publishers may designate those of Philadelphia, Baltimore, New York, Brooklyn, Williamsburgh, &c.

Although the most gratifying evidences of the benefits resulting from the use of this book have been continually received by the publishers, they have yet sought, from competent instructors well acquainted with the subject, suggestions for its improvement. The improvements thus suggested, and many others of importance, are believed to be incorporated in "The First Book of Etymology," by Dr. Joseph Thomas, just issued from the press. The principal distinguishing features of this work, as compared with that of Mr. Lynd, may be briefly stated thus:—

1. The rules for the formation of English derivative words, by means of suffixes, are simplified, and the exercises under them arranged in an improved form.

2. The meanings of the prefixes and suffixes of Latin and other origin are more accurately given and fully explained.

3. The exercises designed to familiarize the pupil with the meanings of the prefixes and suffixes of Latin and other origin are much better adapted for the attainment of the proposed object than those in the work of Mr. Lynd, and will commend themselves to the favor of the thorough teacher.

4. The main part of the work, which contains the principal Latin, Greek, and other roots of our language, arranged in alphabetical order, with the more important English words derived from each placed under it and defined—has been prepared with great care; and it is believed that in every case where the *etymological* or *literal* differs from the *proper* or *usually accepted* meaning of the English derivative, such difference is explained. The great value of this feature will be fully appreciated by every competent instructor. The Latin and Greek roots in this part of the work are arranged *together*, in alphabetical order, as being more easy of reference for the pupil than when placed in two separate parts, as well as for other reasons.

5. By means of *distinctive types*, the portion of the definition corresponding with the prefix and root, or root and suffix respectively, of each illustrative word occurring in the chapter devoted to an explanation of the meanings of prefixes and suffixes, is clearly designated; and, in the same manner, in the main part of the work, containing the English derivatives placed under their appropriate roots, the prefix, root, and suffix occurring in the same word, and the portion of the definition corresponding with each part, is clearly distinguished.

6. The few pages "on the derivation of English words from the Latin through the French" have been transferred to the revised edition of "Lynd's Class Book of Etymology," as being more appropriate for the use of advanced classes than for beginners. They do not, therefore, appear in the work of Dr. Thomas.

7. The *Key* is substantially the same as that in the work of Mr. Lynd.

8. The work of Mr. Lynd is comprised in 215 pages, large duodecimo; that by Dr. Thomas in 261 pages of the same size; the price of the fomer work to teachers is $3.20 per dozen; that of the latter, $4 per dozen.

☞ The publishers will forward a copy of "Thomas's First Book of Etymology," by mail, to such teachers or directors of schools as shall request it for examination, and send with said request postage stamps to prepay the postage on said book; which is, on a copy sent not over 500 miles from Philadelphia, eleven cents; over 500 miles and not over 1,500 miles, twenty-two cents; over 1,500 and not over 2,500 miles, thirty-three cents.

☞ E. C. & J. B. still publish "Lynd's First Book of Etymology," so that teachers using it in their classes may continue its use, if they desire, or may introduce the work by Dr. Thomas, if preferred, as they find it convenient so to do.

Stereotyped by L. Johnson & Co., Philadelphia.
Printed by T. K. & P. G. Collins.

PREFACE.

The present volume is the first of a series of books designed as aids to the student of Etymology. Of this series the succeeding volumes are the Class-Book of Etymology,—which is adapted to the wants of the advanced classes in Grammar Schools,—and Oswald's Etymological Dictionary,—designed as a text-book for High Schools and Academies, or as a work of reference for schools in general. The First Book of Etymology, as its name imports, is intended for the use of those just entering upon the study.

In the Preliminary matter, the compiler has endeavored to impart to the pupil a full conception of the distinction between primitive and derivative, simple and compound words; and, to explain the nature of the prefixes and suffixes, as well as the change they undergo in combining with the root. The pupil should be required to study this portion of the work thoroughly before he is permitted to proceed.

The meaning of the prefixes and suffixes,—an acquaintance with which is indispensable for the successful prosecution of the study of Etymology,—is fully illustrated in Part I. The Exercises contained in this part of the work are believed to be well calculated to fix permanently in the pupil's memory the subject matter contained in them.

Part II. comprises the principal Latin and French roots, arranged in alphabetical order, with the more simple words derived from them, defined and placed under their respective roots.

Part III. is devoted to the Greek roots and their derivatives, defined and arranged as those in Part II.

It has been thought proper thus to separate the Greek from the other roots, because the words derived from them are by no means familiar to the young pupil, and in their combinations with prefixes and suffixes, as well as in the formation of the compounds, present much greater difficulty than the words included in Part II. Having mastered Part II., the pupil, it is presumed, will have become so well acquainted with the study as to be able to proceed through Part III., with comparative ease.

The table showing the changes which Latin words underwent in their transition to French, it is believed, will not be unacceptable to those who may make use of the book. This portion of the work is not designed to be committed to memory by the pupil; but he may refer to it with profit, as he progresses in the study of Part II.

The Key, which is a feature peculiar to this series of Etymological text-books, it is confidently believed, will be found a valuable assistant to those employed in teaching as well as those engaged in studying Etymology.

In the hope that this little volume may prove serviceable to those for whose use it is designed, the compiler submits it to the examination of teachers.

Philadelphia, March, 1847.

In the revision of this work for a second edition, it has been deemed advisable to refer to the text and copious notes of Oswald's Etymological Dictionary, to exhibit the primitive or etymological meaning of the English words defined in Parts II. and III., when the usual acceptation of these words differs from their literal meaning; and to place at the command of the pupil definitions of scientific and technical terms, more full and precise than the limits of this book would allow. These references are made by means of an ° placed after the word whose signification is explained.

Every teacher using the First Book of Etymology or the Class-Book of Etymology as a text-book for his pupils, it is believed will find it advantageous to have in his school, for reference, at least one copy of Oswald's Etymological Dictionary.

THE

FIRST BOOK OF ETYMOLOGY.

PRELIMINARY DEFINITIONS.

ETYMOLOGY is that science which explains the *true origin* and derivation of words, with the view to ascertain their *radical* or *primary* signification.

Through it we learn that *hopeful* is derived from *hope* by affixing *ful*, which means *full of;* that *fearlessly* is derived directly from *fearless*, by affixing the adverbial termination *ly*, and remotely from *fear*, since *fearless* is itself formed by affixing to *fear* the termination *less*, which means *without;* and that *unconsciousness* is formed from *conscious* by prefixing *un*, meaning *not*, and affixing *ness*, which signifies *state of being*.

Etymology of the English Language treats of the *true origin* and *meaning* of English words.

English words are either *Primitive* or *Derivative.*

A *Primitive* word is one that is not derived from any other word; as *sweet, rough, run, take.*

A *Derivative* word is formed from a *Primitive* word by adding or prefixing a syllable; as sweet*en*, rough*ly*, *fore*run, *re*take.

The *Radical* or *Essential* part of a word is called a *Root;* as, *care*, in *care*ful; *see*, in over*see;* *dorm*, in *dorm*ant; *vene*, in con*vene*.

A Root is modified or altered in sense by putting a syllable *before* it or *after* it. Thus, the root *do* becomes *un*do; *hold*, *up*hold; *vide* (L. to see), *pro*vide; *clud-* (L. to shut), *ex*clude; by placing a syllable before the root. And *child* becomes child*less;* *turn*, turn*ing;* *anim-* (L. life), anim*ate;* *reg-* (L. to rule), reg*ent;* by placing a syllable after the root.

When the syllable is placed *before* the root it is called a *Prefix*

When the syllable is placed *after* the root it is called a *Suffix.*

The following exercises are intended for further illustration of the foregoing definitions.

I.

The words in the first column are *primitive* words or *roots;* those in the second are *prefixes;* and those in the third *derivatives,* which result from a combination of the two former.

Sight	fore	foresight.
Bitter	im	imbitter.
Deed	mis	misdeed.
Wear	out	outwear.
Come	over	overcome.
Bar	un	unbar.
Able	un	unable.
Go	under	undergo.
Fix	pre	prefix.
Draw	with	withdraw.
Join	ad	adjoin.
Date	ante	antedate.
Place	dis	displace.
Line	inter	interline.
Build	re	rebuild.
Fine	super	superfine.

II.

In the following exercise the middle column contains *suffixes.*

Civil	ize	civilize.
Child	hood	childhood.
Silk	en	silken.
King	dom	kingdom.
Base	ness	baseness.
Knave	ry	knavery.
Clerk	ship	clerkship.
Abet	or	abettor.
Duck	ling	duckling.
Bond	age	bondage.
Art	ist	artist.
Team	ster	teamster.
Chariot	eer	charioteer.
Find	er	finder.
Drunk	ard	drunkard.
Faith	ful	faithful.
Boy	ish	boyish.
Joy	less	joyless.
War	like	warlike.

III.

In the following list, primitive words, and the two classes of derivative words are mingled. It is expected that the pupil will so study it that, when called upon, he will be able to distinguish the primitive from the derivative words, and also show how the latter are formed.

Full, feel, overhear, runner, childish, fearless, regain, night, gloomy, perilous, cheerful, withstand, unfit, reform, understand, foresee, interview, overlook, blow, soon, heavy, songster, roamer, stealing, disjoin, peerage, prejudge, unhorse, sick, brightness, godlike, home, oar, golden, remove, lordly, troublesome, idolize, mistake, forehead, eye, sand, hearty, underbid, outmarch, overboard, hard, coldness.

RULES

FOR THE FORMATION OF DERIVATIVE WORDS BY MEANS OF SUFFIXES.

In adding suffixes to radical words, as a general rule, no change takes place in the form of the latter. There are instances, however, in which the final letters of the primitive word are omitted or changed, or other letters introduced; and the following rules are given to show the pupil under what circumstances such changes take place.

Rule I.

The final *e* of a radical word is usually rejected, when the suffix commences with a vowel; as, mov*e*-ing, moving; sal*e*-able, salable; pleas*e*-ure, pleasure.

Rule II.

The final consonant of a monosyllable, if preceded by a single vowel, is doubled before a suffix beginning with a vowel; as, ba*g*-age, baggage; spo*t*-ed, spotted.

Rule III.

The final consonant of a word of more than one syllable, if accented on the last syllable and preceded by a single vowel, is doubled before a suffix beginning with a vowel; as, deba*r*-ed, debarred; occu*r*-ence, occurrence.

Rule IV.

The final *y* of a radical word, when preceded by a consonant, is generally changed into *i*, before a suffix, whether beginning with a vowel or a consonant; as, happ*y*-ness, happiness; stor*y*-ed, storied.

Rule V.

The final *y* of a radical word, when preceded by *t*, is generally omitted before a suffix beginning with *a* or *o*; as, purit*y*-an, puritan; felicit*y*-ous, felicitous.

Rule VI.

Words ending in *f* or *fe* often change *f* into *v*, when they receive a suffix beginning with a vowel; as, mischie*f*-ous, mischievous; wi*fe*-es, wives.

EXERCISES

UPON THE FOREGOING RULES.

In the following exercises the roots are placed in the first column; the suffixes in the second; and the third column must be filled up by the pupil with the derivative words formed by combining the words in the first and second columns.

Exercise I.

Rome	an	——	Refuse	al	——
Centre	al	——	Execute	ive	——
Juice	y	——	Lie	ar	——
Globe	ule	——	Serve	ant	——
Sphere	oid	——	Reside	ent	——
Amuse	ing	——	Cure	able	——

Exercise II.

Hope	ing	——	Seize	ure	——
Preside	ent	——	Shine	ing	——
Bake	er	——	Shade	ed	——
Create	or	——	Nerve	ous	——
Pole	ar	——	Irritate	ion	——
Compose	ure	——	Lyre	ist	——

Exercise III.

Run	er	——	Beg	ar	——
Glad	en	——	Rot	en	——
Hop	ing	——	Rag	ed	——
Lug	age	——	Fit	ed	——
Dot	ed	——	Blot	er	——
Mud	y	——	Stop	age	——

Exercise IV.

Commit	ee	———	Crystal	ine	———
Confer	er	———	Intermit	ing	———
Admit	ance	———	Abhor	ence	———
Fulfil	ing	———	Control	er	———
Recur	ence	———	Metal	ic	———
Abet	or	———	Concur	ent	———

Exercise V.

Bounty	ful	———	Embody	ed	———
Dizzy	ness	———	Weary	some	———
Dirty	er	———	Busy	ness	———
Easy	est	———	Pity	less	———
Body	less	———	Glory	ous	———
Likely	hood	———	Gloomy	ly	———

Exercise VI.

Leaf	es	———	Charity	able	———
Loaf	es	———	Calamity	ous	———
Grief	ous	———	Annuity	ant	———
Knife	es	———	Dignity	ary	———
Necessity	ous	———	Iniquity	ous	———

Exercise VII.

This involves all the six rules, and is intended as a final test of the accuracy of the pupil's knowledge.

Ton	age	———	Sum	ary	———
Weighty	ness	———	Fortune	ate	———
Assure	ance	———	Sheaf	es	———
Recur	ed	———	Speculate	ion	———
Pollute	ion	———	Duty	ful	———
Excel	ence	———	Abuse	ive	———
Harmony	ous	———	Occur	ence	———
Wool	en	———	Envy	ous	———
Observe	ant	———	Aspire	ate	———
Wag	ing	———	Happy	er	———
Discipline	ary	———	Slave	ish	———
Verity	able	———	Mystery	ous	———
Early	est	———	Immerse	ion	———
Life	es	———	Felicity	ate	———
Adverse	ary	———	Coral	ine	———
Fop	ish	———	Staff	es	———
Compose	ure	———	Comply	ant	———
Elegy	ac	———	Globe	ule	———

COMPOUND WORDS.

Besides those words consisting of a root, and prefix or suffix, there are a great many in every language, which are formed by combining two or more roots or words. Such words are called *Compound Words.*

Thus, by putting *pen* and *man* together, we have a new word, *penman;* and by joining *whale* and *bone,* we have *whalebone.* In the same way *horseman* is formed from *horse* and *man; goldsmith,* from *gold* and *smith; beehive,* from *bee* and *hive,* &c.

Most of our compound words have been derived from the Latin and Greek languages, and learned men are continually adding to the English tongue words of this class. Thus, *aqua,* water, and *ductum,* to lead, upon being united and slightly changed in form, produce *aqueduct,* a pipe or other construction for *leading* or conveying *water; philos,* a lover, and *anthropos,* a man, produce *philanthropist,* a *lover* of *man* or of *mankind,* &c.

In this process of compounding words, the original form of the root is very seldom preserved. This can be readily seen in the above derivations: *ductum* loses its final syllable *um* and becomes *duct; philos,* suffers a similar loss, and becomes *phil;* and *anthropos* becomes *anthrop,* the *ist* in philanthrop*ist* being merely a suffix. Analogous changes of the form of the root may be observed in *carnivorous,* from *carnis,* (Gen.) flesh, and *voro* to eat; *centipede, centum,* a hundred, and *pedis,* (Gen.) the foot; *chronometer, chronos,* time, and *metrum,* a measure.

Very few English words, even of those that are not compound, retain the forms of their Latin or Greek roots. Thus, the root of *apt,* is *aptus;* of *art, artis* (Gen.); of *sphere, sphæra;* of *scruple, scrupulus,* &c.

For removing the difficulty which this modification of the root occasions to the pupil, a very simple arrangement has been made use of in the present work, as well as in the Class-Book of Etymology and Oswald's Etymological Dictionary. A hyphen (-) is placed between that part of the root which is retained in the English word and that which is rejected. Thus, *aptus* is written *apt-us,* and from it are derived *apt,* un*apt,* ad*apt; angello* is written *angel-lo,* and its derivatives are *angel,* arch*angel,* ev*angel*ical; *lectum* is written *lect-um,* and col*lect,* dia*lect,* e*lect, lect*ure, neg*lect,* are words derived from it.

PREFIXES, SUFFIXES,

AND

LATIN, GREEK, AND OTHER ROOTS

OF THE

ENGLISH LANGUAGE.

PART I.
PREFIXES AND SUFFIXES.

I. PREFIXES.

In illustrating the prefixes and suffixes, the literal signification of the words made use of has been followed very closely. Generally this will lead to their exact meaning, but as there are some words which form an exception to this remark, it is recommended that the pupil be required to give a second definition or an application of each word, so that the teacher may be enabled to correct any misconception on the part of the pupil.

1. OF ENGLISH OR SAXON ORIGIN.

***A*,**

Signifies *on*, *in*, *to*, or *at*.

*A*BOARD'—*on* board.
*A*FIRE'—*on* fire.
*A*FOOT'—*on* foot.
*A*GROUND'—*on* ground.
*A*BED'—*in* bed.
*A*SLEEP'—*in* sleep.
*A*FIELD'—*to* the field.
*A*HEAD'—*to* the head.
*A*STERN'—*to* the stern.
*A*FAR'—*at* a distance.
*A*SIDE'—*at* the side.

Be,

Signifies *to make.*

*Be*CALM'—*to make* calm.
**Be*DAUB'—to daub.
**Be*DECK'—to deck.
*Be*DIM'—*to make* dim.
*Be*FOUL'—*to make* foul.
*Be*NUMB'—*to make* numb.
**Be*SPRINK'LE—to sprinkle.

En,

Signifies, *in, into,* or *on; to make.*

*En*CHAIN'—to put *in* chains.
*En*CIR'CLE—to put *in* a circle.
*En*DAN'GER—to put *in* danger.
*En*ACT'—to make *into* an act.
*En*CAMP'—to form *into* a camp.
*En*SHRINE'—to put *on* a shrine.
*En*THRONE'—to put *on* a throne.
*En*A'BLE—*to make* able.
*En*DEAR'—*to make* dear.
*En*FEE'BLE—*to make* feeble.

Em,

Signifies *to make, to give.*

*Em*BEL'LISH—(*beau*),† *to make* beautiful.
*Em*POV'ERISH—(*pauper*), *to make* poor.
*Em*POW'ER—*to give* power to.
*Em*BOD'Y—*to give* a body to.

Fore,

Signifies *before.*

*Fore'*NOON—the part of day *before* noon.
*Fore*RUN'NER—one who runs *before.*
*Fore*SEE'—to see *before*hand.
*Fore'*SIGHT—a seeing *before*hand.
*Fore*TELL'—to tell *before*hand.

Im,

Signifies *to make.*

*Im*BIT'TER—*to make* bitter.

---

* In the words marked *, the prefix has no force, and as the pupil progresses he will find frequent examples of both prefixes and affixes, which do not modify the signification of the words to which they are attached.

† The words in parentheses are the roots from which the English words are derived. Those marked Gr. will be found in the Part III., the others in Part II.

*Im*BROWN'—*to make* brown.
*Im*POV'ERISH—*to make* poor.

Mis,

Signifies *ill*, *error*, or *defect*.

*Mis*APPLY'—to apply in a *wrong* manner.
*Mis*BELIEF'—*wrong* belief.
*Mis*CAL'CULATE—to make a *wrong* calculation.
*Mis*CON'DUCT—*ill* or *bad* conduct.
*Mis*GUIDE'— to guide *wrong*.
*Mis*PLACE'—to place *wrong*.

Out,

Signifies *beyond*, *more than*.

*Out*BID —to bid *beyond* or *more than* another.
*Out*LIVE'—to live *beyond*.
*Out*NUM'BER—to number *beyond*.
*Out*RUN'—to run *beyond*.

Over,

Signifies *above* or *over*, *too high* or *great*.

*Over*BUR'DEN—to impose *too great* a burden.
*Over*FLOW'—to flow *over*.
*Over*LOAD'—to put on *too great* a load.
*Over*RUN'—to run *over* or *above*.
*Over*SLEEP'—to sleep *too long*, or *over* the usual time.
*Over*SPREAD'—to spread *over* or *above*.
*Over*VAL'UE—to value at *too high* a rate.

Un, before a *verb*,

Signifies *to take off*, *deprive of*.

*Un*BAR'—*to take off* the bar.
*Un*CHAIN'—*to take off* the chain.
*Un*CLOTHE'—*to deprive of* clothes.
*Un*CROWN'—*to deprive of* a crown.
*Un*HINGE'—*to take off* of the hinge.
*Un*HORSE'—*to take off* of a horse.
*Un*PIN'—*to take out* the pin.
*Un*SEAL'—*to take off* the seal.
*Un*STITCH'—*to take out* the stitches.
*Un*YOKE'—*to take off* the yoke.

Un, before an adjectivo,

Signifies *not*

*Un*A'BLE—*not* able.
*Un*AC'TIVE—*not* active.
*Un*ARMED'—*not* armed.

*Un*BORN'—*not* born.
*Un*BRO'KEN—*not* broken.
*Un*CER'TAIN—*not* certain.
*Un*FER'TILE—*not* fertile.
*Un*JUST'—*not* just.
*Un*NAT'URAL—*not* natural.
*Un*POP'ULAR—*not* popular.

Under,

Signifies *beneath* or *under, less than.*

*Under*BID'—to bid *under* or *less than* another.
*Under*GO'—to go *under*, to experience.
*Under*OF'FICER—an officer *under* or *inferior to* another.
*Under*SHER'IFF—one who is *under* or *beneath* the sheriff.
*Under*VAL'UE—to rate *under* its real value.

With,

Signifies *from* or *against.*

*With*DRAW'—to draw *from.*
*With*STAND'—to stand *against.*
*With*HOLD'—to hold *from.*

---

2. OF LATIN ORIGIN.

A,

Signifies *from* or *away.*

*A*VERT'—(*verto*), to turn *from.*
*A*VOCA'TION—(*voco*), a calling *away*—business.
*A*VUL'SION—(*vello*), a tearing *away.*

Ab,

Signifies *from* or *away.*

Ab'DICATE—(*dico*), to speak *from.*
*Ab*ERRA'TION—(*erro*), a wandering *away.*
Ab'JECT—(*jacio*), cast *away.*
*Ab*LU'TION—(*luo*), a washing *away.*
*Ab*RADE'—(*rado*), to rub *away.*
*Ab*RUPT'—(*ruptum*), broken *from* or *off.*
*Ab*SOLVE'—(*solvo*), to loose *from.*
*Ab*SORB'—(*sorbeo*), to suck *from* or *up.*

Abs,

Signifies *from* or *away.*

Ab'SENT—(*ens*), a being *away.*

*Ab*STAIN'—(*teneo*), to hold *from*.
*Ab*STRACT'—(*traho*), to draw *from*.

Ad,

Signifies *to*.

*Ad*APT'—(*aptus*), to fit *to*.
*Ad*DUCE'—(*duco*), to lead *to*.
*Ad'*EQUATE—(*equus*), equal *to*.
*Ad*HERE'—(*hæreo*), to stick *to*.
*Ad*JA'CENT—(*jaceo*), lying *to* or near.
*Ad*JOIN'—(*jungo*), to join *to*.
*Ad*ORE'—(*oro*), to pray *to*.
*Ad*VERT'—(*verto*), to turn *to*.

A,* for *Ad,*

Signifies *to*.

*A*SCEND'—(*scando*), to climb *to*.
*A*SCRIBE'—(*scribo*), to write or impute *to*.
*A*SPERSE'—(*spargo*), to sprinkle *to* or *upon*.
*A*SPIRE'—(*spiro*), to breathe *to*.
*A*V'ENUE—(*venio*), the way of coming *to* (a place).
*A*VOW'—(*votum*), to vow *to*.

Ac,* for *Ad,

Signifies *to*.

*Ac*CEDE'—(*cedo*), to yield *to*.
*Ac*CEPT'—(*capio*), to take *to*.
*Ac*CESS'—(*cedo*), approach *to*.

Af,* for *Ad,

Signifies *to*.

*Af*FIX'—(*fixus*), to fix *to*.
*Af*FLICT'—(*fligo*), to strike *to* or at.
*Af'*FLUX—(*fluo*), a flowing *to*.

Ag,* for *Ad,

Signifies *to*.

*Ag'*GRAVATE—(*gravis*), to make heavy *to*.
*Ag'*GRANDIZE—(*grandis*), to make great *to*.
*Ag*GRESS'—(*gradior*), to go *to* or *against*.

Al,* for *Ad,

Signifies *to*.

*Al*LE'VIATE—(*levis*), to make light *to*.

---

* For the sake of euphony, the form of the prefix is frequently changed. Thus, we have *a*scend, for *ad*scend; *a*venue, for *ad*venue; *ac*cept, for *ad*cept, *af*firm for *ad*firm; *col*lect, for *con*lect, &c.

*Al*LUDE'—(*ludo*), to play or advert *to*.
*Al*LU'VIAL—(*luo*), washing *to*.
*Al*LY'—(*ligo*), to bind *to*.

An, for **Ad**,
Signifies *to*.

*An*NEX'—(*necto*), to tie *to*.
*An*NI'HILATE—(*nihil*), to make *to* nothing.
*An*NOUNCE'—(*nuncio*), to tell *to*.
*An*NUL'—(*nullus*), to reduce to nothing.

Ap, for **Ad**,
Signifies *to*.

*Ap*PA'RENT—(*pareo*), becoming visible *to*.
*Ap*PEND'—(*pendeo*), to hang *to*.
*Ap*PERTAIN'—to pertain *to*.
*Ap*PROX'IMATE—(*prope*), near *to*.

Ar, for **Ad**,
Signifies *to*.

*Ar*RANGE'—(*rang*), to put *to* or *in* order.
Ar'ROGATE'—(*rogo*), to ask or assume *to* (one's self).

As, for **Ad**,
Signifies *to*.

*As*SAIL'—(*salio*), to jump *to* or *against*.
*As*SID'UOUS—(*sedeo*), sitting *to*.
*As*SIGN'—(*signum*), to mark or allot *to*.
*As*SIM'ILATE—(*similis*), to make like *to*.
*As*SIST'—(*sisto*), to stand *to*.
*As*SO'CIATE—(*socio*), to join *to*.
*As*SUME'—(*sumo*), to take *to*.

At, for **Ad**,
Signifies *to*.

*At*TAIN'—(*tango*), to touch *to*.
*At*TEND'—(*tendo*), to stretch *to*
*At*TEST'—(*testis*), to bear witness *to*.
*At*TRACT'—(*traho*), to draw *to*.
*At*TRIB'UTE—(*tribuo*), to give or ascribe *to*.

Am,
Signifies *round* or *about*.

*Am*BITI'ON—(*eo*), a going *about*.
Am'PUTATE—(*puto*), to cut *round* or *off*

Ante,

Signifies *before.*

*Ante*CE'DENT—(*cedo*), going *before.*
*An'te*CHAMBER—a chamber *before* the main one
*Ante*DATE'—to date *before.*
*Ante*DILU'VIAN—(*diluvium*), *before* the flood.
*Ante*MERID'IAN—(*meridies*), *before* midday.
*Ante*MUN'DANE—(*mundus*), *before* the world.

Circum,

Signifies *about* or *round.*

*Circum*JA'CENT—(*jaceo*), lying *round.*
*Circum*NAV'IGATE—to navigate *round.*
*Circum*PO'LAR—(*polus*), *about* the pole.
*Circum*ROTA'TION—(*rota*), a whirling *round.*
*Circum*SCRIBE'—(*scribo*), to write *round.*
*Cir'cum*SPECT—(*specio*), looking *round.*

Cis,

Signifies *on this side.*

*Cis'*ALPINE—*on this side* of the Alps.
*Cis'*ATLANTIC—*on this side* of the Atlantic.

Con, (CUM,)

Signifies *together* or *with.*

*Con*CAT'ENATE—(*catena*), to link *together.*
*Con*CEN'TRATE—(*centrum*), to center *together*
*Con*CUR'—(*curro*), to run *together.*
*Con*FED'ERATE—(*fedus*), leagued *together.*
*Con*FLICT'—(*fligo*), to strike *together.*
*Con'*FLUENCE—(*fluo*), a flowing *together.*
*Con*G'REGATE—(*grex*), to flock *together.*
*Con*NECT'—(*necto*), to tie *together.*
*Con*SPIRE'—(*spiro*), to breathe *together.*
*Con*STRUCT'—(*struo*), to build *together.*
*Con'*TACT—(*tango*), touch *together.*
*Con*TEND'—(*tendo*), to stretch or strive *together.*
*Con*TOR'TION—(*tortum*), a twisting *together.*
*Con*TRIB'UTE—(*tributum*), to give *together.*
*Con*VENE'—(*venio*), to come *together.*
*Con*VERGE'—(*vergo*), to tend *together*
*Con*VOKE'—(*voco*), to call *together.*

Co, for ***Con,***

Signifies *together* or *with.*

*Co*E'QUAL—equal *with.*

*Co*E'VAL—(*ævum*), of the same age *with*.
*Co*EXIST'—to exist *together*.
*Co*HEIR'—one who is heir *with* another.
*Co*HERE'—(*hæreo*), to stick *together*.
Co-OP'ERATE—(*opera*), to work *with*.

Cog, for **Con,**
Signifies *together* or *with*.

*Cog'*NATE—(*nascor*), born *together* or *with*.

Col, for **Con,**
Signifies *together* or *with*.

*Col*LAPSE'—(*labor*), a falling *together*.
*Col*LATE'—(*latum*), to bring *together*.
*Col*LECT'—(*lego*), to gather *together*.
*Col'*LOCATE—(*locus*), to place *together*.
*Col'*LOQUY—(*loquor*), a speaking *together*.
*Col*LU'SION—(*ludo*), a playing *together*.

Com, for **Con,**
Signifies *together* or *with*.

*Com*BINE'—(*bini*), to put two or more things *together*
*Com*MEN'SURATE—(*mensura*), measured *with*.
*Com'*MERCE—(*mercor*), a trading *together*.
*Com*MIX'—to mix *together*.
*Com*MO'TION—(*moveo*), a moving *together*.
*Com*PA'TRIOT—a patriot *with* another.
*Com*PEL'—(*pello*), to drive *with*.
*Com*POSE'—(*pono*), to put *together*.
*Com*PRESS'—(*premo*), to press *together*.

Cor, for **Con,**
Signifies *together* or *with*.

*Cor*REL'ATIVE—relative *with*.
*Cor*ROB'ORATE—(*robur*), to make strong *together*.
*Cor*RODE'—(*rodo*), to gnaw *together*.

Contra,
Signifies *against*.

*Contra*DICT'—(*dico*), to speak *against* or *contrary to*.
*Contra*POSITI'ON—a position *against* or *opposite to*.
*Contro'*VERT—(*verto*), to turn *against*.

Counter, for **Contra,**
Signifies *against*.

*Counter*BAL'ANCE—to balance *against*.
*Counter*MARCH'—to march in an *opposite* direction.

De,

Signifies *down* or *from*.

*De*cline'—(*clino*), to bend *down*.
*De*duce'—(*duco*), to lead *from*.
*De*fend'—(*fendo*), to strike *down*.
*De*fer'—(*fero*), to bear *from*.
*De*grade'—(*gradior*), to cause to go *down*.
*De*ject'—(*jacio*), to cast *down*.
*De*pend'—(*pendeo*), to hang *from*.
*De*pose'—(*pono*), to put *down*.
*De*pre'ciate—(*precium*), to put the price *down*.
*De*r'ogate—(*rogo*), to ask or take *from*.
*De*scend'—(*scando*), to climb *down*.
*De*scribe'—(*scribo*), to write *down*.
*De*spair'—(*spero*), to be *from* or *out of* hope.
*De*tain'—(*teneo*), to hold *from*.
*De*throne'—to take *from* a throne.
De'viate—(*via*), to go *from* or *out of* the way.
*De*volve'—(*volvo*), to roll *down*.

Dis,

Signifies *to take from*, *away*, *off*, or *out*; *not*.

*Dis*a'ble—to render *un*able.
*Dis*arm'—*to take away* arms.
*Dis*believe'—*not* to believe.
*Dis*bur'den—*to take off* a burden.
*Dis*hon'est—*not* honest.
*Dis*loy'al—*not* loyal.
*Dis*or'der—*to take away* order.

Dis,

Signifies *asunder*.

*Dis*pel'—(*pello*), to drive *asunder*.
*Dis*sect'—(*seco*), to cut *asunder*.
*Dis*solve'—(*solvo*), to loose *asunder*.
*Dis*tend'—(*tendo*), to stretch *asunder*.
*Dis*tort'—(*tortum*), to twist *asunder*.
*Dis*tract'—(*traho*), to draw *asunder*.
*Dis*trib'ute—(*tributum*), to give *asunder*.

Di, for *Dis*,

Signifies *asunder*.

*Di*sperse'—(*spargo*), to sprinkle *asunder*.
*Di*verge'—(*vergo*), to tend *asunder*.

*Di*VERT'—(*verto*), to turn *asunder.*
*Di*GRESS'—(*gradior*), to go *asunder.*
*Di*LUTE'—(*luo*), to wash *asunder.*
*Di*MEN'SION—(*mensura*), the measure *asunder.*

Dif, for Dis,

Signifies *asunder.*

*Dif'*FER—(*fero*), to bear *asunder.*
*Dif*FUSE—(*fundo*), to pour *asunder.*

Ex (εξ),

Signifies *out, out of.*

*Ex*ACT'—(*ago*), to take or force *out of.*
*Ex*CEPT'—(*capio*), to take *out.*
*Ex*CITE'—(*cito*), to call *out.*
*Ex*CLAIM'—(*clamo*), to cry *out.*
*Ex*CLUDE'—(*claudo*), to shut *out.*
*Ex*CUL'PATE—(*culpa*), to put *out of* fault.
*Ex*EMPT'—(*emo*), to buy *out of.*
*Ex*HALE'—(*halo*), to breathe *out.*
*Ex*HAUST'—(*haustum*), to draw *out.*
*Ex*HUME'—(*humus*), to take *out of* the earth.
*Ex*PAND'—(*pando*) to spread *out.*
*Ex*PEL'—(*pello*), to drive *out.*
*Ex*PEND'—(*pendo*), to weigh *out.*
*Ex*PORT'—(*porto*), to carry *out.*
*Ex*POSE'—(*pono*), to put *out.*
*Ex*TEND'—(*tendo*), to stretch *out.*
*Ex*TORT'—(*tortum*), to twist *out.*
*Ex*TRACT'—(*traho*), to draw *out.*

E, for Ex,

Signifies *out, out of.*

*E*BULLITI'ON—(*bulla*), a bubbling *out.*
*E'*DICT—(*dico*), what is spoken *out.*
*E*DUCE'—(*duco*), to lead *out.*
*E'*GRESS—(*gradior*), a going *out.*
*E*JECT'—(*jacio*), to cast *out.*
*E*LATE'—(*latum*), carried *out.*
*E*LECT'—(*lego*), to choose *out.*
*El'*OQUENT—(*loquor*), speaking *out.*
*Em'*ANATE—(*mano*), to flow *out.*
*E*MERGE'—(*mergo*), to rise *out of.*
*E*MIT'—(*mitto*), to send *out.*
*E*MO'TION—(*moveo*), a moving *out.*
*E*RAD'ICATE—(*radix*), to root *out.*

*E*RASE'—(*rado*), to rub *out*.
*E*RUP'TION—(*rumpo*), a breaking *out*.

Ec (εκ), for **Ex**,
Signifies *out*, *out of*.

*E*CCEN'TRIC—(*centrum*, Gr.), *out of* the center.
Ec'LOGUE—(*logos*, Gr.), something spoken *out*.
Ecs'TASY—(*stasis*, Gr.), a standing *out of* (one's mind for joy)

Ef, for **Ex**,
Signifies *out*, *out of*.

*Ef*FACE'—(*facies*), to take *out* the face or form.
Ef'FLUX—(*fluo*), a flowing *out*.
*Ef*FUL'GENCE—(*fulgeo*), a shining *out*.
IN*ef*'FABLE—(*fari*), not to be spoken *out*.

Extra,
Signifies *beyond*.

*Extra*MUN'DANE—(*mundus*), *beyond* the world.
*Extra*OR'DINARY—*beyond* ordinary.

In, before a *verb*,
Signifies *in* or *into*, *on* or *upon*.

*In*CLINE'—(*clino*), to lean *into*.
*In*CLUDE'—(*claudo*), to shut *in*.
*In*CUL'CATE—(*culco*), to tread *in*.
*In*CUM'BENT—(*cubo*), leaning *upon*.
*In*CUR'—(*curro*), to run *upon*.
*In*DUCT'—(*duco*), to lead *into*.
*In*FLICT'—(*fligo*), to strike *upon*.
In'FLUX—(*fluo*), a flowing *in*.
*In*FUSE'—(*fundo*), to pour *into*.
*In*HALE'—(*halo*), to breathe *in*.
*In*HERE'—(*hæreo*), to stick *in*.
*In*HUME'—(*humus*), to put *into* the ground.
*In*JECT'—(*jacio*), to throw *into*.
*In*SPECT'—(*specio*), to look *into*.
*In*SPIRE'—(*spiro*), to breathe *into*.
*In*SULT'—(*salio*), to leap *upon*.
*In*TER'—(*terra*), to put *into* the earth.
*In*VENT'—(*venio*), to come *upon*.
*In*VOKE'—(*voco*), to call *upon*.

Il, for **In**,
Signifies *in* or *on*.

*Il*LU'MINATE—(*lumen*), to put light *into*.

Im, for **In,**

Signifies *in* or *into*, *on* or *upon*.

*Im*MERSE'—(*mergo*), to plunge *into*.
*Im*MURE'—(*murus*), to put *into* or *within* walls.
*Im*PEL'—(*pello*), to drive *on*.
*Im*PEND'—(*pendeo*), to hang *upon* or *over*.
*Im*PORT'—(*porto*), to carry *into*.
*Im*POSE'—(*pono*), to put *upon*.
*Im'*PRECATE—(*precor*), to pray *upon*.
*Im*PRIS'ON—to put *in* prison.

Ir, for **In,**

Signifies *in* or *on*.

*Ir*RA'DIATE—(*radius*), to throw rays *on* or *upon*.
*Ir'*RITATE—(*ira*), to put *in* anger.
*Ir*RUP'TION—(*ruptum*), a breaking *in* or *into*.

In, before an adjective.

Signifies *not*.

*In*AC'TIVE—*not* active.
*In*AN'IMATE—(*anima*), *not* having life.
*In*AR'ABLE—(*aro*), *not* to be ploughed.
*In*CAU'TIOUS—*not* cautious.
*In*COM'PETENT—*not* competent.
*In*CRED'IBLE—(*credo*), *not* to be believed.
*In*EV'ITABLE—(*vito*), *not* to be avoided.
*In*FAL'LIBLE—(*fallo*), *not* to be deceived.
*In'*FINITE—(*finis*), *not* or *without* bounds.
*In*SANE'—*not* sane.
*In*SIP'ID—(*sapio*), *not* having taste.
*In*TES'TATE—(*testis*), *not* having a will.

Ig, for **In,**

Signifies *not*.

*Ig*NO'BLE—*not* noble.
*Ig*NOMIN'IOUS—(*nomen*), *not* having a name or reputation.

Il, for **In,**

Signifies *not*.

*Il*LE'GAL—*not* legal.
*Il*LEG'IBLE—(*lego*), *not* to be read.
*Il*LIB'ERAL—*not* liberal.
*Il*LIC'IT—(*liceo*), *not* permitted.
*Il*LIT'ERATE—(*litera*), *not* having letters or knowledge.

Im, for **In,**

Signifies *not*.

*Im*MAC'ULATE—(*macula*), *not* having a spot.

*Im*MATURE'—(*maturus*), *not* ripe.
*Im*MOR'AL—*not* moral.
*Im*MOR'TAL—*not* mortal.
*Im*MU'TABLE—(*muto*), *not* to be changed.
*Im*PAR'TIAL—*not* partial.
*Im*PA'TIENT—*not* patient.
*Im*PER'FECT—*not* perfect.
*Im*PER'VIOUS—(*via*), *not* having a way through.
*Im'*PUDENT—(*pudeo*), *not* having shame.

Ir, for *In*,

Signifies *not*.

*Ir*RATI'ONAL—*not* rational.
*Ir*REFU'TABLE—*not* to be refuted.
*Ir*REG'ULAR—*not* regular.
*Ir*RELIGI'ON—*not* or *want of* religion.
*Ir*RESIST'IBLE—*not* to be resisted.
*Ir'*RESOLUTE—*not* resolute.
*Ir*REV'OCABLE—(*voco*), *not* to be called back.

Inter,

Signifies *between* or *among*.

*Inter*FERE'—(*ferio*), to strike *between*.
*Inter*JA'CENT—(*jaceo*), lying *between*.
*Inter*JEC'TION—(*jacio*), a throwing *between*.
*Inter*LINE'—to make lines *between*.
*In'ter*LUDE—(*ludo*), a part *between* plays.
*Inter*MIX'—to mix *among*.
*Inter*POSE'—(*pono*), to place *between*.
*Inter*REG'NUM—(*rego*), the time *between* two reigns
*Inter'*ROGATE—(*rogo*), to ask *between*.
*Inter*RUPT'—(*ruptum*), to break *between*.
*Inter*SECT'—(*seco*), to cut *between*.
*Inter*VENE'—(*venio*), to come *between*.

Intro,

Signifies *within*.

*Intro*DUCE'—(*duco*), to lead *within*.

Ob,

Signifies *in the way*, *against*, *out*.

*Ob'*JECT—(*jacio*), something cast *in the way* or *against*
*Ob*LIT'ERATE—(*litera*), to rub *out* the letters.
*Ob'*LOQUY—(*loquor*), something spoken *against*.
*Ob'*STACLE—(*sto*), something standing *in the way*.
*Ob*TRUDE'—(*trudo*), to thrust *against*.
*Ob'*VIATE—(*via*), to put *out of* the way.

Oc, for *Ob*,

Signifies *in the way*, *up*, *down.*

*Oc*CA'SION—(*cado*), a falling *in the way*.
Oc'CUPY—(*capio*), to take *up*.
*Oc*CUR'—(*curro*), to run *against* or *in the way*.

Of, for *Ob*,

Signifies *in the way*, *against*

*Of*FEND'—(*fendo*), to strike *against*.
Of'FER—(*fero*), to bear *in the way*.

Op, for *Ob*,

Signifies *in the way*, *against*.

*Op*POSE'—(*pono*), to place *in the way*.
*Op*PRESS'—(*premo*), to press *against*.
*Op*PUGN'—(*pugna*), to fight *against*.

Per,

Signifies *through* or *thoroughly*.

*Per*AM'BULATE—(*ambulo*), to walk *through*.
*Per*EN'NIAL—(*annus*), lasting *through* the year.
Per'FECT—(*facio*), made *thoroughly*.
Per'FORATE—(*foro*), to bore *through*.
Per'MANENT—(*maneo*), abiding *thoroughly*.
Per'SECUTE—(*sequor*), to follow *through*.
*Per*SPIRE'—(*spiro*), to breathe *through*.
*Per*VADE'—(*vado*), to go *through*.
*Per*USE'—(*utor*), to use *through*.

Post,

Signifies *after*.

*Post*DILU'VIAN—(*diluvium*), *after* the flood.
Post'HUMOUS—(*humus*), *after* one is put in the ground.
*Post*MERID'IAN—(*meridies*), *after* midday.
*Post*PONE'—(*pono*), to put *after* or *off*.
Post'SCRIPT—(*scribo*), something written *after*.

Pre,

Signifies *before*.

*Pre*CEDE'—(*cedo*), to go *before*.
*Pre*CUR'SOR—(*curro*), a *fore*runner.
*Pre*DICT'—(*dico*), to *fore*tell.
*Pre*FER'—(*fero*), to bear or esteem *before*.
*Pre*FIX—(*fixus*), something fixed *before*.
*Pre*L'UDE—(*ludo*), something *before* the play.

*Pre*MATURE'—(*maturus*), ripe *before* or too soon.
*Pre*PON'DERATE—(*pondus*), to weigh *before* or *more than.*
*Pre*SIDE'—(*sedeo*), to sit *before.*
*Pre*VENT'—(*venio*), to come *before.*

Preter,

Signifies *beyond* or *past.*

*Pre'ter*ITE—(*eo*), gone *past.*
*Preter*NAT'URAL—*beyond* or *more than* natural.

Pro,

Signifies *for*, *forward*, *forth*, or *out.*

*Pro*CON'SUL—one who acts *for* a consul.
*Pro'*NOUN—a word standing *for* a noun.
*Pro*X'Y—(*cura*), one who does the care or business *for* another
*Pro*CEED'—(*cedo*), to go *forward.*
*Pro*MOTE'—(*moveo*), to move *forward.*
*Pro*PEL'—(*pello*), to drive *forward.*
*Pro*S'PECT—(*specio*), the look or appearance *forward.*
*Pro*DUCE'—(*duco*), to lead *forth.*
*Pro*F'FER—(*fero*), to bear or hold *forth.*
*Pro*FUSE'—(*fundo*), poured *forth.*
*Pro*CLAIM'—(*clamo*), to cry *out.*
*Pro*TRACT'—(*traho*), to draw *out.*
*Pro*VOKE'—(*voco*), to call *out.*

Re,

Signifies *back* or *again, anew.*

*Re*AC'TION—action *back* or in return.
*Re*BEL'—(*bellum*), to war *back.*
*Re*CEDE'—(*cedo*), to go *back.*
*Re*CLAIM'—(*clamo*), to call *back.*
*Re*CLINE'—(*clino*), to lean *back.*
*Re*CUM'BENT—(*cubo*), lying *back.*
*Re'*FLUX—(*fluo*), a flowing *back.*
*Re*FUSE'—(*fundo*), to pour *back.*
*Re*PULSE'—(*pello*), to beat *back.*
*Re*VOKE'—(*voco*), to call *back.*
*Re*AN'IMATE—to animate *again.*
*Re*CON'QUER—to conquer *again.*
*Re*COUNT'—to count *again.*
Re-ELECT'—to elect *again.*
*Re*ORDAIN'—to ordain *again.*
*Re*PUB'LISH—to publish *again.*
*Re*SUME'—(*sumo*), to take *again.*
*Re*TAKE'—to take *again.*

Retro,

Signifies *back* or *backwards.*

*Retro*CESSI'ON—(*cedo*), a yielding *back.*
*Ret'ro*GRADE—(*gradior*), stepping *backwards.*
*Ret'ro*SPECT—(*specio*), a looking *backwards.*

Se,

Signifies *aside* or *apart.*

*Se*CEDE'—(*cedo*), to go *aside.*
*Se*CLU'SION—(*claudo*), a shutting *apart.*
*Se*DUCE'—(*duco*), to lead *aside.*
*Se*DIT'ION—(*eo*), a going *aside.*

Sine,

Signifies *without.*

*Sim'*PLE—(*plico*), *without* fold.
*Sin*CERE'—(*cera*), *without* wax.
*Sin'e*CURE—(*cura*), a situation *without* care.

Sub,

Signifies *under.*

*Sub*CUTA'NEOUS—(*cutis*), *under* the skin.
*Sub*JA'CENT—(*jaceo*), lying *under.*
*Sub*MARINE'—(*mare*), *under* the sea.
*Sub*SCRIBE'—(*scribo*), to write *under.*
*Sub*TRACT'—(*traho*), to draw *under* or *from.*
*Sub*BEA'DLE—an *under* beadle.
*Sub*DEA'CON—an *under* deacon.

Suc, for Sub,

Signifies *under, up.*

*Suc*CEED'—(*cedo*), to go *under* or *after.*
*Suc'*COUR—(*curro*), to run *under.*
*Suc*CUMB'—(*cubo*), to lean *under.*

Suf, for Sub,

Signifies *under.*

*Suf'*FER—(*fero*), to bear *under.*
*Suf*FUSE'—(*fundo*), to pour *under.*

Sup, for Sub,

Signifies *under, up.*

*Sup*PORT'—(*porto*), to bear *up.*
*Sup*POSE'—(*pono*), to put *under.*
*Sup*PRESS'—(*premo*), to press *under.*

Subter,

Signifies *under* or *beneath.*

*Sub'ter*FUGE—(*fugio*), a flying *under*.

Super,

Signifies *above* or *over*, *upon.*

*Super*ABOUND'—to *over*abound.
*Super*ADD'—to add *over* and *above.*
*Super*FINE'—*over*fine.
*Super'*FLUOUS—(*fluo*), flowing *over* or *above.*
*Super*NAT'URAL—*above* or *more than* natural.
*Super*SEDE'—(*sedeo*), to sit *above.*
*Super*VI'SOR—(*video*), an *over*seer.
*Super*FICI'AL—(*facies*), *upon* the face or outside.
*Super*SCRIBE'—(*scribo*), to write *upon.*
*Super*STRUCTURE—(*struo*), what is reared *upon.*

Sur, (Fr. cont. of *Super,*)

Signifies *above*, *over*, *upon.*

*Sur*CHARGE'—to *over*charge.
*Sur*MOUNT'—to mount *above.*
*Sur*TOUT'—(*totus*), *over* all.
*Sur*VIVE'—(*vivo*), to live *over* or *after.*
*Sur'*FACE—(*facies*), *upon* the face.
*Sur*VEY'—(*video*), to look *upon.*

Sus, for *Sub,* or *Sursum,*

Signifies *under*, *up*, *upwards.*

*Sus*PECT'—(*specio*), to look *under.*
*Sus*PEND'—(*pendeo*), to hang *up.*
*Sus*TAIN'—(*teneo*), to hold *up.*

Trans,

Signifies *across*, *over* or *beyond*, *through.*

*Tra*DUCE'—(*duco*), to lead *across.*
*Tra*DITI'ON—(*do*), a giving *across.*
*Tra*JECT'—(*jacio*), to throw *across.*
*Trans*AL'PINE—*across* the Alps.
*Trans*CEND'—(*scando*), to climb *beyond.*
*Trans*FER'—(*fero*), to carry *over.*
*Trans*GRESS'—(*gradior*), to go *over* or *beyond.*
*Trans*LATE'—(*latum*), to carry *over.*
*Trans'*MIGRATE—(*migro*), to remove *beyond.*
*Trans*MIT'—(*mitto*), to send *over.*
*Trans*PA'RENT—(*pareo*), appearing *through.*
*Trans*PORT'—(*porto*), to carry *over.*

*Trans*POSE'—(*pono*), to put *across*.
*Trans*VERSE'—(*verto*), turned *across*.
*Tres'*PASS—(*passus*), a passing *over* or *across*.

Ultra,

Signifies *beyond*.

*Ultra*IST'—one who is *beyond*.
*Ultra*MON'TANE—(*mons*), *beyond* the mountains.
*Ultra*MUN'DANE—(*mundus*), *beyond* the world.

II. SUFFIXES.

Ac,

Signifies *of* or *belonging to*.

CAR'DI*ac*—(*cardia*, Gr.), *belonging to* the heart.
ELEGI'*ac*—(*elegia*, Gr.), *belonging to* elegy.
DEMO'NI*ac*—*belonging to* a demon.

Aceous,

Denotes *of* or *consisting of*, *like* or *resembling*.

ARENA'*ceous*—(*arena*), *consisting of* sand.
ARGILLA'*ceous*—(*argilla*), *consisting of* clay.
FARINA'*ceous*—(*farina*), *consisting of* meal.
FOLIA'*ceous*—(*folium*), *consisting of* leaves.
HERBA'*ceous*—(*herba*), *consisting of* herbs.
ARUNDINA'*ceous*—(*arundo*), *resembling* reeds.
BUTYRA'*ceous*—(*butyrum*), *resembling* butter.
CORIA'*ceous*—(*corium*), *resembling* leather.
SAPONA'*ceous*—(*sapo*), *resembling* soap.

Acy,

Denotes *being*, or *state of being*; *office of*.

AC'CUR*acy*—*a being* accurate.
DEL'IC*acy*—*a being* delicate.
OB'STIN*acy*—*a being* obstinate.
CEL'IB*acy*—(*cælebs*), *the state of being* single.
LU'N*acy*—(*luna*), *the state of being* a lunatic.
CU'R*acy*—the *office of* a curate.
MAG'ISTR*acy*—the *office of* a magistrate.
PRI'M*acy*—the *office of* a primate.

Age,

Denotes a *collection of; state of being; an allowance for.*

BAG'G*age*—a *collection of* bags or bundles.
CORD'*age*—a *collection of* cords.
FOL'I*age*—(*folium*), a *collection of* leaves.
HERB'*age*—a *collection of* herbs.
BOND'*age*—*state of being* in bonds.
OR'PHAN*age*—*state of being* an orphan.
PEER'*age*—*state of being* a peer.
CAR'RI*age*—*an allowance for* the thing carried.
MINT'*age*—*an allowance for* minting or coining.
POST'*age*—*an allowance for* the post or letter carrier.
POR'TER*age*—*an allowance for* a porter's services.
WHARF'*age*—*an allowance for* the use of a wharf.

Al,

Denotes *of, belonging, relating* or *pertaining to; befitting* or *becoming.*

CELES'TI*al*—(*cœlestis*), *relating to* heaven.
FIL'I*al*—(*filius*), *relating to* or *becoming* a son.
FLO'R*al*—(*flos*), *relating to* flowers.
FRATER'N*al*—(*frater*), *relating to* or *becoming* a brother.
MAN'U*al*—(*manus*), *relating to* the hand.
MATER'N*al*—(*mater*), *relating to* or *becoming* a mother.
MENT'*al*—(*mens*), *relating to* the mind.
NA'TION*al*—*belonging* or *relating to* a nation.
PAREN'T*al*—*belonging* or *relating to* a parent.
PEC'TOR*al*—(*pectus*), *relating to* the breast.
PER'SON*al*—*pertaining* or *relating to* a person.
RE'G*al*—(*rego*), *relating to* a king.
RU'R*al*—(*rus*), *relating to* the country.
TEM'POR*al*—(*tempus*), *relating to* time.
VER'B*al*—(*verbum*), *relating to* words.
VO'C*al*—(*vox*), *relating to* the voice.

An, Ian,

Signifies *belonging, relating* or *pertaining to.*

AGRA'RI*an*—(*ager*), *relating to* the fields.
CHRIS'T*ian*—*relating to* Christ.
DILU'VI*an*—(*diluvium*), *relating to* the flood.
EUROPE'*an*—*relating to* Europe.
GRE'CI*an*—*belonging* or *relating to* Greece.
HYMENE'*an*—(*hymen*, Gr.), *relating to* marriage.
PLEBEI'*an*—(*plebs*), *relating to* the people.
SYL'V*an*—(*sylva*), *relating to* the woods.

An, Ian,

Denotes *one who*, or *the person that.*

ARTISan'—*one who* is skilled in an art.
CHRIS'TIan—*one who* believes in Christ.
COLLE'GIan—*one who* studies at a college.
EPISCOPA'LIan—*one who* belongs to the Episcopal church.
EUROPE'an—*one who* lives in Europe.
HISTO'RIan—*one who* writes history.
LIBRA'RIan—*one who* has charge of a library.
MAGICI'an—*one who* practices magic.
PARTISan'—*one who* is attached to a party.
REPUB'LICan—*one who* advocates a republic.
VET'ERan—(*vetus*), *one who* is old.

Ance, Ancy,

Denotes *being* or *state of being; 'ing.'*

CON'SONance—*state of being* consonant.
CON'STancy—*state of being* constant.
IG'NORance—*state of being* ignorant.
MAIN'TENance—(*manus, teneo*), *state of being* held by the hand or supported.
RA'DIancy—*state of being* radiant.
VIG'ILance—*state of being* vigilant.
ACCEPT'ance—(*capio*), a tak*ing* to.
AR'ROGancy—(*rogo*), an ask*ing* to or for.
ASSIST'ance—(*sisto*), a stand*ing* to.
CONVEY'ance—(*veho*), a carry*ing* together.
RELUC'Tance—(*luctor*), a fight*ing* back.
VAG'Rancy—(*vagus*), a wander*ing*.

Ant,

Denotes *one who*, or *the person that.*

AD'JUTant—(*juvo*), *one who* aids.
ASSAIL'ant—*one who* assails.
ASSIST'ant—*one who* assists.
CLAIM'ant—*one who* claims.
COM'BATant—*one who* combats.
DEFEND'ant—*one who* defends.
DIS'PUTant—*one who* disputes.
LIEUTEN'ant—(*lieu, teneo*), *one who* holds the place of another
MER'CHant—(*mercor*), *one who* trades.
SER'vant—*one who* serves.
TEN'ant—(*teneo*), *one who* holds.
VA'GRant—(*vagus*), *one who* wanders.
VIS'ITant –*one who* visits.

Ant,

Signifies '*ing*.'

ATTEN'D*ant*—attend*ing*.
BRIL'LI*ant*—(*briller*), shin*ing*.
CON'SON*ant*—(*sonus*), sound*ing* together.
DEPEN'D*ant*—(*pendeo*), hang*ing* down.
DIS'T*ant*—(*sto*), stand*ing* apart.
EXTRAV'AG*ant*—(*vagus*), wander*ing* beyond.
IG'NOR*ant*—(*gnorus*), not know*ing*.
MIL'IT*ant*—(*miles*), fight*ing*.
OBSER'V*ant*—observ*ing*.
PLEAS'*ant*—pleas*ing*.
PLI'*ant*—(*plico*), fold*ing* or bend*ing*.
RA'DI*ant*—(*radius*), throw*ing* out rays.
REPUG'N*ant*—(*pugna*), fight*ing* back.
SIGNIF'IC*ant*—signify*ing*.
VIG'IL*ant*—(*vigil*), watch*ing*.

Ar,

Signifies *belonging*, *relating*, or *pertaining to ; having*

CIR'CUL*ar*—(*circulus*), *relating to* a circle.
GLOB'UL*ar*—(*globus*), *relating to* a globe.
IN'SUL*ar*—(*insula*), *relating to* an island.
JU'GUL*ar*—(*jugulum*), *relating to* the throat.
LU'N*ar*—(*luna*), *relating to* the moon.
OC'UL*ar*—(*oculus*), *relating to* the eyes.
PO'L*ar*—(*polus*), *relating to* the poles.
SO'L*ar*—(*sol*), *relating to* the sun.
TIT'UL*ar*—(*titulus*), *relating to* a title.
AN'GUL*ar*—(*angulus*), *relating to* an angle.
CEL'LUL*ar*—(*cella*), *having* cells.
CURVILIN'E*ar*—(*curvus, linea*), *having* curved lines.
MUS'CUL*ar*—(*musculus*), *having* muscles.
RECTAN'GUL*ar*—(*rectus, angulus*), *having* right-angles
RECTILIN'E*ar*—(*rectus, linea*), *having* straight lines.

Ar,

Signifies *one who*.

BEG'G*ar*—*one who* begs.
LI'*ar*—*one who* lies.
SCHOL'*ar*—*one who* goes to school.

Ard,

Denotes *one who*.

DRUNK'*ard*—*one who* gets drunk.
SLUG'G*ard*—*one who* is sluggish.

Ary,

Denotes *one who*, or *the person that.*

AD'VERS*ary*—*one who* is adverse or opposed to.
AN'TIQU*ary*—*one who* studies antiquity.
COTEM'POR*ary*—(*tempus*), *one who* lives at the same time.
DIG'NIT*ary*—*one who* has a dignity.
EM'ISS*ary*—*one who* is sent out.
LAP'ID*ary*—(*lapis*), *one who* deals in precious stones.
MIS'SION*ary*—(*mitto*), *one who* is sent.
PEN'SION*ary*—*one who* receives a pension.
PLENIPOTEN'TI*ary*—(*plenus, posse*), *one who* has full power.
TRIB'UT*ary*—*one who* pays a tribute.
VOLUP'TU*ary*—(*voluptas*), *one who* is given up to pleasure.

Ary,

Denotes *the place where*, or *the thing that.*

API*ary*—(*apis*), *the place where* bees are kept.
DIC'TION*ary*—(*dico*), *the place where* words are collected.
GRAN'*ary*—(*granum*), *the place where* grain is stored.
LI'BR*ary*—(*liber*), *the place where* books are kept.
SANC'TU*ary*—(*sanctus*), *the place where* sacred things are kept.
BOUND'*ary*—*the thing that* bounds.
LU'MIN*ary*—(*lumen*), *the thing that* gives light.
PRELIM'IN*ary*—(*limen*), *something that* is before the threshold, or at the very beginning.
VAG*a'ry*—(*vagus*), *the thing that* wanders; a wandering thought.

Ary,

Signifies *belonging, relating*, or *pertaining to.*

ALIMEN'T*ary*—*pertaining* or *relating to* aliment.
AR'BOR*ary*—(*arbor*), *pertaining* or *relating to* trees.
EPIS'TOL*ary*—(*epistola*), *pertaining* or *relating to* a letter.
HON'OR*ary*—*pertaining* or *relating to* honor.
LIT'ER*ary*—(*litera*), *pertaining* or *relating to* letters.
MIL'IT*ary*—(*miles*), *pertaining* or *relating to* soldiers.
PLAN'ET*ary*—*pertaining* or *relating to* planets.
PUL'MON*ary*—(*pulmo*), *pertaining* or *relating to* the lungs.
TEM'POR*ary*—(*tempus*), *pertaining* or *relating to* time.
TRADITI'ON*ary*—*pertaining* or *relating to* tradition.

Ate,

Denotes *having; being.*

COR'POR*ate*—(*corpus*), *having* a body.
FOR'TUN*ate*—*having* fortune.
INAN'IM*ate*—(*anima*), not *having* life.

INTES'T*ate*—(*testis*), not *having* a will.
PASSI'ON*ate*—*having* passion.
TEM'PER*ate*—*having* temper or restraint.
AD'EQU*ate*—(*equus*), *being* equal to.
CONFED'ER*ate*—(*fedus*), *being* leagued together.
DES'PER*ate*—(*spero*), *being* out of hope.
ILLIT'ER*ate*—(*litera*), *being* without letters.
INSA'TI*ate*—(*satis*), *being* without enough.

Ate,

Denotes *one who*, or *the person that.*

CONFED'ER*ate*—(*fedus*), *one who* is leagued with.
CU'R*ate*—(*cura*), *one who* has the care.
DEL'EG*ate*—(*lego*), *one who* is sent from.
GRAD'U*ate*—(*gradior*), *one who* takes a degree.
LEG'*ate*—(*lego*), *one who* is sent.
LICEN'TI*ate*—*one who* has a license.
PO'TENT*ate*—(*posse*), *one who* has power.
PRI'M*ate*—(*primus*), *one who* is first.

Ate,

Denotes *to make*, *to give*, *to put*, or *to take.*

ANNI'HIL*ate*—(*nihil*), *to make* to nothing.
AN'TIQU*ate*—(*antiquus*), *to make* ancient
ASSIM'IL*ate*—(*similis*), *to make* like to.
AUTHEN'TIC*ate*—*to make* authentic.
DEBIL'IT*ate*—(*debilis*), *to make* feeble.
FACIL'IT*ate*—(*facilis*), *to make* easy.
FRUS'TR*ate*—(*frustra*), *to make* vain.
ME'LIOR*ate*—(*melior*), *to make* better.
REN'OV*ate*—(*novus*), *to make* new again.
AN'IM*ate*—(*anima*), *to give* life.
DEC'OR*ate*—(*decor*), *to give* ornament.
REG'UL*ate*—(*rego*), *to give* rules.
RETAL'I*ate*—(*talis*), *to give* back like for like.
STIM'UL*ate*—(*stimulus*), *to give* a spur.
DEPOP'UL*ate*—(*populus*), *to take* out or destroy the people.
DIS'LOC*ate*—(*locus*), *to put* out of place.
ENER'V*ate*—(*neuron*), *to put* out of nerve.
ERAD'IC*ate*—(*radix*), *to take* out the roots.
EXFO'LI*ate*—(*folium*), *to put* out leaves.
ILLU'MIN*ate*—(*lumen*), *to put* light into.
INCAR'CER*ate*—(*carcer*), *to put* into prison.
INOC'UL*ate*—(*oculus*), *to put* an eye in or upon.
INSIN'U*ate*—(*sinus*), *to put* into the bosom.

Ble, Able, Ible,

Denotes *may be* or *can be; worthy of.*

ACCES'SI*ble*—(*cedo*), that *can be* approached.
ATTAIN'*able*—that *can be* attained.
BLAM'*able*—that *may be* blamed.
UNAN'SWER*able*—that *can*not *be* answered.
DISCER'NI*ble*—that *can be* discerned.
FLEX'I*ble*—(*flecto*), that *can be* bent.
INHAB'IT*able*—that *can be* inhabited.
INNU'MER*able*—(*numerus*), that *can* not *be* numbered.
INVIS'I*ble*—(*video*), that *can* not *be* seen.
CONTEMP'T*ible*—*worthy of* contempt.
PUN'ISH*able*—*worthy of* punishment.
RESPEC'T*able*—*worthy of* respect.

Cle,

Signifies *little* or *small.*

CAN'TI*cle*—(*cano*), a *little* song.
I'CI*cle*—a *small* stick of ice.
PED'I*cle*—(*pes*), a *little* flower stem.
VEN'TRI*cle*—(*venter*), a *little* belly.

Dom,

Signifies *the place where; state of being.*

DUKE'*dom*—*the place where* a duke reigns.
KING'*dom*—*the place where* a king reigns.
POPE'*dom*—*the place where* the pope governs.
FREE'*dom*—*the state of being* free.
WIS'*dom*—*the state* or *quality of being* wise.

Ee,

Denotes *one who,* or *one to whom.*

ABSENT*ee'*—*one who* is absent.
GUARANT*ee'*—*one who* guarantees.
REFUG*ee'*—(*fugio*), *one who* flies.
ASSIGN*ee'*—*one to whom* any thing is assigned.
DON*ee'*—(*do*), *one to whom* any thing is given.
GRANT*ee'*—*one to whom* a grant is made.
LESS*ee'*—*one to whom* a lease is made.
TRUST*ee'*—*one to whom* a trust is given.

Eer,

Signifies *one who,* or *the person that.*

AUCTION*eer'*—*one who* has an auction.
CHARIOT*eer'*—*one who* drives a chariot.
ENGIN*eer'*—*one who* has charge of an engine.

MOUNTAINeer'—*one who* lives on a mountain
MUTINeer'—*one who* is guilty of mutiny.
SONNETTeer'—*one who* writes sonnets.

En,

Denotes *made of.*

BRA'zen—*made of* brass.
HEM'Pen—*made of* hemp.
WOOD'en—*made of* wood.
WOOL'Len—*made of* wool.

En,

Denotes *to make.*

DEEP'en—*to make* deep.
FAS'Ten—*to make* fast.
GLAD'Den—*to make* glad.
HAR'Den—*to make* hard.
SHAR'Pen—*to make* sharp.
SHOR'Ten—*to make* short.

Ence, Ency,

Denotes *being* or *state of being; 'ing.'*

AB'sence—a *being* away.
EQUIV'ALence—a *being* equivalent.
IM'POTence—(*posse*), *state of being* without power
IM'PUDence—(*pudeo*), *state of being* without shame
IN'NOcency—(*noceo*), *state of being* innocent.
ADHE'Rence—(*hæreo*), a stick*ing* to.
CA'Dence—(*cado*), a fall*ing*.
CONCUR'Rence—(*curro*), a runn*ing* together.
CON'FLUence—(*fluo*), a flow*ing* together.
EL'OQUence—(*loquor*), a speak*ing* out.
INTERFE'Rence—(*ferio*), a strik*ing* between.
PRE'SCIence—(*scio*), a know*ing* beforehand.
REFUL'Gence—(*fulgeo*), a shin*ing* back.

Ent,

Denotes *one who*, or *the person that.*

ADHE'Rent—(*hæreo*), *one who* sticks to.
A'Gent—(*ago*), *one who* acts.
DELIN'QUent—(*linquo*), *one who* leaves out or omits
PA'TIent—(*patior*), *one who* suffers.
PEN'ITent—(*peniteo*), *one who* repents.
PRES'IDent—*one who* presides.
RECIP'Ient—(*capio*), *one who* receives.
RE'Gent—(*rego*), *one who* governs.
STU'Dent—(*studeo*), *one who* studies.

Ent,

Denotes '*ing*,' or *being*.

ANTECE'D*ent*—(*cedo*), go*ing* before.
AR'D*ent*—(*ardeo*), burn*ing*.
BENEV'OL*ent*—(*bene, volo*), wish*ing* well.
BELLIG'ER*ent*—(*bellum, gero*), wag*ing* war.
COHE'R*ent*—(*hæreo*), stick*ing* together.
CONCUR'R*ent*—(*curro*), runn*ing* together.
CON'SEQU*ent*—(*sequor*), follow*ing* with or after.
EFFUL'G*ent*—(*fulgeo*), shin*ing* forth.
PEN'D*ent*—(*pendeo*), hang*ing*.
TRANSPA'R*ent*—(*pareo*), appear*ing* through.
AB'S*ent*—(*ens*), *being* away.
EQUIV'AL*ent*—(*equus, valeo*), *being* of equal value.
IM'POT*ent*—(*potens*), *being* without power.
IM'PUD*ent*—(*pudeo*), *being* without shame.
PO'T*ent*—(*potens*), *being* powerful.

Er,

Denotes *one who*, or *the person that*.

ARCH'*er*—(*arcus*), *one who* uses a bow.
BEHOLD'*er*—*one who* beholds.
BUILD'*er*—*one who* builds.
BUY'*er*—*one who* buys.
COMMAND'*er*—*one who* commands.
FISH'*er*—*one who* fishes.
INQUI'R*er*—*one who* inquires.
LEC'TUR*er*—*one who* lectures.
OF'FIC*er*—*one who* has an office.
ROB'B*er*—*one who* robs.
TEACH'*er*—*one who* teaches.
TREAS'UR*er*—*one who* keeps treasure.
VIL'LAG*er*—*one who* lives in a village.

Escence,

Denotes *state of growing* or *becoming*.

ADOL*es'cence*—(*oleo*), *state of growing* to or up to (manhood).
CONVAL*es'cence*—(*valeo*), *state of growing* well.
EFFLOR*es'cence*—(*flos*), *state of growing* or putting out flowers
PUTR*es'cence*—(*putris*), *state of becoming* rotten.
QUI*es'cence*—(*quies*), *state of becoming* quiet.

Escent,

Denotes *growing* or *becoming*.

CONVAL*es'cent*—*growing* well.
EXCR*es'cent*—*growing* out.

PUTRES'*cent*—(*putris*), *growing* or *becoming* rotten.
QUIES'*cent*—(*quies*), *becoming* quiet.

Ful,

Denotes *full of.*

CARE'*ful*—*full of* care.
DOUBT'*ful*—*full of* doubt.
FEAR'*ful*—*full of* fear.
HOPE'*ful*—*full of* hope.
MER'CI*ful*—*full of* mercy.
PIT'I*ful*—*full of* pity.
SIN'*ful*—*full of* sin.
WON'DER*ful*—*full of* wonder.

Fy,

Denotes *to make.*

DIVER'SI*fy*—*to make* diverse or various.
FOR'TI*fy*—(*fortis*), *to make* strong.
MAG'NI*fy*—(*magnus*), *to make* great.
NUL'LI*fy*—(*nullus*), *to make* null or void.
PU'RI*fy*—(*purus*), *to make* pure.
REC'TI*fy*—(*rego*), *to make* right.
SANC'TI*fy*—(*sanctus*), *to make* sacred.
VER'I*fy*—(*verus*), *to make* true.

Hood,

Denotes *the state of.*

BOY'*hood*—*the state of* a boy.
CHILD'*hood*—*the state of* a child.
KNIGHT'*hood*—*the state of* a knight.

Ic, Ical,

Denotes *of, belonging, relating,* or *pertaining to.*

ACADEM'*ical*—*belonging* or *relating to* an academy.
ANGEL'*ical*—*belonging* or *relating to* an angel.
GIGAN'TIC—(*gigas*), *belonging* or *relating to* a giant.
HERO'*ic*—*belonging* or *relating to* a hero.
METAL'LIC—*belonging* or *relating to* metals.
OCEAN'*ic*—*belonging* or *relating to* the ocean.
POET'*ical*—*belonging* or *relating to* a poet.
RUS'TIC—(*rus*), *belonging* or *relating to* the country.

Ice,

Denotes *a being,* or *thing that.*

AV'ARICE—(*avarus*), *a being* fond of money.
JUS'TICE—*a being* just.

MAL'*ice*—(*male*), *a being* evil.
SER'*vice*—*the thing that* is served.
No'TICE—(*nosco*), *the thing that* makes known.

Ics,

Denotes *the doctrine, science,* or *art of.*

ETH'*ics*—(*ethos*, Gr.), *the science of* manners.
OP'TICS—(*opto*, Gr.), *the science of* vision.
PNEUMAT'*ics*—(*pneuma*, Gr.), *the science of* air.
ECONOM'*ics*—(*eceo, nomos*, Gr.), *the doctrine of* household management.
PYROTECH'NICS—(*pyr, techne*, Gr.), *the art of* making fireworks.
TAC'TICS—(*tactos*, Gr.), *the science* or *art of* military arrange ments.

Id,

Denotes *being*, or '*ing*.'

AC'RID—(*acris*), *being* sharp.
FRIG'*id*—(*frigus*), *being* cold.
TIM'*id*—(*timeo*), fear*ing*.
FER'VID—(*ferveo*), burn*ing*.
PEL'LUCID—(*luceo*), shin*ing* through.
SPLEN'DID—(*splendeo*), shin*ing*.
TOR'RID—(*torreo*), parch*ing*.
TUR'GID—(*turgeo*), *being* swollen.
VIV'*id*—(*vivo*), liv*ing*.

Ile,

Denotes *belonging to; may* or *can be; easily.*

FE'BRILE—(*febris*), *belonging to* a fever.
HOS'TILE—(*hostis*), *belonging to* an enemy.
JUV'ENILE—(*juvenis*), *belonging to* youth.
PU'ERILE—(*puer*), *belonging to* a boy.
VI'RILE—(*vir*), *belonging to* a man.
DOC'*ile*—(*doceo*), that *may be* taught, or *easily* taught.
DUC'TILE—(*duco*), that *may be* lead.
FRAG'*ile*—(*frango*), *easily* broken.
PROJEC'TILE—(*jacio*), that *can be* thrown forward.
TRAC'TILE—(*traho*), that *may be* drawn out.

Ine,

Denotes *of* or *belonging to.*

ADAMAN'TINE—*belonging to* adamant.
CA'NINE—(*canis*), *belonging to* dogs.
CRYS'TALLINE—*belonging to* a crystal.
DIVINE'—(*divus*), *belonging to* God.
FEM'ININE—(*femina*), *belonging to* woman.

IN'FANT*ine*—*belonging to* an infant.
MAR*ine'*—(*mare*), *belonging to* the sea.
MAS'CUL*ine*—(*masculus*), *belonging to* a male.
SER'PENT*ine*—*belonging to* a serpent.

Ion,

Denotes *the act of; state of being; 'ing.'*

ABERRA'T*ion*—(*erro*), *the act of* wandering away.
ADDIT*i'on*—(*do*), *the act of* giving to or adding.
CONTOR'T*ion*—(*tortum*), *the act of* twisting together.
EXPUL'S*ion*—(*pello*), *the act of* driving out.
INSPEC'T*ion*—(*specio*), *the act of* looking into.
PRODUC'T*ion*—(*duco*), *the act of* leading forth.
RETEN'T*ion*—(*teneo*), *the act of* holding back.
ANIMA'T*ion*—the *state of being* animate.
CORRUP'T*ion*—the *state of being* corrupt.
PRECIS*i'on*—the *state of being* precise.
SALVA'T*ion*—(*salvus*), the *state of being* safe.
SUBORDINA'T*ion*—the *state of being* subordinate.
COHE'S*ion*—(*hæreo*), a stick*ing* together.
COMMO'T*ion*—(*moveo*), a mov*ing* together.
DISSOLU'T*ion*—(*solvo*), a loos*ing* together.
ELEC'T*ion*—(*lego*), a choos*ing*.
EXPAN'S*ion*—(*pando*), a spread*ing* out.
FRIC'T*ion*—(*frico*), a rubb*ing*.
IMMER'S*ion*—(*mergo*), a plung*ing* in.
INVA'S*ion*—(*vado*), a go*ing* into.

Ise, Ize,

Denotes *to make; to give.*

CIV'IL*ize*—*to make* civil.
FAMIL'IAR*ize*—*to make* familiar.
FER'TIL*ize*—*to make* fertile.
FRAN'CH*ise*—(*franc*), *to make* free.
LE'GAL*ize*—*to make* legal.
MOD'ERN*ize*—*to make* modern.
PUL'VER*ize*—(*pulvis*), *to make* to powder.
SOL'EMN*ize*—*to make* solemn.
AU'THOR*ize*—*to give* authority.
CHAR'ACTER*ize*—*to give* character.
CRIT'IC*ise*—(*crites*, Gr.), *to give* judgment or opinion.
DOG'MAT*ize*—(*dogma*, Gr.), *to give* an opinion.
PARTIC'ULAR*ize*—*to give* the particulars.
STIG'MAT*ize*—(*stigma*, Gr.), *to give* a stigma or blot.
SYSTEM'AT*ize*—*to give* system.

Ish,

Denotes *somewhat; belonging to; like.*

BLACK'*ish*—*somewhat* black.
GREEN'*ish*—*somewhat* green.
SCOT'T*ish*—*belonging to* Scotland.
SPAN'*ish*—*belonging to* Spain.
BOY'*ish*—*like* a boy.
CHILD'*ish*—*like* a child.
FOOL'*ish*—*like* a fool.
FOP'P*ish*—*like* a fop.

Ish,

Denotes *to make.*

CHER'*ish*—(*carus*), *to make* dear.
EMBEL'L*ish*—(*beau*), *to make* beautiful.
EMPOV'ER*ish*—(*pauper*), *to make* poor.
FIN'*ish*—(*finis*), *to make* an end.
PUB'L*ish*—(*vulgus*), *to make* public.
REPLEN'*ish*—(*plenus*), *to make* full again.
VAN'*ish*—(*vanus*), *to make* empty.

Ism,

Denotes *state of being; an idiom; doctrine of*

BAR'BAR*ism*—*state of being* barbarous.
FANAT'IC*ism*—*state of being* a fanatic.
HER'O*ism*—*state of being* a hero.
ID'IOT*ism*—*state of being* an idiot.
PA'GAN*ism*—*state of being* a pagan.
PAR'ALLEL*ism*—*state of being* parallel.
AN'GLIC*ism*—an English *idiom.*
GAL'LIC*ism*—(*Gallia*), a French *idiom.*
HEB'RA*ism*—a Hebrew *idiom.*
HEL'LEN*ism*—(*Hellen*, Gr.), a Greek *idiom.*
A'THE*ism*—(*theos*, Gr.), *the doctrine* that there is no God
CAL'VIN*ism*—*the doctrines of* Calvin.
CATHOL'IC*ism*—*the doctrines of* a Catholic.
EP'ICUR*ism*—*the doctrines of* Epicurus.
SCEP'TIC*ism*—*the doctrines of* the sceptics.
TO'RY*ism*—*the doctrines of* a tory.

Ist,

Denotes *one who,* or *the person that.*

AN'NAL*ist*—(*annus*), *one who* writes annals.
ART'*ist*—*one who* practices an art.
A'THE*ist*—(*theos*, Gr.), *one who* believes there is no God.
BOT'AN*ist*—*one who* studies botany.
DRAM'AT*ist*—(*drama*, Gr.), *one who* writes dramas.

FAB'UList—(*fabula*), *one who* writes fables.
FLO'RIst—(*flos*), *one who* cultivates flowers.
HU'MORist—*one who* is fond of humor.
JU'RIst—(*jus*), *one who* is learned in law.
LING'UIst—(*lingua*), *one who* studies languages.
NOV'EList—*one who* writes novels.
OC'ULIst—(*oculus*), *one who* treats diseases of the eye.
PSALMist—*one who* writes psalms.
TOBAC'CONist—*one who* sells tobacco.

Ite,

Denotes *one who*, or *the person that.*

CAN'AANite—*one who* dwells in Canaan.
FA'VORite—*one who* is favored.
LE'vite—*one who* is descended from Levi.

Ity, or *Ty*,

Denotes *being* or *state of being.*

ABIL'ity—*state of being* able.
AM'ity—(*amicus*), *state of being* friends.
ANTIQ'UIty—(*antiquus*), *state of being* ancient.
BREV'ity—(*brevis*), *state of being* short.
CAPTIV'ity—*state of being* a captive.
DIVIN'ity—*state of being* divine.
DOCIL'ity—*state of being* docile.
EQ'UIty—(*equus*), *state of being* just.
FELIC'ity—(*felix*), *state of being* happy.
FERTIL'ity—*state of being* fertile.
GENEROS'ity—*state of being* generous.
HOSTIL'ity—*state of being* hostile.
IMBECIL'ity—*state of being* imbecile.
INFIRM'ity—*state of being* infirm.
LOY'ALty—*state of being* loyal.
MATU'RIty—*state of being* mature.
NOV'ELty—*state of being* novel.
POPULAR'ity—*state of being* popular.
PUERIL'ity—*state of being* puerile.
SUBLIM'ity—*state of being* sublime.
SINCER'ity—*state of being* sincere.
TIMID'ity—*state of being* timid.
VELOC'ity—(*velox*), *state of being* swift.

Ive,

Denotes *one who*, or *the person that.*

CAP'TIve—(*capio*), *one who* is taken.
FU'GITive—(*fugio*), *one who* flies.

OP'ERATive—(*opera*), *one who* works.
NA'Tive—(*nascor*), *one who* is born.

Ive,

Denotes *having power*, or '*ing*.'

CORREC'Tive—*having power* to correct.
CORRO'sive—(*rodo*), *having power* to eat away.
DESTRUC'Tive—(*struo*), *having power* to destroy.
INVEN'Tive—*having power* to invent.
LEG'ISLATive—(*lex, latum*), *having power* to make laws.
LO'COMOTive—(*locus, moveo*), *having power* to move from its place.
ABU'sive—abus*ing*.
AC'Tive—act*ing*.
ADHE'sive—(*hæreo*), stick*ing* to.
AMU'sive—amus*ing*.
ATTRACT'ive—attract*ing*.
IMPER'ATive—(*impero*), command*ing*.
IMPUL'sive—(*pello*), driv*ing* on.
INCLU'sive—(*claudo*), shutt*ing* in.
PAS'sive—(*patior*), suffer*ing*.

Less,

Denotes *without*.

ART'*less*—*without* art.
CHILD'*less*—*without* a child.
DEFENCE'*less*—*without* defence.
FRUIT'*less*—*without* fruit.
POW'ER*less*—*without* power.
THOUGHT'*less*—*without* thought.
WORTH'*less*—*without* worth.

Like,

Denotes *like* or *resembling*

GOD'*like*—*like* or *resembling* God.
MAN'*like*—*like* or *resembling* man.
WAR'*like*—*like* or *resembling* war.

Ling,

Denotes *little, young*.

DAR'*ling*—a *little* dear.
DUCK'*ling*—a *little* or *young* duck.
GOS'*ling*—a *little* or *young* goose.
LORD'*ling*—a *little* or *young* lord.

Ly, for *Like*,

Denotes *like* or *resembling.*

BEAST'*ly*—*like* or *resembling* a beast.
COW'ARD*ly*—*like* or *resembling* a coward.
FA'THER*ly*—*like* or *resembling* a father.
GEN'TLEMAN*ly*—*like* or *resembling* a gentleman.
PRINCE'*ly*—*like* or *resembling* a prince.
WORLD'*ly*—*like* or *resembling* the world.

Ment,

Denotes *being* or *state of being; act of; the thing that.*

ABASE'*ment*—*state of being* abased.
CONCEAL'*ment*—*state of being* concealed.
EMBAR'RASS*ment*—*state of being* embarrassed.
ENTAN'GLE*ment*—*state of being* entangled.
EXCITE'*ment*—*state of being* excited.
REFINE'*ment*—*state of being* refined.
RETIRE'*ment*—*state of being* retired.
ACCOM'PLISH*ment*—*act of* accomplishing.
ACKNOWL'EDG*ment*—*act of* acknowledging.
ADJOURN'*ment*—*act of* adjourning.
CHASTISE'*ment*—*act of* chastising.
IMPEACH'*ment*—*act of* impeaching.
IMPRIS'ON*ment*—*act of* imprisoning.
INFRINGE'*ment*—*act of* infringing.
MAN'AGE*ment*—*act of* managing.
PAY'*ment*—*act of* paying.
PUN'ISH*ment*—*act of* punishing
SET'TLE*ment*—*act of* settling.
ABRIDG'*ment*—*the thing* abridged.
ACQUIRE'*ment*—*the thing* acquired.
AL'I*ment*—(*alo*), *the thing* that nourishes.
FRAG'*ment*—(*frango*), *the thing* broken.
INDUCE'*ment*—*the thing* which induces.
LIG'A*ment*—(*ligo*), *the thing* which binds.
NOUR'ISH*ment*—*the thing* that nourishes.
TEN'E*ment*—(*teneo*), *the thing* holden.

Mony,

Denotes *the state of being; thing that.*

AC'RI*mony*—(*acris*), *the state of being* sharp.
MAT'RI*mony*—(*mater*), *the state of being* a mother.
SANC'TI*mony*—(*sanctus*), *the state of being* sacred.
AL'I*mony*—(*alo*), the *thing that* is allowed for nourishment
PAT'RI*mony*—(*pater*), the *thing* or estate inherited from a father
TES'TI*mony*—(*testis*), the *thing that* is affirmed by a witness.

Ness,

Denotes *a being* or *state of being.*

BASE'*ness*—the *state of being* base.
BOLD'*ness*—the *state of being* bold.
COOL'*ness*—the *state of being* cool.
FAITH'FUL*ness*—the *state of being* faithful.
FOND'*ness*—the *state of being* fond.
GLAD'*ness*—the *state of being* glad.
HAP'PI*ness*—the *state of being* happy.
HAU'GHTI*ness*—the *state of being* haughty.
I'DLE*ness*—the *state of being* idle.
WEA'RI*ness*—the *state of being* weary.
WORTH'LESS*ness*—the *state of being* worthless.

Or,

Denotes *one who*, or *the person that.*

ACT'*or*—*one who* acts.
AGGRES'S*or*—(*gradior*), *one who* attacks.
AU'DIT*or*—(*audio*), *one who* hears.
BENEFAC'T*or*—(*bene, facio*), *one who* does good.
COLLEC'T*or*—*one who* collects.
CON'FESS*or*—*one who* confesses or hears another's confession.
CONSPIR'AT*or*—*one who* conspires.
CREA'T*or*—*one who* creates.
DEBT'*or*—*one who* is in debt.
DIREC'T*or*—*one who* directs.
DOC'T*or*—(*doceo*), *one who* teaches.
DO'N*or*—(*donum*), *one who* gives.
GLADIA'T*or*—(*gladius*), *one who* uses a sword.
IM'ITAT*or*—*one who* imitates.
INSPEC'T*or*—*one who* inspects.
INTER'ROGAT*or*—*one who* interrogates.
JU'R*or*—(*juro*), *one who* swears.
MI'N*or*—(*minuo*), *one who* is younger.
PREDIC'T*or*—*one who* predicts.
SPECTA'T*or*—(*specio*), *one who* beholds.
SUPERVI'S*or*—(*video*), *one who* overlooks
VIC'T*or*—(*vinco*), *one who* conquers.

Ory,

Denotes *the place where; thing that.*

AR'M*ory*—*the place where* arms are kept.
DEPOSI'T*ory*—*the place where* things are deposited.
DOR'MIT*ory*—(*dormio*), *a place where* persons sleep.
FAC'T*ory*—(*facio*), *a place where* articles are made.
OBSER'VAT*ory*—*the place where* observations are made.
PUR'GAT*ory*—(*purgo*), *the place where* souls are purged.

AU'DITory—(*audio*), *the thing that*, or those who hear.
DIREC'Tory—*the thing that*, or those who direct.
JU'DICATory—(*judico*), *the thing that*, or those who judge.
MEM'ory—*the thing* or faculty *that* remembers.

Ory,

Denotes *of; belonging* or *relating to; 'ing.'*

CONSOL'ATory—*belonging* or *relating to* consolation.
INTERROG'ATory—*belonging* or *relating to* an interrogatioı
PIS'CATory—(*piscis*), *belonging* or *relating to* fishes.
PREF'ATory—*belonging* or *relating to* a preface.
PROM'ISSory—*belonging* or *relating to* a promise.
VALEDIC'Tory—(*vale, dico*), *relating to* a farewell.
AD'ULATory—(*adulatum*), flatter*ing*.
COMPUL'sory—(*pello*), compell*ing*.
DECLAR'ATory—declar*ing*.
EXPLAN'ATory—explain*ing*.
INFLAM'MATory—inflam*ing*.
PROHIB'ITory—prohibit*ing*.
SATISFAC'Tory—satisfy*ing*.
TRAN'SITory—(*eo*), pass*ing* away.

Ose,

Denotes *full of.*

JOCose'—(*jocus*), *full of* jokes.
OPERose'—(*opera*), *full of* work.
VERBose'—(*verbum*), *full of* words.

Ous,

Denotes *full of; consisting of*, or *belonging to; 'ing.'*

CLAM'ORous—(*clamor*), *full of* clamor.
DAN'GERous—*full of* danger.
DU'BIous—(*dubius*), *full of* doubt.
GLO'RIous—*full of* glory.
GRIE'vous—*full of* grief.
LABO'RIous—*full of* labor.
LOQUA'CIous—(*loquor*), *full of* talk.
PER'ILous—*full of* peril.
POP'ULous—(*populus*), *full of* people.
A'QUEous—(*aqua*), *consisting of* or *belonging to* water.
BIL'Ious—(*bilis*), *consisting of* or *belonging to* bile.
CARTILAG'INous—*consisting of* cartilage.
CUTA'NEous—(*cutis*), *belonging to* the skin.
FI'BRous—(*fibra*), *consisting of* threads.
IG'NEous—(*ignis*), *consisting of* or *belonging to* fire.
LIG'NEous—(*lignum*), *consisting of* or *belonging to* wood
SONO'ROUS—(*sonus*), *consisting of* or *belonging to* sound.

VIT'REO*us*—(*vitrum*), *consisting of* or *belonging to* glass.
AMBITI'*ous*—(*eo*), go*ing* about.
CONTIG'U*ous*—(*tango*), touch*ing* together.
FALLA'CI*ous*—(*fallo*), deceiv*ing*.
LANIG'ER*ous*—(*lanis*, *gero*), bear*ing* wool.
MUR'DER*ous*—murder*ing*.
PERSPIC'U*ous*—(*specio*), appear*ing* through.
PISCIV'OR*ous*—(*piscis*, *voro*), devour*ing* fish.
TENA'CI*ous*—(*teneo*), hold*ing*.
TIM'OR*ous*—(*timeo*), fear*ing*.

Ry,

Denotes *a being; the art of; the place where.*

BRA'VE*ry*—*a being* brave.
GAL'LANT*ry*—*a being* gallant.
SLA'VE*ry*—*a being* a slave.
CHEM'IST*ry*—*the art* or *science of* the chemist.
COOK'E*ry*—*the art of* a cook.
RO'GUE*ry*—*the art of* a rogue.
SOPH'IST*ry*—*the art of* a sophist.
SUR'GE*ry*—*the art of* a surgeon.
COL'LIE*ry*—*the place where* coals are dug.
FISH'E*ry*—*the place where* fish are caught.
NURS'E*ry*—*the place where* the young are nursed

Ship,

Denotes *office of; state of.*

CLERK'*ship*—*the office of* a clerk.
DICTA'TOR*ship*—*the office of* a dictator.
HORSE'MAN*ship*—*the office of* a horseman.
PROFES'SOR*ship*—*the office of* a professor.
STEW'ARD*ship*—*the office of* a steward.
APPREN'TICE*ship*—*the state of* an apprentice.
BACH'ELOR*ship*—*the state of* a bachelor.
FRIEND'*ship*—*the state of* a friend.
RI'VAL*ship*—*the state of* a rival.
WARD'*ship*—*the state of* a ward.

Some,

Denotes *somewhat; full of.*

BLITHE'*some*—*somewhat* blythe.
DARK'*some*—*somewhat* dark.
GLAD'*some*—*somewhat* glad.
LONE'*some*—*somewhat* lone.
WEA'RI*some*—*somewhat* weary.
BUR'DEN*some*—*full of* burden.
FROL'IC*some*—*full of* frolic.

PLAY'*some*—*full of* play.
TOIL'*some*—*full of* toil.

Ster,

Denotes *one who.*

GAME'*ster*—*one who* games or gambles.
SONG'*ster*—*one who* sings.
YOUNG'*ster*—*one who* is young.

Tude, Ude,

Denotes *being* or *state of being.*

AL'TI*tude*—(*altus*), the *state of being* high.
AP'TI*tude*—(*aptus*), the *state of being* fit.
BEAT'I*tude*—(*beatus*), the *state of being* blessed.
FOR'TI*tude*—(*fortis*), the *state of being* brave.
GRATI'*tude*—(*gratia*), the *state of being* grateful.
LAS'SI*tude*—(*lassus*), the *state of being* weary.
MUL'TI*tude*—(*multus*), the *state of being* many.
QUI'ET*ude*—(*quies*), the *state of being* quiet.
REC'TI*tude*—(*rectus*), the *state of being* right.
SER'VI*tude*—(*servio*), the *state of being* a slave.
SOLIC'IT*ude*—(*solicitus*), the *state of being anxious.*
SOL'I*tude*—(*solus*), the *state of being* alone.
TUR'PI*tude*—(*turpis*), the *state of being* shameful.
DECREP'IT*ude*—the *state of being* decrepit.

Ule,

Denotes *little* or *small.*

ANIMAL'*cule*—a *little* animal.
GLOB'*ule*—a *little* globe.
GRAN'*ule*—(*granum*), a *little* grain.
RET'I*cule*—(*rete*), a *little* net or bag.
SPHER'*ule*—a *little* sphere.

Ure,

Denotes *the thing; state of being; act of.*

CREA'T*ure*—*the thing* created.
CUR'VAT*ure*—*the thing* that is curved.
ENCLO'*sure*—*the thing* that is enclosed.
MANUFAC'T*ure*—(*manus, facio*), *the thing* made by the hand
PIC'T*ure*—(*pingo*), *the thing* painted.
SCRIP'T*ure*—(*scribo*), *the thing* written.
TEX'T*ure*—(*textus*), *the thing* woven.
COMPO'*sure*—the *state of being* composed.
DISPLEAS'*ure*—the *state of being* displeased.
EXPO'*sure*—the *state of being* exposed.
PRIMOGEN'IT*ure*—(*primus, genus*), the *state of being* first born.
RAP'T*ure*—(*rapio*), the *state of being* seized (with pleasure)

CAP'*ture*—(*capio*), the *act of* taking.
DEPAR'*ture*—the *act of* departing.
DISCLO'*sure*—the *act of* disclosing.
INTERMIX'*ture*—the *act of* intermixing.
RUP'*ture*—(*ruptum*), the *act of* breaking.
SEIZ'*ure*—the *act of* seizing.

Ward,

Denotes *in the direction of*, or *looking toward.*

EAST'*ward*—*in the direction of* the east.
HEAV'EN*ward*—*in the direction of* heaven.
HOME'*ward*—*in the direction of* or *looking towards* home.
WIND'*ward*—*in the direction of* or *looking towards* the wind.

Y,

Denotes *the being; state of being; 'ing.'*

AN'ARCH*y*—(*arche*, Gr.), *state of being* without government.
ANTIP'ATH*y*—(*pathos*, Gr.), a feel*ing* against.
AP'ATH*y*—(*pathos*, Gr.), *state of being* without feeling.
HON'EST*y*—*state of being* honest.
MAS'TER*y*—*state of being* master.
MOD'EST*y*—*state of being* modest.
APOS'TAS*y*—(*stasis*, Gr.), a stand*ing* from or away.
CHIRO'MANC*y*—(*chir*, *mancia*, Gr.), a divin*ing* by the hand.
COL'LOQU*y*—(*loquor*), a talk*ing* together.
EU'PHON*y*—(*eu*, *phone*, Gr.), a sound*ing* well.
SYM'PATH*y*—(*pathos*, Gr.), a feel*ing* with.

Y,

Denotes *full of; consisting* or *made of.*

BLOOD'*y*—*full of* blood.
BRI'N*y*—*full of* brine.
DEW'*y*—*full of* dew.
DIRT'*y*—*full of* dirt.
DUST'*y*—*full of* dust.
GLOOM'*y*—*full of* gloom.
GUM'M*y*—*full of* gum.
HEALTH'*y*—*full of* health.
KNOT'T*y*—*full of* knots.
OIL'*y*—*consisting of* oil.
CHALK'*y*—*consisting of* chalk.
CLAY'E*y*—*consisting of* clay.
FLESH'*y*—*consisting of* flesh.
FLINT'*y*—*made* or *consisting of* flint.
HORN'*y*—*made* or *consisting of* horn.
ROCK'*y*—*made* or *consisting of* rock.
SAND'*y*—*made* or *consisting of* sand.
SLA'T*y*—*made* or *consisting of* slate.
SPON'G*y*—*made* or *consisting of* sponge.

EXERCISES

UPON THE

PREFIXES AND SUFFIXES.

As it is of great importance that the pupil should have a thorough knowledge of the signification of the Prefixes and Suffixes, before he commences the general analysis of words, it has been deemed proper to devote a further portion of the "First Book of Etymology" to this subject.

In Part I., the prefixes and suffixes have been pointed out, and their meaning, with copious illustrations, given; and the pupil should now be able to tell the force of any prefix or suffix that may be presented to him. But, in the general course of etymological study, the prefixes and suffixes are not *pointed out*, and the pupil will be obliged first to determine what they are—and in view of this fact the following exercises have been prepared. They comprise two lists of words, arranged in alphabetical order, one applying to the prefixes, the other to the suffixes. Care has been taken to select those words in which the root suffers little change in its combination with the prefix or suffix. Words formed immediately from foreign roots, or immediately from the words already existing in our own language, have been admitted indiscriminately into the list; both equally answer the purposes for which they are designed. In each case the original word is given, and, in that of foreign roots, the meaning accompanies it, so that the pupil may be supplied with every aid that is necessary in ascertaining the root, and may give up his whole time and attention to the consideration of the prefix or suffix.

I. PREFIXES.

Abbreviate—*brev-is*, short.
Abjure—*jur-o*, to swear.
Ablative—*lat-um*, to carry.
Aboriginal—*origo*, *origin-is*, the beginning.
Abrogate—*rogo*, *rogat-um*, to say.
Abscind—*scind-o*, to cut.
Absolution—*solvo*, *solut-um*, to loose.
Abstinence—*ten-eo*, to hold.
Abstruse—*trudo*, *tru-sum*, to thrust.
Absurd—*surd-us*, deaf.
Accelerate—*celer*, swift.
Accident—*cad-o*, to fall.
Acclivity—*cliv-us*, a slope.
Accuse—*caus-a*, a cause.
Accustom—custom.

Addict—*dico, dict-um*, to say.
Adhesion—*hæreo, hæs-um*, to stick.
Adjourn—*jour*, a day.
Adjudge—judge.
Adjunct—*jungo, junct-um*, to join.
Adjure—*jur-o*, to swear.
Administer—minister.
Admix—mix.
Advocate—*voc-o, vocat-um*, to call.
Adult—*ol-eo*, to grow.
Adverb—verb.
Affiance—*fid-es*, faith.
Affiliate—*fili-us*, a son.
Affront—*frons, front-is*, the forehead.
Afront—front.
Aggregate—*grex, greg-is*, a flock.
Allege—*leg-o*, to say.
Allure—*lure*, an enticement.
Anhelation—*halo*, to breathe.
Annihilate—*nihil*, nothing.
Antepenult—penult.
Apace—pace.
Appeal—*pel-lo*, to call.
Appear—*par-eo*, to become visible.
Applaud—*plaud-o*, to praise.
Apportion—portion.
Apposite—*posit-us*, placed.
Appreciate—*preci-um*, a price.
Approximate—*proxim-us*, next.
Ascend—*scand-o*, to climb.
Aslant—slant.
Aspire—*spir-o*, to breathe.
Assent—*sent-io*, to think.
Assume—*sum-o*, to take.
Attend—*tend-o*, to stretch.
Attenuate—*tenuis*, thin.
Attract—*traho, tract-um*, to draw.
Attrition—*trit-us*, rubbed.
Bedew—dew.
Bemoan—moan.
Besiege—siege.
Bethink—think.
Bewitch—witch.
Circumambulate—*ambul-o*, to walk.
Circumference—*fer-o*, to carry.
Circumflex—*flecto, flex-um*, to bend.
Circumfluent—*flu-o*, to flow.
Circumfuse—*fundo, fus-um*, to pour.
Circumlocution—*loquor, locut-us*, to speak.
Circumposition—position.
Circumstance—*st-o*, to stand.
Circumvent—*venio, vent-um*, to come.
Circumvolution—*volvo, volut-um*, to roll.
Coaction—action.
Coefficient—efficient.
Coessential—essential.
Coeval—*æv-um*, age.
Coextend—extend.
Cohesion—*hæreo, hæs-um*, to stick.
Combine—*bin-i*, two.
Commingle—mingle.
Compare—*par*, like.
Compassion—*patior, pass-us*, to suffer.
Compendium—*pend-o*, to weigh.
Compete—*pet-o*, to seek.
Complete—*plet-us*, filled.
Complicate—*plic-o*, to fold.
Component—*pon-o*, to put.
Compress—*premo, press-um*, to press.
Compulsion—*pello, puls-um*, to drive.
Compute—*put-o*, to think.
Concatenate—*caten-a*, a chain.
Concentre—*centr-um*, the centre.
Concise—*cædo, cæs-um*, to cut.
Concoct—*coquo, coct-um*, to cook.
Concord—*cor, cord-is*, the heart.
Concourse—*curro, curs-um*, to run.

Concussion—*cutio, cuss-um*, to strike.
Condense—*dens-us*, thick.
Condole—*dole-o*, to grieve.
Conduce—*duc-o*, to lead.
Confer—*fer-o*, to carry.
Confess—*fess-um*, to declare.
Confine—*fin-is*, a limit.
Conflagration—*flagr-o*, to burn.
Conflux—*fluo, flux-um*, to flow.
Confound—*fund-o*, to pour.
Confront—*frons, front-is*, the forehead.
Confuse—*fundo, fus-um*, to pour.
Congress—*gradior, gress-us*, to go by steps.
Conjecture—*jacio, ject-um*, to cast.
onjoin—join.
Conjugate—*jug-um*, a yoke.
Conjunct—*junct-us*, joined.
Conjure—*jur-o*, to swear.
Connect—*nect-o*, to bind.
Consanguinity—*sanguis, sanguin-is*, blood.
Conscript—*script-us*, written.
Consecutive—*sequor, secut-um*, to follow.
Consent—*sent-io*, to feel.
Consequent—*sequ-or*, to follow.
Consolidate—*solid-us*, solid.
Consonant—*son-o*, to sound.
Constant—*st-o*, to stand.
Constellation—*stell-a*, a star.
Constrain—*string-o*, to bind.
Construe—*stru-o*, to build.
Consume—*sum-o*, to take.
Contain—*ten-eo*, to hold.
Conterminous—*termin-us*, a boundary.
Context—*text-us*, woven.
Contingent—*tang-o*, to touch.
Continue—*ten-eo*, to hold.
Contract—*traho, tract-um*, to draw.
Contradistinguish—distinguish.
Contravene—*ven-io*, to come.
Controvert—*vert-o*, to turn.
Converge—*verg-o*, to verge.
Convert—*vert-o*, to turn.
Convey—*veh-o*, to carry.
Convivial—*viv-o*, to live.
Convulse—*vuls-us*, torn.
Copartner—partner.
Correspond—respond.
Counteract—act.
Countercharm—charm.
Countermand—*mand-o*, to order.
Counterpart—part.
Counterplot—plot.
Countersign—sign.
Decapitate—*caput, capit-is*, the head.
Declaim—*clam-o*, to shout.
Defame—fame.
Define—*fin-is*, the end.
Dedicate—*dico, dicat-um*, to set apart.
Deduct—same; *duco, duct-um*, to lead.
Deform—form.
Degenerate—*genus, gener-is*, a race.
Degree—*gradi-or*, to go by steps.
Deject—*jacio, jact-um*, to cast.
Delineate—*line-a*, a line.
Delinquent—*linqu-o*, to leave.
Delusive—*ludo, lus-um*, to play.
Demonstrate—*monstr-o*, to show.
Denote—*nota*, a mark.
Denounce—*nuncio*, to call.
Depict—*pingo, pict-um*, to paint.
Depopulate—*popul-us*, people.
Deprecate—*prec-or*, to pray.
Deposit—*pono, posit-um*, to put.
Depredate—*præd-a*, plunder.
Depress—*premo, press-um*, to press.
Derange—*rang*, order.
Deride—*ride-o*, to laugh.
Descend—*scand-o*, to climb.

Design—*sign-um*, a mark.
Desist—*sist-o*, to stand.
Desperate—*sper-o*, to hope.
Detect—*tego*, *tect-um*, to cover.
Determine—*termin-us*, a boundary.
Detrude—*trud-o*, to thrust.
Diffidence—*fid-es*, faith.
Digest—*gero*, *gest-um*, to carry.
Dilacerate—*lacer*, torn.
Dilapidation—*lapis*, *lapid-is*, a stone.
Disadvantageous — advantageous.
Disagree—agree.
Disappear—appear.
Disapprove—approve.
Disarrange—arrange.
Disbelieve—believe.
Disclose—*claudo*, *claus-um*, to shut.
Discomfort—comfort.
Discontent—content.
Discolor—color.
Discredit—credit.
Discourse—*curro*, *curs-um*, to run.
Discriminate—*crimen*, *crimin-is*, a crime.
Discursive—*curro*, *curs-um*, to run.
Discuss—*cutio*, *cuss-um*, to strike.
Disease—ease.
Disembark—embark.
Disengage—engage.
Disentangle—entangle.
Disfigure—figure.
Dishonor—honor.
Disingenuous—ingenuous.
Dislike—like.
Dislocate—*loc-us*, a place.
Dismember—member.
Dismount—mount.
Dismiss—*mitto*, *miss-um*, to send.
Dispense—*pendo*, *pens-um*. to weigh.
Disobliging—obliging.
Displace—place.
Dispose—*pono*, *posit-um*, to put.
Disproportion—proportion.
Dispute—*put-o*, to think.
Disqualify—qualify.
Disregard—regard.
Dissatisfy—satisfy.
Dissect—*seco*, *sect-um*, to cut.
Dissent—*sent-io*, to feel.
Dissimilar—similar.
Dissolve—*solv-o*, to loose.
Dissonant—*son-us*, a sound.
Dissuade—*suade-o*, to advise.
Distemper—temper.
Distil—*still-a*, a drop.
Distinguish—*stinguo*, to mark.
Disuse—use.
Divert—*vert-o*, to turn.
Divide—*vidu-o*, to part.
Ecstasy—*st-o*, to stand.
Eclectic—*lego*, *lect-um*, to choose.
Edition—*do*, *dat-um*, to give.
Educate—*duc-o*, to lead.
Effluence—*flu-o*, to flow.
Effusion—*fundo*, *fus-um*, to pour.
Ejaculate—*jacul-um*, a dart.
Elaborate—*labor*, labor.
Elapse—*labor*, *laps-us*, to slide.
Elect—*lego*, *lect-um*, to choose.
Elevate—*lev-o*, to lift.
Eligible—*leg-o*, to choose.
Elude—*lud-o*, to play.
Emanate—*man-o*, to flow.
Embowel—bowel.
Embroil—broil.
Empassion—passion.
Empurple—purple.
Emission—*mitto*, *miss-um*, to send.
Encage—cage.
Encourage—courage.
Enforce—force.
Engulf—gulf.
Enkindle—kindle.
Ennoble—noble.

Enormous—*norm-a*, a rule.
Enrage—rage.
Enslave—slave.
Entangle—tangle.
Entomb—tomb.
Entitle—title.
Eruption—*rumpo, rupt-um*, to break.
Evade—*vad-o*, to go.
Evident—*vid-eo*, to see.
Eviscerate—*viscus, viscer-is*, an entrail.
Exaggerate—*agger*, a heap.
Exalt—*alt-us*, high.
Excavate—*cav-us*, hollow.
Exceed—*ced-o*, to go.
Exclude—*claud-o*, to shut.
Excoriate—*cori-um*, the hide.
Excrescent—*cresc-o*, to grow.
Excursion—*curro, curs-um*, to run.
Execute—*sequor, secut-us*, to follow.
Exfoliate—*foli-um*, a leaf.
Exit—*eo, it-um*, to go.
Exonerate—*onus, oner-is*, a burden.
Exorable—*or-o*, to pray.
Expanse—*pando, pans-um*, to spread.
Expect—*specio, spect-um*, to look.
Expectorate—*pectus, pector-is*, the breast.
Expire—*spir-o*, to breathe.
Explicit—*plic-o*, to fold.
Explore—*plor-o*, to weep.
Explode—*plaudo*, to make a noise.
Export—*port-o*, to carry.
Expostulate—*postul-o*, to demand.
Expound—*pono*, to place.
Express—*premo, press-um*, to press.
Expulsion—*pello, puls-um*, to drive.
Expurgation—*purg-o, purgat-um*, to make clean.
Extempore—*tempus, tempor-is*, time.
Extend—*tend-o*, to stretch.
Exterminate—*termin-us*, a limit.
Extinct—*stinguo, stinct-um*, to mark.
Extirpate—*stirps, stirp-is*, a root.
Extol—*toll-o*, to raise.
Extrajudicial—judicial.
Extraprovincial—provincial.
Extravagance—*vag-or*, to wander.
Extrude—*trud-o*, to thrust.
Exult—*salio, salt-um*, to spring.
Forearm—arm.
Foredoom—doom.
Forefather—father.
Foreknow—know.
Forementioned—mentioned.
Forepart—part.
Foreshow—show.
Foretaste—taste.
Forethought—thought.
Forewarn—warn.
Ignominious—*nomen, nomin-is*, a name.
Illegal—legal.
Illegible—legible.
Illiberal—liberal.
Illicit—*lic-eo*, to be lawful.
Illimited—limited.
Illiterate—*liter-a*, a letter.
Illogical—logical.
Illumine—*lumen, lumin-is*, light.
Illustrate—*lustr-um*, a survey.
Imbibe—*bib-o*, to drink.
Imbody—body.
Imbosom—bosom.
Imbower—bower.
Immaterial—material.
Incorporeal—corporeal.
Immeasurable—measurable.
Immediate—*medi-us*, the middle.
Immerge—*merg-o*, to dip.

Immense—*metior*, *mens-us*, a measure.
Imminent—*min-eo*, to jut out.
Immobility—mobility.
Immoderate—moderate.
Immodest—modest
Immovable—movable.
Immure—*mur-us*, a wall.
Impalpable—*palp-o*, to touch softly.
Impart—*pars*, *part-is*, a part.
Impartial—partial.
Impatience—patience.
Impede—*pes*, *ped-is*, the foot.
Impel—*pel-lo*, to drive.
Impenetrable—penetrable.
Impenitence—penitence.
Imperishable—perishable.
Impersonal—personal.
Impious—pious.
Implacable—*plac-o*, to appease.
Implicate—*plic-o*, to fold.
Implore—*plor-o*, to cry.
Impolite—polite.
Imponderous—ponderous.
Import—*port-o*, to carry.
Impossible—possible.
Impost—*pono*, *posit-um*, to put.
Impotency—*potens*, powerful.
Impress—*premo*, *press-um*, to press.
Imprison—prison.
Improper—proper.
Impugn—*pugn-a*, a fight.
Impulse—*pello*, *puls-um*, to drive.
Impunity—*puni-o*, to punish.
Impure—pure.
Impute—*put-o*, to think.
Inaccurate—accurate.
Inaction—action.
Inalienable—alienable.
Inanimate—animate.
Inaptitude—aptitude.
Inattentive—attentive.
Inaudible—audible.
Incantation—*cano*, *cant-um*, to sing
Incapacitate—capacitate.
Incarcerate—*carcer*, a prison.
Incarnate—*caro*, *carn-is*, flesh.
Incertitude—*cert-us*, sure.
Incessant—*cedo*, *cess-um*, to yield.
Incidental—*cad-o*, to fall.
Incision—*cædo*, *cæs-um*, to cut.
Incivility—civility.
Inclement—*clemens*, *clement-is*, mild.
Incline—*clino*, to bend.
Inclusive—*claudo*, *claus-um*, to shut.
Incomplete—complete.
Inconvenient—convenient.
Incorporate—*corpus*, *corpor-is*, a body.
Incredulous—credulous.
Inculcate—*calco*, to tread.
Inculpable—culpable.
Incursion—*curro*, *curs-um*, to run.
Indecent—decent.
Indemnity—*damn-um*, loss.
Indent—*dens*, *dent-is*, a tooth.
Independent—dependent.
Index—*dic-o*, to set apart.
Indicate—*dic-o*, to speak.
Indignity—*dign-us*, worthy.
Indistinct—distinct.
Indocile—*doc-eo*, to teach.
Indolence—*dole-o*, to grieve.
Indubitable—dubitable.
Induce—*duc-o*, to lead.
Ineffectual—effectual.
Ineptitude—*apt-us*, fit.
Inequality—equality.
Inexperience—experience.
Infectious—*faci-o*, to make.
Infer—*fer-o*, to bear.
Infidel—*fid-es*, faith.
Infirm—firm.
Inflame—*flamm-a*, a flame.
Inflate—*flat-us*, a puff of wind
Inflection—*flect-o*, to bend.
Inflict—*fligo*, *flict-um*, to strike
Influx—*fluo*, *flux-um*, to flow.

Infraction—*frango, fract-um*, to break.
Infrangible—*frang-o*, to break.
Infrequent—frequent.
Infringe—*frang-o*, to break.
Inglorious—glorious.
Ingrate—*grat-us*, grateful.
Ingratiate—*grati-a*, favor.
Ingress—*gradior, gress-us*, to go.
Inharmonious—harmonious.
Inherent—*hær-eo*, to stick.
Inhuman—*hom-o*, a man.
Inject—*jacio, jact-um*, to cast.
Inimical—*amic-us*, a friend.
Iniquitous—*æqu-us*, right.
Injurious—*jus, jur-is*, law.
Injustice—*just-us*, just.
Innate—*nat-us*, born.
Innocent—*noc-eo*, to hurt.
Innovate—*nov-us*, new.
Innoxious—*noxi-us*, hurtful.
Innumerable—*numer-us*, number.
Inoffensive—offensive.
Inordinate—*ordo, ordin-is*, order.
Inquietude—quietude.
Inquire—*quær-o*, to seek.
Insatiate—*satis*, enough.
Inscribe—*scrib-o*, to write.
Insecure—secure.
Insensate—*sentio, sens-um*, to feel.
Insert—*sert-um*, to knit.
Insincere—sincere.
Insinuate—*sin-us*, the bosom.
Insipid—*sapi-o*, to taste of.
Insist—*sist-o*, to stand.
Insociable—sociable.
Insolvent—solvent.
Inspect—*specio, spect-um*, to look.
Inspire—*spir-o*, to breathe.
Instant—*st-o*, to stand.
Instigate—*stig-o*, to spur.
Instil—*still-a*, a drop.
Instruct—*struo, struct-um*, to build.
Insuperable—*super*, above.
Insurmountable—surmountable.
Insurrection—*surgo, surrect-um*, to rise.
Intemperate—temperate.
Intend—*tend-o*, to stretch.
Intercede—*ced-o*, to go.
Intercept—*capi-o*, to take.
Intercostal—*cost-a*, a rib.
Intercourse—*curro, curs-um*, to run.
Interdict—*dico, dict-um*, to say.
Intermediate—*medi-us*, the middle.
Intermeddle—meddle.
Interminable—*termin-us*, end.
Intermingle—mingle.
Intermission—*mitto, miss-um*, to send.
Intersperse—*spargo, spars-um*, to scatter.
Interstice—*st-o*, to stand.
Intervene—*ven-io*, to come.
Interweave—weave.
Intestate—*test-is*, a witness.
Intimidate—*tim-eo*, to fear.
Intolerant—tolerant.
Intomb—tomb.
Intrepid—*trepid-us*, trembling.
Introduce—*duc-o*, to lead.
Intrude—*trud-o*, to thrust.
Inundation—*undo, undat-um*, to rise in waves.
Invade—*vad-o*, to go.
Invalid—*valid-us*, strong.
Invaluable—valuable.
Invasion—*vado, vas-um*, to go
Invective—*veho, vect-um*, to carry.
Invert—*vert-o*, to turn.
Investigate—*vestigi-um*, a trace
Invest—*vest-is*, a garment.
Invigorate—*vigor*, strength.
Invincible—*vinc-o*, to conquer.
Invisible—visible.
Inviolable—*viol-o*, to hurt.
Invoke—*voc-o*, to call.
Involve—*volv-o*, to roll.

Involuntary—voluntary.
Irradiate—*radi-us*, a ray.
Irrational—rational.
Irremovable—removable.
Irresolute—resolute.
Irreverent—reverent.
Misadvised—advised.
Misbegotten—begotten.
Misbehave—behave.
Misbeliever—believer.
Miscal—call.
Mischance—chance.
Misdeed—deed.
Misemploy—employ.
Misfortune—fortune.
Misgovernment—government.
Misjudge—judge.
Mislead—lead.
Mismanage—manage.
Misproportion—proportion.
Misspend—spend.
Misreckon—reckon.
Misrule—rule.
Misshape—shape.
Misunderstand—understand.
Obligate—*lig-o*, to bind.
Obliterate—*liter-a*, a letter.
Obsequious—*sequ-or*, to follow.
Obstinate—*ten-eo*, to hold.
Obstruct—*struo*, *struct-um*, to build.
Obtain—*ten-eo*, to hold.
Obtrusion—*trudo*, *trus-um*, to thrust.
Obtuse—*tundo*, *tus-um*, to blunt.
Occur—*curr-o*, to run.
Offence—*fendo*, *fens-um*, to strike.
Omit—*mitt-o*, to send.
Opponent—*pon-o*, to put.
Oppress—*premo*, *press-um*, to press.
Oppugn—*pugn-a*, a fight.
Outbound—bound.
Outdare—dare.
Outfrown—frown.
Outguard—guard.
Outlaw—law.
Outmeasure—measure.
Outpour—pour.
Outshine—shine.
Outspread—spread.
Outwalk—walk.
Outweigh—weigh.
Overawe—awe.
Overbalance—balance.
Overcloud—cloud.
Overhang—hang.
Overhear—hear.
Overleap—leap.
Overmatch—match.
Overpower—power.
Overreach—reach.
Oversight—sight.
Overthrow—throw.
Overwrought—wrought.
Perception—*capio*, *capt-um*, to take.
Percussion—*cutio*, *cuss-um*, to strike.
Perdition—*do*, *dat-um*, to give.
Peregrinate—*ager*, *agri*, a field.
Perennial—*ann-us*, a year.
Permit—*mitt-o*.
Pernicious—*nex*, *nec-is*, death.
Perplex—*plic-o*, to fold.
Persecute—*sequor*, *secut-us*, to follow.
Persist—*sist-o*, to stand.
Perspicuous—*speci-o*, to see.
Persuade—*suad-eo*, to advise.
Pertain—*ten-eo*, to hold.
Pervade—*vad-o*, to go.
Pervert—*vert-o*, to turn.
Precaution—caution.
Preclude—*claud-o*, to shut.
Predetermine—determine.
Predispose—dispose.
Predominance — *domin-us*, a lord.
Preeminence—eminence.
Preface—*fari*, to speak.
Prejudice—*judic-o*, to judge.
Premeditate—meditate.
Premonitory—*moneo*, *monit-um*, to advise.

Preordain—ordain.
Preponderance—*pondus*, *ponder-is*, weight.
Prerequisite—requisite.
Presage—*sag-us*, wise.
Prescription—*scribo*, *script-um*, to write.
Present—*ens*, *ent-is*, being.
Presume—*sum-o*, to take.
Presumption—*sumo*, *sumpt-um*, to take.
Presuppose—suppose.
Pretense—*tendo*, *tens-um*, to stretch.
Prevalent—*val-eo*, to be strong.
Previous—*vi-a*, a way.
Procession—*cedo*, *cess-um*, to go.
Procure—*cur-a*, care.
Profane—*fan-um*, a temple.
Profess—*fess-um*, to declare.
Profit—*faci-o*, to make.
Prognosticate—*gnost-os*, known.
Progress—*gradior*, *gress-us*, to step.
Project—*jacio*, *jact-um*, to throw.
Progenitor—*genitor*, a father.
Prominent—*min-eo*, to jut out.
Promise—*mitto*, *miss-um*, to send.
Promontory—*mons*, *mont-is*, a mountain.
Promotion—*moveo*, *mot-um*, to move.
Pronounce—*nunci-o*, to tell.
Propagate—*ag-o*, to drive.
Propose—*pono*, *posit-um*, to put.
Propulsion—*pello*, *puls-um*, to drive.
Prorogation—*rogo*, *rogat-um*, to say.
Proscribe—*scrib-o*, to write.
Prosecute—*sequor*, *secut-us*, to follow.
Prostitute—*st-o*, to stand.
Prostrate—*sterno*, *strat-um*, to throw down.
Protect—*tego*, *tect-um*, to cover.
Protract—*traho*, *tract-um*, to draw.
Protrude—*trud-o*, to thrust.
Protuberance—*tuber*, a swelling.
Proverb—*verb-um*, a word.
Provide—*vid-eo*, to see.
Readmit—admit.
Reanimate—animate.
Reascend—ascend.
Reassure—assure.
Rebaptize—baptize.
Rebuild—build.
Recant—*cano*, *cant-um*, to sing.
Receive—*capi-o*, to take.
Recommit—commit.
Reconsecrate—consecrate.
Recreate—create.
Recriminate—*crimen*, *crimin-is*, a crime.
Recur—*curr-o*, to run.
Reddition—*do*, *dat-um*, to give.
Redeem—*em-o*, to buy.
Redeliver—deliver.
Redemption—*emo*, *empt-um*, to buy.
Reduce—*duc-o*, to lead.
Re-enforce—enforce.
Refer—*fer-o*, to carry.
Reflect—*flect-o*, to bend.
Refraction—*frango*, *fract-um*, to break.
Refrain—*fræn-um*, a bit.
Refrigerate—*frigus*, *frigor-is*, cold.
Refuge—*fugi-o*, to flee.
Refulgent—*fulg-eo*, to shine.
Refuse—*fundo*, *fus-um*, to pour.
Refute—*fut-o*, to disprove.
Regenerate—*genus*, *gener-is*, a family.
Reinspire—inspire.
Reject—*jacio*, *jact-um*, to throw.
Relapse—*laps-us*, fallen.
Relate—*fero*, *lat-um*, to carry.
Relinquish—*linq-uo*, to leave.
Reluctant—*luct-or*, to struggle

Remit—*mitt-o*, to send.
Remonstrate — *monstr-o*, to show.
Remove—move.
Remunerate—*munus*, *muner-is*, a gift.
Renovate—*nov-us*, new.
Repel—*pell-o*, to drive.
Repent—*pœn-a*, punishment.
Replete—*pleo*, *plet-um*, to fill.
Repose—*pono*, *posit-um*, to put.
Repugnance—*pugna*, a fight.
Repurchase—purchase.
Rescind—*scind-o*, to cut.
Reserve—*serv-o*, to keep.
Reside—*sed-eo*, to sit.
Resplendent—*splend-eo*, to shine.
Respond—*spond-eo*, to answer.
Restrain—*string-o*, to hold fast.
Restrict—*strict-um*, to hold fast.
Result—*salio*, *salt-um*, to leap.
Retain—*ten-eo*, to hold.
Retaliate—*tal-is*, such.
Retention—*teneo*, *tent-um*, to hold.
Retrace—trace.
Retract—*traho*, *tract-um*, to draw.
Retribution—*tribuo*, *tribut-um*, to give back.
Retrogression—*gradior*, *gress-us*, to go by steps.
Retrospect—*specio*, *spect-um*, to look.
Reunite—unite.
Revert—*vert-o*, to turn.
Revisit—visit.
Revival—*viv-o*, to live.
Revolve—*volvo*, to roll.
Revomit—vomit.
Secession—*cedo*, *cess-um*, to go.
Seclude—*claud-o*, to shut.
Select—*lego*, *lect-um*, to choose.
Simple—*plic-o*, to fold.
Sincere—*cer-a*, wax.
Sinecure—*cur-a*, care.
Subdivide—divide.
Subdue—*duc-o*, to lead.
Subject—*jacio*, *jact-um*, to throw.
Subjugate—*jug-um*, a yoke.
Sublingual—*lingu-a*, the tongue.
Sublunary—*lun-a*, the moon.
Submarine—marine.
Submit—*mitt-o*, to send.
Subordinate—ordinate.
Subscription—*scribo*, *script-um*, to write.
Subsequent—*sequ-or*, to follow
Subservience—*servi-o*, to serve.
Subside—*sed-eo*, to sit.
Subsist—*sist-o*, to stand.
Substance—*st-o*, to stand.
Subtract—*traho*, *tract-um*, to draw.
Subtend—*tend-o*, to stretch.
Subterraneous—*terr-a*, earth.
Subtrahend—*trah-o*, to draw.
Subvert—*vert-o*, to turn.
Success—*cedo*, *cess-um*, to go.
Succinct—*cingo*, *cinct-um*, to bind.
Suffuse—*fundo*, *fus-um*, to pour.
Suggest—*gero*. *gest-um*, to carry.
Superabundant—abundant.
Superadd—add.
Superannuate—*ann-us*, a year.
Superexcellent—excellent.
Superlative—*lat-um*, to bear.
Supernatural—natural.
Supernumerary—*numerus*, a number.
Superstructure—*struo*, *struct-um*, to build.
Supervene—*ven-io*, to come.
Supervise—*video*, *vis-um*, to look.
Supplant—plant.
Support—*port-o*, to carry.
Suppurate—*pus*, *pur-is*, the matter from sores.
Surmise—*mitto*, *miss-um*, to send.
Surname—name.
Surplice—*plic-o*, to fold.

Survive—*viv-o*, to live.
Suspense—*pendeo*, *pens-um*, to hang.
Suspire—*spir-o*, to breathe.
Sustenance—*ten-eo*, to hold.
Traduce—*duc-o*, to lead.
Transatlantic—atlantic.
Transcribe—*scrib-o*, to write.
Transfer—*fer-o*, to carry.
Transfix—fix.
Transfuse—*fundo*, *fus-um*, to pour.
Transgress—*gradior*, *gress-us*, to go.
Transient—*iens*, *ient-is*, going.
Translucent—*lux*, *luc-is*, light.
Transmission—*mitto*, *miss-um*, to send.
Transmute—*mut-o*, to change.
Transpire—*spir-o*, to breathe.
Transplant—plant.
Unabashed—abashed.
Unbolt—bolt.
Unbecoming—becoming.
Unbuckle—buckle.
Unblemished—blemished.
Unburthen—burthen.
Unbought—bought.
Uncase—case.
Uncharitable—charitable.
Unclose—close.
Uncommon—common.
Undeceive—deceive.
Underclerk—clerk.
Underhand—hand.
Undermine—mine.
Underrate—rate.
Undersecretary—secretary
Underwood—wood.
Undutiful—dutiful.
Unfetter—fetter.
Unforbidden—forbidden
Unharness—harness.
Unholy—holy.
Unkennel—kennel.
Unknown—known.
Unlatch—latch.
Unlawful—lawful.
Unmuffle—muffle.
Unpolished—polished.
Unriddle—riddle.
Unrighteous—righteous.
Unsettle—settle.
Unsuitable—suitable.
Untwist—twist.
Unwarlike—warlike.
Unwind—wind.
Unworthy—worthy.

II. SUFFIXES.

Absurdity—absurd.
Accountant—account.
Accumulation—accumulate.
Acerbity—*acerb-us*, sour.
Achievement—achieve.
Acrimony—*acr-is*, sharp.
Action, Active, Actor—act.
Activity—active.
Acuteness—acute.
Adoption—adopt.
Adversity—adverse.
Advisable advise.
Affectionate—affection.
Afflictive—afflict.
Agency—*ag-o*, to do or act.
Agent—the same.
Algebraist—algebra.
Aliment—*al-o*, to nourish.
Alimentary—aliment.
Allegorical—allegory.
Alterable—*alter*, another.
Altitude—*alt-us*, high.
Amicable—*amic-us*, a friend
Amorous—*amor*, love.
Amplitude—*ampl-us*, large
Amplify—*ampl-us*, large.

Anatomist—anatomy.
Angular—*angul-us*, a corner.
Animalcule—animal.
Animate—*anim-a*, life.
Annual—*ann-us*, a year.
Annuitant—annuity.
Antiquary—*antiqu-us*, old, ancient.
Antiquity—the same.
Apiary—*ap-is*, a bee.
Appearance—appear.
Applauder—applaud.
Aptitude—*apt-us*, fit.
Appointment—appoint.
Aquatic—*aqua*, water.
Arable—*ar-o*, to plough.
Architecture—architect.
Ardent—*ard-eo*, to burn.
Ardency—the same.
Arenaceous—*aren-a*, sand.
Aridity—*arid-us*, dry.
Arithmetician—arithmetic.
Armory—*arm-a*, arms.
Artful—art.
Asperity—*asper*, rough.
Assessor—assess.
Association—associate.
Astral—*astr-on*, a star.
Atheistical—atheist.
Atrocious—*atrox*, *atroc-is*, fierce.
Atrocity—the same.
Attendant—attend.
Audacious—*audax*, *audac-is*, bold.
Audible—*audi-o*, to hear.
Audience—the same.
Auditor—the same.
Austerity—*auster-us*, severe.
Autumnal—autumn.
Available—avail.
Aviary—*av-is*, a bird.
Baptist—*bapt-o*, to dip.
Bandage—band.
Banishment—banish.
Barbarian—*barbar-us*, rude.
Barbarism—the same.
Barrenness—barren.
Beatitude—*beat-us*, blessed.
Bedlamite—bedlam.
Beggarly—beggar.
Believer—believe.
Benignity—*benign-us*, kind.
Bigotry—bigot.
Blameless—blame.
Blindness—blind.
Botanical—botany.
Bountiful—bounty.
Brevity—*brev-is*, short.
Brighten—bright.
Brotherhood—brother.
Brutal, Brutish—brute.
Brutalize, Brutality—brutal.
Business—busy.
Calculate—*calcul-us*, a pebble.
Calculator—calculate.
Calumniator—calumniate.
Calvinist—Calvin.
Canine—*can-is*, a dog.
Canticle—*cant-us*, a song.
Captive—*capt-um*, to take.
Capture—the same.
Captivate, Captivity—captive.
Careless—care.
Carelessness—careless.
Carnal—*caro*, *carn-is*, flesh.
Cautionary—caution.
Cavity—*cav-us*, hollow.
Celebrate—*celebr-is*, renowned.
Celerity—*celer*, swift.
Celibacy—*cæleb-s*, single.
Cellarage—cellar.
Censor—*cens-eo*, to judge
Censorship—censor.
Certify—*cert-us*, sure.
Cession—*cedo*, *cess-um* to yield.
Changeable—change.
Chastity—chaste.
Cheerful—cheer.
Chorister—*chor-us*, a band of singers.
Christian—Christ.
Chronologist, Chronological—chronology.
Circular—*circul-us*, a circle.

Circulate—the same.
Citation—*cito, citat-um*, to call.
Civility, Civilize—civil.
Claimant—claim.
Clamorous—*clamor*, noise.
Clamorously—clamorous.
Clarify—*clar-us*, clear.
Cleanliness—cleanly.
Climber—climb.
Coinage—coin.
Collection—collect.
Commentary—comment.
Committee—commit.
Compliance—comply.
Conductor—conduct.
Confectionary—confection.
Conference—confer.
Copartnership—copartner.
Copious—*copi-a*, plenty.
Copiously—copious.
Coralline—coral.
Cordiality—cordial.
Coriaceous—*cori-um*, leather.
Coronation—*coron-a*, a crown.
Coronet—the same.
Corporate—*corpus, corpor-is*, a body.
Corporeal—the same.
Corpuscle—the same.
Correspondence, Correspondent —correspond.
Corruptible—corrupt.
Cottager—cottage.
Courageous—courage.
Courtship—court.
Creator—create.
Credible—*cred-o*, to believe.
Credulity—*credul-us*, easy of belief.
Criminal—*crimen, crimin-is*, a crime.
Critic—*crit-es*, a judge.
Criticise—critic.
Crookedness—crooked.
Cruelty—cruel.
Crystallize—crystal.
Culpable—*culp-a*, fault.
Culture—*colo, cult-um*, to till.

Curious—*cura*, care.
Current—*curr-o*, to run.
Currency—the same.
Curricle—the same.
Customary—custom.
Deafen—deaf.
Debauchee—debauch.
Decorate—*decor*, grace.
Defrauder—defraud.
Deify—*de-us*, God.
Deism—the same.
Deist—the same.
Deistical—deist.
Deliberative—deliberate.
Delightful—delight.
Density—dense.
Dental—*dens, dent-is*, a tooth.
Dentist—the same.
Dependence—depend.
Depositary—deposit.
Despotism, Despotic—despot.
Derogatory—derogate.
Detestable—detest.
Devotion—devote.
Diabolical—*diabol-us*, the devil.
Diary—*di-es*, a day.
Dictate—*dict-um*, a word.
Dictator—dictate.
Difference—differ.
Diffusive—diffuse.
Dignity—*dign-us*, worthy.
Dispensary—dispense.
Discomposure—discompose.
Discovery—discover.
Dissenter—dissent.
Disturbance—disturb.
Divergent—diverge.
Doctor—*doct-us*, taught.
Dominant—*domin-us*, a lord.
Dominion—the same.
Donation—*don-o, donat-um*, to give.
Donee—the same.
Donor—the same.
Dormant—*dorm-io, dormit-um* [to sleep.
Dormitory—the same.
Doubtless—doubt.
Dramatic—*drama*, a play.

Dreadful—dread.
Druggist—drug.
Drunkenness—drunken.
Dubious—*dubi-um*, doubt.
Dwarfish—dwarf.
Earldom—earl.
Earthen—earth.
Edition, Editor—edit.
Election, Elective—elect.
Elephantine—elephant.
Enchantment—enchant.
Envious—envy.
Epicurean—epicure.
Episcopalian—episcopal.
Epistolary—*epistol-a*, a letter.
Equality, Equalize—equal.
Equity—*equ-us*, just.
Errant—*err-o*, *errat-um*, to wander.
Erratic—the same.
Erroneous—the same.
Estimate—*æstim-o*, to value.
Ethics—*eth-os*, manners.
Etymological—etymology.
Executor, Executive—execute.
Executorship—executor.
Exhaustible—exhaust.
Existent—exist.
Expectancy—expect.
Extraction—extract.
Fabrication—*fabric-o*, *fabricat-um*, to make or frame.
Fabulous—*fabula*, a fable.
Facilitate—facility.
Facility—*facil-is*, easy.
Factor—*facio*, *fact-um*, to do or make.
Fallible—*fall-o*, *fals-um*, to deceive.
Fallacy—the same.
Falsify—the same.
Familiar—family.
Famous—*fam-a*, fame.
Farinaceous—*farin-a*, meal.
Farmer—farm.
Fatherless—father.
Faulty—fault.
Fellowship—fellow.
Feminine—*femin-a*, a woman.
Fertility, Fertilize—fertile.
Fervency—*ferv-eo*, to be warm.
Fervid—the same.
Festive—*fest-um*, a feast.
Festivity—festive.
Feverish—fever.
Fibrous—*fibr-a*, a thread.
Fidelity—*fidel-is*, faithful.
Fierceness—fierce.
Filial—*fili-us*, a son.
Filthy—filth.
Final—*fin-is*, the end.
Finery—fine.
Finish—*fin-is*, the end.
Finite—the same.
Fissure—*findo*, *fiss-um*, to cleave or cut.
Flagrancy—*flagr-o*, to burn.
Flattery—flatter.
Flaxen—flax.
Flexible—*flecto*, *flex-um*, to bend.
Floral—*flos*, *flor-is*, a flower.
Florist—the same.
Flourish—the same.
Fluctuate—*fluct-us*, a wave.
Fluctuation—fluctuate.
Fluent—*flu-o*, to flow.
Fluid—the same.
Fluidity—fluid.
Foliage—*foli-um*, a leaf.
Fondling—fond.
Forbearance—forbear.
Foreigner—foreign.
Formal—form.
Formality—formal.
Formidable—*formid-o*, fear
Fortify—*fort-is*, strong.
Fortitude—the same.
Fortunate—fortune.
Fraction—*frang-o*, *fract-um*, to break.
Fracture—the same
Fragile—the same
Fragment—the same.
Fragmentary—fragment.
Frailty—frail.

Fragrance—*fragr-o*, to smell sweetly.
Fraternal—*frater*, a brother.
Friction—*frico*, *frict-um*, to rub.
Friendless—friend.
Frightful—fright.
Frigid—*frig-us*, cold.
Frigidity—frigid.
Frontal—*frons*, *front-is*, the forehead.
Frustrate—*frustr-a*, in vain.
Fugitive—*fugio*, *fugit-um*, to flee.
Fulgency—*fulg-eo*, to shine.
Fulness—full.
Fusible—*fundo*, *fus-um*, to pour, to melt.
Fusion—the same.
Gazetteer—gazette.
Geographer—geography.
Girlish—girl.
Gladiator—*gladi-us*, a sword.
Glandule—gland.
Globule—globe.
Globular—globule.
Glorious—glory.
Golden—gold.
Goodly—good.
Government—govern.
Governor—govern.
Graduate—*grad-us*, a step.
Grammarian—grammar.
Granary—*gran-um*, a grain of corn.
Granule—the same.
Gratitude—*grat-us*, grateful.
Gratuity—the same.
Gravity—*grav-is*, heavy.
Grocery—grocer.
Groundless—ground.
Guardian—guard.
Guardianship—guardian.
Guiltiness—guilty.
Habitable—*habit-o*, to dwell in; to inhabit.
Hairy—hair.
Hasten—haste.
Harmonious—*harmoni-a*, agreement.
Hazardous—hazard.
Healthful—health.
Heavenly—heaven.
Herbage—*herb-a*, an herb.
Heretical—heretic.
Heroic—hero.
Heroism—hero.
Hinderance—hinder.
Historian, Historic—history.
Honorary—honor.
Horrible—*horr-eo*, to be dreadful.
Horrid—the same.
Hostile—*host-is*, an enemy.
Houseless—house.
Humiliate—*humil-is*, humble.
Humility—the same.
Humorsome—humor.
Igneous—*ign-is*, fire.
Illness—ill.
Illustrative—illustrate.
Imagery—image.
Imaginary, Imaginable—imagine.
Imitation, Imitator—imitate.
Immortality, Immortalize—immortal.
Impurity—impure.
Indenture—indent.
Induction, Inductive—induct.
Indulgence—indulge.
Infantile—infant.
Inferiority—inferior.
Informant—inform.
Inhabitant—inhabit.
Inheritor—inherit.
Insinuation—insinuate.
Insular—*insul-a*, an island.
Integrity—*integer*, whole.
Interpreter—interpret.
Interrogative, Interrogatory—interrogate.
Intrepidity—intrepid.
Introductory—introduce.
Invention—invent.
Jealousy—jealous.

Jocose—*joc-us*, a joke.
Journalist—journal.
Joyful—joy.
Junction—*jungo, junct-um*, to join.
Juncture—the same.
Jurist—*jus, jur-is*, law.
Juror—*jur-o*, to swear.
Justice, Justify—just.
Kindness—kind.
Knavery, Knavish—knave.
Laboratory—*laboro, laborat-um*, to labor.
Ladyship—lady.
Lapidary—*lapis, lapid-is*, a stone.
Lassitude—*lass-us*, weary.
Lateral—*latus, later-is*, a side.
Latinism, Latinist—Latin.
Latitude—*lat-us*, broad.
Laudable—*laud-o*, to praise.
Lawyer—law.
Leaden—lead.
Leakage—leak.
Lecture—*lego, lect-um*, to read.
Lecturer—lecture.
Legal—*lex, leg-is*, law.
Legality, Legalize—legal.
Legate—*leg-o*, to send as an ambassador.
Legible—*leg-o*, to read.
Legionary—legion.
Leisurely—leisure.
Levity—*lev-is*, light.
Liberal, Liberty—*liber*, free.
Liberality—liberal.
Library—*liber, libr-i*, a book.
Librarian—library.
Ligament—*lig-o, ligat-um*, to bind.
Ligature—the same.
Ligneous—*lign-um*, wood.
Likelihood—likely.
Lineal—*line-a*, a line.
Literary—*litera*, a letter.
Loathsomeness—loathsome.
Local—*loc-us*, a place.
Locate—the same.
Longitude—*long-us*, long.
Lucid—*lux, luc-is*, light.
Luminary—*lumen, lumin-is*, light.
Luminous—the same.
Lunar—*lun-a*, the moon.
Luxurious—luxury.
Magician—magic.
Magistracy—*magister, magistr-i*, a master.
Magnetism—magnet.
Magnify—*magn-us*, great.
Magnitude—the same.
Maidenly—maiden.
Malice—*mal-us*, bad.
Malleable—*malle-us*, a hammer.
Mandate—*mand-o*, to command.
Mansion—*maneo, mans-um*, to stay.
Marine—*mar-e*, the sea.
Mariner—marine.
Marriage—marry.
Marshy—marsh.
Martial—*mars, mart-is*, the god of war.
Martyrdom—martyr.
Marvellous—marvel.
Masculine—*mascul-us*, a male.
Matchless—match.
Maternal—*mater, matr-is*, a mother.
Matrimony—the same.
Maturity—*matur-us*, ripe.
Measurement—measure.
Mechanics—*mechan-ao*, to invent.
Mediation, Mediator—mediate.
Meditation, Meditative—meditate.
Meekness—meek.
Meliorate—*melior*, better.
Mendicant—*mendic-us*, a beggar.
Mensuration—*mensur-a*, a measure.
Mental—*mens, ment-is*, the mind.

Merchant—*merc-or*, to buy and sell.
Merriment—merry.
Microscopic—microscope.
Migration—*migro, migrat-um*, to change one's abode.
Military—*miles, milit-is*, a soldier.
Minor—*minor*, less.
Minuend—*minu-o*, to lessen.
Misery—*miser*, wretched.
Miserable—the same.
Mission—*mitto, miss-um*, to send.
Missionary—mission.
Mitigation—mitigate.
Moderator—moderate.
Moisture—moist.
Momentary—moment.
Moneyless—money.
Monitor—*moneo, monit-um*, to advise.
Monkish—monk.
Moral—*mos, mor-is*, custom.
Moralist, Morality—moral.
Morbid—*morb-us*, a disease.
Motherly—mother.
Motion—*moveo, mot-um*, to move.
Mouldy—mould.
Mournful—mourn.
Multitude—*mult-us*, many.
Mutable—*mut-o, mutat-um*, to change.
Mutation—the same.
Nakedness—naked.
Narrative—narrate.
Natal, Native—*nat-us*, born.
Natural—nature.
Naturalist, Naturalize—natural.
Nautical—*naut-a*, a sailor.
Naval—*nav-is*, a ship.
Navigator—navigate.
Negation—*neg-o, negat-um*, to deny.
Negotiate—*negoti-um*, business.
Negotiator—negotiate.
Neighborhood—neighbor.
Nervous—nerve.
Notice—*nosco, not-um*, to know.
Notify—the same.
Novel—*nov-us*, new.
Novelist, Novelty—novel.
Nullify—*null-us*, none.
Numberless—number.
Numerical, Numerous—*numer-us*, number.
Oaken—oak.
Obligee—oblige.
Observance—observe.
Occupancy, Occupant—occupy.
Occurrence—occur.
Ocular—*ocul-us*, the eye.
Odious—*odi*, to hate.
Offender—offend.
Operate—*opus, oper-is*, work.
Operative—operate.
Operose—*opus, oper-is*, work.
Optics—*opt-o*, to see.
Oral—*or-o, orat-um*, to ask.
Oration—the same.
Orator—the same.
Orderly—order.
Ornament—*orn-o*, to deck.
Osseous—*os, oss-is*, a bone.
Outrageous—outrage.
Pacify—*pax, pac-is*, peace.
Painful—pain.
Pamphleteer—pamphlet.
Parent—*par-io*, to bring forth.
Parentage—parent.
Parsimony—*parco, pars-um*, to spare.
Particle—*pars, part-is*, a part.
Partition—the same.
Partial—the same.
Partisan—the same.
Pasture—*pasco, past-um*, to feed.
Passive—*patior, pass-us*, to suffer.
Patentee—patent.
Paternal—*pater*, a father.
Patience—*pati-or*, to suffer.
Patient—the same.

Patrimony—*pater*, a father.
Patron—the same.
Pavement—pave.
Peaceableness—peaceable.
Peasantry—peasant.
Pecuniary—*pecuni-a*, money.
Peerage—peer.
Penal—*pœn-a*, punishment.
Penance—the same.
Pendent—*pend-eo*, to hang.
Penetration—penetrate.
Penitence—*pœnit-eo*, to repent.
Penitent—the same.
Pension—*pendo*, *pens-um*, to [weigh.
Pensioner—pension.
Perfidious—perfidy.
Periodical—period.
Persecutor—persecute.
Personate—person.
Petition—*pet-o*, to beg.
Physical—*phys-is*, nature.
Physics—the same.
Planetary—a planet.
Piety—*pi-us*, religious.
Pilgrimage—pilgrim.
Pitiless—pity.
Pleasantry—pleasant.
Pleasure—please.
Plenary—*plen-us*, full.
Plenitude—the same.
Plenteous, Plentiful—plenty.
Plumage—*plum-a*, a feather.
Pneumatics—*pneuma*, *pneumat-os*, air.
Poetry—poet.
Poisonous—poison.
Politeness—polite.
Pollution—pollute.
Ponderous—*pondus*, *ponder-is*, weight.
Popular—*popul-us*, the people.
Populous—the same.
Portable—*port-o*, to carry.
Portage—the same.
Porter—the same.
Posterior—*poster-us*, coming after.
Posterity—the same.
Possessor—possess.
Posture—*pon-o*, *posit-um*, to place.
Potation—*pot-o*, *potat-um*, to [drink.
Potion—the same.
Potentate—potent.
Precedence, Precedent—precede.
Predatory—*præd-a*, booty.
Preferment—prefer.
Pressure—press.
Preventive—prevent.
Priesthood—priest.
Primary—*prim-us*, first.
Princedom—prince.
Private—*priv-us*, one's own.
Privacy—the same.
Probationary—probation.
Prophetic—prophet.
Propitiatory—propitiate.
Proportionate—proportion.
Probity—*prob-us*, approved.
Protector—protect.
Protestant—protest.
Providence—provide.
Publisher—publish.
Puerile—*puer*, a boy.
Pulverize—*pulvis*, *pulver-is*, dust.
Punster—pun.
Purify—pure.
Puritanism—puritan.
Purity—pure.
Putrescence—*putr-is*, rotten.
Quarrelsome—quarrel.
Questionable—question.
Quickness—quick.
Quiescence—*quies*, quiet.
Quietude—quiet.
Radiance—*radi-us*, the spoke of a wheel, a ray.
Radical—*radix*, *radic-is*, a root.
Ramify—*ram-us*, a branch.
Rapidity—rapid.
Reconcilement—reconcile.
Rectify—*rect-us*, straight.
Rectitude—*rect-us*, straight.
Reflection, Reflective—reflect.

Regal—*rex, reg-is*, a king.
Regardless—regard.
Regent—*rex, reg-is*, a king.
Regency—the same.
Regular—*regul-a*, a rule.
Regularity—regular.
Repentance, Repentant—repent.
Reproachful—reproach.
Reptile—*repo, rept-um*, to creep.
Resident, Residence—reside.
Respondent—respond.
Reticule—*rete*, a net.
Revelry—revel.
Reversionary—reversion.
Rewarder—reward.
Rhetorician—rhetoric.
Rigid—*rig-eo*, to be stiff.
Rigidity—rigid.
Ripeness—ripe.
Rivalry—rival.
Romish—Rome.
Rotary—*rot-a*, a wheel.
Rotation—the same.
Royalist, Royalty—royal.
Rupture—*rumpo, rupt-um*, to break.
Rural—*rus, rur-is*, the country.
Rustic—the same.
Rusty—rust.
Sacrament—*sacer, sacr-i*, sacred.
Sagacity — *sagax, sagac-is*, wise.
Salutary—*salus, salut-is*, health.
Salutation—*saluto, salutat-um*, to greet.
Salvation—*salvus*, safe.
Sanctify—*sanct-us*, holy.
Sanctimony—the same.
Sanctuary—the same.
Sanguinary—*sanguis, sanguin-is*, blood.
Sanity—*san-us*, sound.
Satiety—*sat-is*, enough.
Scholar—*schol-a*, a school.
Scholarship—scholar.
Scornful—scorn.
Scripture—*scribo, script-um*, to write.
Sculptor—*sculpo, sculpt-um*, to carve.
Sculpture—the same.
Section—*seco, sect-um*, to cut.
Security—secure.
Sedentary—*sed-eo*, to sit.
Sediment—the same.
Sentient—*senti-o, sens-um*, to feel.
Sentiment—the same.
Sensual—the same.
Sequel—*sequ-or*, to follow.
Serpent—*serp-o*, to creep.
Serpentine—serpent.
Serrate—*serr-a*, a saw.
Servant—*serv-io*, to serve.
Service—the same.
Servile—the same.
Servility—servile.
Servitude—*serv-io*, to serve.
Session—*sedeo, sess-um*, to sit.
Setacious—*set-a*, a bristle.
Severity—severe.
Shadowy—shadow.
Shameful—shame.
Sharpness—sharp.
Shelterless—shelter.
Sidereal—*sidus, sider-is*, a star
Signalize—signal.
Silken—silk.
Similarity—similar.
Singularity—singular.
Smuggler—smuggle.
Sociable—*soci-us*, a companion.
Social—the same.
Society—the same.
Solar—*sol*, the sun.
Solidity—solid.
Solitude—*sol-us*, alone.
Soluble—*solv-o, solut-um*, to loose.
Solvent—the same.
Sonorous—*sonus, sonor-is*, a sound.
Sophism—*soph-ia*, wisdom.
Sophist—the same.

Sophistry—sophist.
Sorrowful—sorrow.
Spectator—*specto*, *spectat-um*, to look.
Speculation—speculate.
Spinster—spin.
Spiritualize—spiritual.
Stiffen—stiff.
Stormy—storm.
Stricture—*stringo*, *strict-um*, to bind.
Structure—*struo*, *struct-um*, to build.
Suavity—*suav-is*, sweet.
Subservient—subserve.
Subsistence—subsist.
Supremacy—supreme.
Surveyor—survey.
Sylvan—*sylv-a*, a wood.
Tangible—*tang-o*, to touch.
Temporal—*tempus*, *tempor-is*, time.
Temporary—the same.
Temporize—the same.
Tenable—*ten-eo*, to hold.
Tenant—the same.
Tenement—the same.
Tendency—*tend-o*, *tens-um*, to stretch.
Tension—the same.
Tenure—*ten-eo*, to hold.
Terminate—*termin-us*, a limit.
Testament—*test-is*, a witness.
Testamentary—testament.
Testator—*test-is*, a witness.
Testify—the same.
Texture—*texo*, *text-um*, to weave.
Theological—theology.
Timid—*tim-eo*, to fear.
Timidity—timid.
Torrid—*torr-eo*, to parch.
Township—town.
Tradition—*trado*, *tradit-um*, to give.
Transgressor—transgress.
Translation—translate.
Treatment—treat.
Tributary—*tribuo*, *tribut-um*, to give.
Triumphal, Triumphant—triumph.
Troublesome—trouble.
Turpitude—*turp-is*, ugly.
Ultimate—*ultim-us*, last.
Uniformity—uniform.
Unity—*un-us*, one.
Union—the same.
Usage, Useful—use.
Utterance—utter.
Vacancy—*vac-o*, to be empty.
Vacate—the same.
Vassalage—vassal.
Vehicle—*veh-o*, to carry.
Ventricle—*venter*, *ventr-is*, the belly.
Verbal—*verb-um*, a word.
Verbose—the same.
Verify—*ver-us*, true.
Verity—the same.
Veteran—*vetus*, *veter-is*, old.
Vigilance—*vigil-o*, to watch.
Vinous—*vin-um*, wine.
Visible—*video*, *vis-um*, to see.
Vision—the same.
Visionary—vision.
Vital—*vit-a*, life.
Vivacity—*viv-o*, to live.
Vivid—the same.
Vivify—the same.
Vocal—*vox*, *voc-is*, voice.
Voluntary—*volunt-as*, will.
Votary—*vot-um*, a vow.
Warmness—warm.
Waxen—wax.
Weaponless—weapon.
Widen—wide.
Widowhood—widow.
Woolly—wool.
Workmanship—workman.
Worldliness—worldly.
Yellowish—yellow.
Yeomanry—yeoman.
Youthful—youth.
Zealous—zeal.

PART II

LATIN AND OTHER ROOTS.

GENERAL OBSERVATIONS.

PRONUNCIATION. The rules to be observed in the pronunciation of Latin and Greek, differ but slightly from those laid down for our own language. It is important, however, to bear in mind:

1. That every vowel or diphthong must be enunciated. Accordingly, *miles* is pronounced *mi-les; mare, mar-e; arche, arch-e; botane, botan-e.*

2. That the diphthongs *æ* and *œ* have the sound of *e*. *Ædes* is pronounced *Edes; ævum, evum; pœna, pena; fœdus, fedus.*

3. That *ch* is always sounded like *k*: as, *achos*, pronounced *akos; echeo, ekeo; chir, kir; chylos, kylos.*

4. That in the Latin *c* and *g* are hard before *a*, *o*, and *u*, and soft before *e* (*æ, œ*), *i* and *y*. *Calo* is pronounced *kalo; colo, kolo; cura, kura; cedo, sedo; civis, sivis.* In *Gallia, lego, gutta, the g* is sounded like the same letter in the English word *go;* in *gelu* and *gibbus*, like *g* in *giant*. In the Greek roots *c* (κ) and *g* are always sounded hard.

5. That dissyllables have the accent on the *first* syllable: *a'lo a'ger, ca'nis.*

For the pronunciation of the roots from the French and other languages, we do not deem it necessary to make any provision. The roots of this character are so few, and, in regard to the French especially, all written instruction is so unserviceable, that, if the pupil feels any desire for such information, he must seek it in the proper books or from proper teachers.

In prosecuting the study of Etymology, it should be noticed that the form of the Latin or Greek word is subject to great variation, in order to express its number and case, or voice, mood, &c.; and, as our words are derived sometimes from one, and sometimes from another of these forms, two or more derivatives may differ very much in their appearance, although they spring from the same root. Thus, *core, courage,* and *encourage* come from *cor* (the *Nom.* of the Lat. for heart); while *accord, cordial,* and *discordant* come from *cordis* (the *Gen*). *Component* and *postpone* come from *pono* (*Ind. pres.*); *compose* and *position* from *positum* (*Supine*). In the same manner from *corpus* (*Nom.*), we have *corpse* and *corpuscle*, and from *corporis* (*Gen.*), *corporeal* and *incorporate;* from *ago* (*Ind. pres.*), *agent, cogent,* and *exigency*, and from *actum* (*Supine*), *action, actual,* and *exact.*

A slight modification in the form of the derivative arises from the change of *e* and of *a* the primitives into *i* in the compounds and derivatives. Thus, *teneo*, when it takes *con*, *per*, or any other prefix, becomes *contineo*, *pertineo*, and the corresponding English derivatives are *tenant*, *continent*, and *pertinent*. From *sapio* we have *sapid*, *sapient*, and *insipid*, *insipience*.

Also *æ* is sometimes changed into *i;* as, from *lædo*, *læsum*, come *collido*, *collisum:* *au* into *u;* as, from *claudo* come *concludo*, *conclusum*, &c.

Ace-o, to be sour or acid. **Acet-um**, vinegar.

ACES'CENT, tending to sourness. | ACE'TOUS, like vinegar.

Acerb-us, bitter, sour.

ACER'BITY, bitterness. | EXAC'ERBATE, to imbitter.

Acid-us, tart, sharp.

ACID'ULATE, to tinge with acid. | ACID'ITY, sourness.

Acr-is, sharp.

AC'RID, sharp. | AC'RIMONY, sharpness, severity.

Acu-o, acut-um, to sharpen.

ACU'MEN, sharpness of intellect. | ACUTE', penetrating.

Adulat-um (ab **adulor**), to flatter. ADULA'TION, flattery.

Agger, a heap. EXAG'GERATE, to heighten ; to magnify.

Agil-is, nimble.

AG'ILE, quick ; active. | AGIL'ITY, nimbleness.

Agit-o, to drive, to stir.

AG'ITATE, to put in motion ; to disturb.
AGITA'TION, disturbance ; emotion.
COG'ITATE, to think.
INCOG'ITATIVE, wanting the power of thought.

Ag-o, act-um, to do, to act.

ACT, to do ; to perform.
AC'TIVE, busy ; quick,
AC'TOR, a stage-player.
AC'TION, a deed ; an operation.
AC'TUATE, to put in action.
AGENT, a substitute ; a factor.
CIRCUMNAV'IGATE, to sail round.
COACT', to act together.
CO'GENT, forcible.
COUNTERACT,' to oppose ; to hinder.
ENACT', to perform ; to decree.
EXACT', strict ; accurate.
INAC'TION, rest.
IN'DIGENT, poor ; needy.
NAV'IGABLE, fit for the passage of vessels.
PROD'IGAL, a spendthrift.
REACT', to act again ; to resist.
TRANSACT', to perform ; to manage.

Ager, agri, a field.

AGRA'RIAN, relating to the field.
AGRICUL'TURAL, relating to agriculture.
AGRICUL'TURE, the art of cultivating the ground.
PER'EGRINATE, to travel.

Ali-us, alien-us, another, foreign.

A'LIEN, a foreigner.
A'LIAS, otherwise.
INA'LIENABLE, that cannot be transferred.

Al-o, alit-um, to nourish.

AL'IMENT, food; nourishment.
AL'IMONY, the allowance to a divorced woman.
AL'MONER, an officer who distributes alms.
ALMS, gifts to the poor.
COALITI'ON, union; league.

Alp-es, the Alps.

AL'PINE, pertaining to the Alps.
CISAL'PINE, on this side of the Alps.

Alter, another, change.

AL'TER, to change.
UNAL'TERABLE, unchangeable.

Altern-us, by turns.

ALTER'NATE, by turns; in succession.
ALTER'NATIVE, a choice of two things.

Alt-us, high.

AL'TITUDE, height; elevation.
ALTIL'OQUENCE, lofty speech.
ALTIS'ONANT, high-sounding.
EXALT', to raise; to elevate.

Ambul-o, to walk.

AM'BLE, a gentle trot.
PERAM'BULATE, to walk through

Amic-us, a friend.

AM'ITY, friendship.
AM'ICABLE, friendly; kind.
EN'MITY, hatred.
INIM'ICAL, unfriendly; hostile.

Am-o, to love. ***Amor,*** love.

A'MIABLE, worthy of love.
AMOUR', an affair of love; an intrigue.
AM'OROUS, inclined to love.
AMATEUR', a lover of the fine arts.
AM'ATORY, relating to love.
ENAM'OR, to inflame with love.

Ampl-us, large.

AM'PLE, full; wide.
AM'PLIFY, to enlarge; to exaggerate.
AMPLIFICA'TION, enlargement.
AM'PLITUDE, largeness; extent.

Ang-o (anxi), to vex.

AN'GUISH, intense pain.
AN'GER, resentment; rage.
ANXI'ETY, concern; solicitude.
ANX'IOUS, solicitous; concerned

Angul-us, an angle.

ANG'LE, a corner.
AN'GULAR, having angles.
MULTANG'ULAR, many cornered.
PENTANG'ULAR, five cornered.
QUAD'RANGLE, a square.
REC'TANGLE, a right-angled parallelogram.
SEPTANG'ULAR, having seven angles.
TRI'ANGLE, a figure of three angles

Anim-a, wind, the vital air.

AN'IMAL, a living creature.
ANIMAL'CULE, a minute animal.
ANIMAL'ITY, animal existence.
AN'IMATE, to make alive.
EXAN'IMATE, lifeless; dead.
INAN'IMATE, void of life.
REAN'IMATE, to restore to life.

Anim-us, the mind.

ANIMADVERT', to consider; to pass censure.
ANIMADVER'SION, reproof; censure.
ANIMOS'ITY, hatred; malignity.
EQUANIM'ITY, evenness of mind.
MAGNANIM'ITY, greatness of mind.
MAGNAN'IMOUS, brave; noble.
PUSILLANIM'ITY, cowardice.
UNANIM'ITY, agreement.
UNAN'IMOUS, of one mind.

Ann-us, a year.

AN'NALS, yearly records.
AN'NALIST, a writer of annals.
ANNIVER'SARY, a stated day, coming once in every year.
AN'NUAL, yearly.
ANNU'ITY, a yearly allowance.
ANNU'ITANT, one who has an annuity.
BIEN'NIAL, in every two years.
CENTEN'NIAL, occurring every hundred years.
MILLEN'NIUM, a thousand years.
OCTEN'NIAL, in every eighth year.
PEREN'NIAL, lasting through the year; perpetual.
SEPTEN'NIAL, happening every seven years.
SUPERAN'NUATE, to impair by age.
TRIEN'NIAL, happening every third year.

Annul-us, a ring. AN'NULAR, having the form of a ring.

Antiqu-us, old or ancient.

AN'TIQUARY, one versed in antiquity.
AN'TIQUARIAN, relating to antiquity.
AN'TIQUATE, to make obsolete.
ANTIQUE', ancient; of old fashion.
ANTIQ'UITY, old times.
AN'CIENT, old; antique.
AN'TIC, odd; fanciful.

Aperi-o, apert-um, to open.

APE'RIENT, gently purgative.
AP'ERTURE, an opening; a hole.

Apis, a bee. API'ARY, a place where bees are kept.

Apt-us, fit, meet.

ADAPT', to fit; to adjust.
APT, fit; ready.
AP'TITUDE, fitness.
INAP'TITUDE, unfitness.

Aqua, water.

AQUAT'IC, pertaining to water.
A'QUEDUCT, a channel for water.
A'QUEOUS, watery.
TERRA'QUEOUS, composed of land and water.

Aquil-a, an eagle. AQ'UILINE, resembling an eagle ; hooked.

Ar-o, to plough.

AR'ABLE, fit for tillage.
INAR'ABLE, not arable.

Arbiter, arbitr-i, an umpire or judge.

AR'BITER, a judge ; an umpire.
ARBIT'RAMENT, will ; award.
AR'BITRATE, to decide ; to judge of.
AR'BITRARY, despotic; unlimited.

Arbor, a tree.

AR'BOR, a bower.
AR'BORARY, belonging to trees.
AR'BORIST, one who makes trees his study.

Arc-us, a bow.

ARCH, a hollow structure supported by its own curve.
ARCH'ER, he that shoots with a bow.

Ard-eo, ars-um, to burn.

AR'DENT, hot ; passionate.
AR'DENCY, eagerness ; heat.
AR'DOR, passion ; zeal.
ARS'ON, the crime of houseburning.

Aren-a, sand.

ARENA'CEOUS, sandy.
ARENOSE', full of sand.

Are-o, to be dry.

AREFAC'TION, a drying.
AR'ID, dry ; parched.

Argu-o, to argue.

AR'GUE, to reason ; to dispute.
AR'GUMENT, a reason alleged.

Arm-a, arms.

ARM, to furnish with arms.
ARMA'DA, a fleet of war.
AR'MAMENT, a force equipped for war.
AR'MISTICE, a cessation of hostilities ; a truce.
AR'MOR, defensive arms.
AR'MORY, a place for arms.
ARMS, weapons.
AR'MY, a large body of armed men.
DISARM', to deprive of weapons.

Ars, art-is, art, skill.

ART, skill ; cunning.
AR'TIFICE, trick ; fraud
ARTISAN', a mechanic ; a workman.
ART'IST, one skilled in any art.
INARTIFICI'AL, plain ; artless.
INERT', inactive ; sluggish.
UNART'FUL, without craft.

Articul-us, a little joint.

AR'TICLE, a part of speech ; a single thing.
ARTIC'ULATE, distinct ; jointed.
INARTIC'ULATE, not distinct.

Asin-us, an ass.

As'inine, resembling an ass.
Ass, an animal of burden.

Asper, rough.

Asper'ity, roughness, harshness.
Exas'perate, to enrage; to vex.

Atra, black.

Atrabila'rian, affected with melancholy, or black bile.

Atrox, atroc-is, fierce, cruel.

Atro'cious, enormous; outrageous.
Atroci'ty, great wickedness.

Audax, audac-is, daring.

Auda'cious, bold; impudent.
Audac'ity, effrontery; boldness.

Audi-o, audit-um, to hear.

Au'dible, that can be heard.
Au'dience, a hearing; an auditory.
Au'dit[illegible], those assembled to hear.
Disobey', to break commands.
Inau'dible, not to be heard.
Obey', to comply with commands
Obe'dience, submission.

Aug-eo, auct-um, to increase.

Auc'tion, a public sale of property to the highest bidder.
Augment', to increase.
Au'thor, originator; maker.
Author'itative, having authority; positive.
Au'thorize, to give authority.

Augur, a soothsayer.

Au'gur, to foretell; to predict.
Au'gury, prediction by omens.
Inau'gurate, to lead into office with suitable ceremonies

Aur-is, the ear.

Au'ricle, the external ear.
Auric'ular, told in secret.

Auster-us, severe, rigid.

Austere', severe, harsh.
Auster'ity, severity; rigor.

Auxili-um, aid, help.

Auxil'iar, assisting.
Auxil'iary, a helper.

Avant (Fr.), before, forward.

Avant'guard, the van.
Advance,' to go forward.
Advantage, superiority; gain.
Disadvan'tage, loss; injury.
Van, the front of an army.
Van'courier, a light-armed soldier.

Avid-us, greedy. Avid'ity, eagerness; greediness.

Av-is, a bird. A'viary, a place for birds

Babel (Heb.), confusion.

BA'BEL, confusion; disorder.
BAB'YLON, an ancient empire.

Bacch-us, the god of wine.

BACCHANA'LIAN, relating to revelry.
DEBAUCH', to corrupt; to ruin.
DEBAUCHEE', a rake; a drunkard.
DEBAUCH'ERY, intemperance.

Barb-a, a beard. BAR'BER, one who shaves the beard.

Barbar-us, rude, savage.

BAR'BAROUS, rude; uncivilized.
BARBA'RIAN, a savage.
BARBAR'IC, foreign, rude.
BAR'BARISM, inhumanity; ignorance of arts.
BARBAR'ITY, brutality.

Barre (Fr.), a bar, a stop.

BAR, a long piece of wood or metal.
BARRICADE', to fortify.
BAR'RIER, a boundary; a stop.
EMBAR'RASS, to perplex.

Beat-us, happy.

BEAT'IFY, to bless; to make happy.
BEAT'ITUDE, blessedness; perfect felicity.

Beau, belle (Fr.), fair, beautiful.

BEAU, a man of dress.
BEAU'TY, fairness; elegance.
BELLE, a gay young lady.
EMBEL'LISH, to adorn.

Bell-um, war.

BELLIG'ERENT, waging war.
BELLIP'OTENT, mighty in war.
REBEL', to rise against lawful authority.

Bene, good, well.

BENEDIC'TION, blessing.
BENEFAC'TION, a benefit conferred.
BENEFAC'TOR, he who confers a benefit.
BENEF'ICENT, kind; doing good.
BENEFICI'AL, advantageous.
BENEFIC'IARY, a person benefitted.
BENEV'OLENCE, good will; charity.

Benign-us, kind, liberal.

BENIGN', kind; generous.
BENIG'NITY, actual kindness.

Bib-o, to drink.

BIB'BER, a tippler; a sot.
IMBIBE', to drink in, to admit.

Bil-is, the bile.

BIL'IOUS, pertaining to the bile
ANTIBIL'IOUS, remedying bilious disorders.

Bin-i, two by two. ***Bis***, two.

BIEN'NIAL, in every two years.
BIG'AMY, the having two wives at once.
BIG'AMIST, one guilty of bigamy.
BI'NARY, two ; double.
BINOC'ULAR, having two eyes.
BI'PED, an animal with two feet.
BIS'CUIT, a kind of bread.
BISECT', to divide into two equal parts.
COMBINE', to join together.

Bland-us, soothing, gentle.

BLAND, soft ; mild.
BLAN'DISH, to smooth ; to soften.

Bon-us, good.

BOUN'TY, liberality.
BOUN'TEOUS, liberal ; kind.

Brachi-um, an arm. BRACH'IAL, belonging to the arm.

Brev-is, short, brief.

ABBRE'VIATE, to shorten.
ABRIDGE', to abbreviate.
BREV'IARY, an abridgment.
BREV'ITY, conciseness ; shortness.
BRIEF, short ; concise.

Brill-er (Fr.), to sparkle.

BRILL'IANT, shining ; sparkling.
BRILL'IANCY, lustre ; splendor.

Brut-us, brute, senseless.

BRU'TAL, like a brute.
BRU'TISH, bestial ; ferocious.

Bull-a, a bubble in water.

BOIL, to bubble from heat.
EBULLITI'ON, act of boiling.

Cad-o, cas-um, to fall.

AC'CIDENT, casualty ; chance.
CA'DENCE,° the tone or sound.
CASCADE', a waterfall.
CASE, condition ; state.
CAS'UAL,° accidental,
COINCIDE', to agree.
DECAY', to rot ; to decline.
DECID'UOUS, falling ; dying.
IN'CIDENT, an event.
OCCA'SION, to cause ; to produce.
OC'CIDENT, the west.

Cæd-o, cæs-um, to cut, to kill.

CONCISE', brief ; short.
DECIDE', to determine.
DECISI'ON, determination.
DECI'SIVE, conclusive ; final.
EXCISE', a tax.
FRAT'RICIDE, the murder of a brother.
HOM'ICIDE, manslaughter.
HOMICI'DAL, murderous.
INCISED', cut ; made by cutting.
INCISI'ON, a cut ; a gash.
INFAN'TICIDE, the murder of an infant.
PAR'RICIDE, the murder of a parent.
PRECISE', exact ; strict.
PRECISI'ON, exactness.
REG'ICIDE, the murder of a king.
SU'ICIDE, self-murder.

Calamit-as, a misfortune.

CALAM'ITY, misfortune.
CALAM'ITOUS, full of woe.

Calcul-us,° a small stone, a pebble.

CAL'CULATE, to compute; to reckon.
INCAL'CULABLE, that cannot be calculated.

Cale-o, to be warm. **Calor,** heat.

CALEFAC'TION, the act of heating.
CAL'DRON, a pot; a boiler.
CALOR'IC, heat.
CALORIF'IC, causing heat.
INCALES'CENCE, a growing warm.
SCALD, to burn with a hot fluid.

Calumni-a, calumny.

CAL'UMNY, slander; false accusation.
CALUM'NIOUS, slanderous.
CALUM'NIATE, to slander.

Camp-us, a plain; tents in the field.

CAMP, the place of an army.
CAMPAIGN', a military year.
DECAMP', to shift a camp.
ENCAMP', to pitch tents.

Cande-o, to be white, to glow.

CAN'DOR, frankness; openness.
CAN'DID, fair; open.
CAN'DIDATE,* one proposed for office, or preferment.
CAN'DLE, a light made of tallow, &c.
EXCANDES'CENCE, white heat.
CHANDELIER', a branch for candles.
INCEN'DIARY, one who maliciously sets houses, &c., on fire.
INCENSE', to enrage; to provoke.
INCEN'TIVE, a motive; a spur.

Can-is, a dog. CAN'INE, relating to the dog.

Cano, cant-um, to sing.

AC'CENT, a stress of voice.
ACCENT'UATE, to mark or pronounce with accents.
CANT, affected manner of speech; slang.
CAN'TICLE, a song.
CAN'TO, a section of a poem.
CHANT, to sing.
DECANT', to pour off gently.
DESCANT', to sing; to discourse.
ENCHANT', to charm.
INCANTA'TION, an enchantment.
RECANT,' to retract.

Capi-o, capt-um, to take.

ACCEPT', to take; to receive.
ACCEPT'ABLE, grateful; pleasing.
ANTIC'IPATE, to take or do beforehand; to foretaste.
CAPA'CIOUS, wide; large.
CAP'TIVATE, to take prisoner.
CAP'TIVE, one taken in war.
CAP'TOR, he who takes prisoners.
CAP'TURE, a seizure; a prize.
CONCEIT', fancy; opinion.
CONCEIVE', to think.
CONCEP'TION, notion; thought.
DECEIVE', to cheat; to mislead.
DECEIT', fraud; a cheat.
DECEP'TION, act of deceiving.
EMAN'CIPATE, to free from servitude.
EXCEPT', to leave out.
IMPERCEP'TIBLE, not to be perceived.

* Those who sought preferments among the Romans, were called *Candidati*, from a white robe (*toga candida*) worn by them, which was rendered shining (*candens*) by the art of the fuller.

INCA'PABLE, unable ; unfit.
INCAPAC'ITY, inability.
INTERCEPT', to stop ; to seize.
MISCONCEP'TION, a false opinion.
OC'CUPANCY, a holding.
OC'CUPY, to possess.
PARTIC'IPATE,°to share.
PAR'TICIPLE, a part of speech.
PERCEIVE', to see ; to know.
PRE'CEPT, a rule ; a mandate.
PRECONCEIVE', to imagine beforehand.
PREOC'CUPY, to occupy previously.
PRINCE, a sovereign ; a ruler.
PRIN'CIPLE, cause ; motive.
RECEIVE', to take ; to admit.
RECEIPT', an acknowledgment for money paid.
RECEPT'ACLE, that which receives or contains.
RECEP'TION, a receiving.
REC'IPE,* a medical prescription.
RECIP'IENT, a receiver.

Capill-us, the hair. CAP'ILLARY, like hair ; minute.

Caput, capit-is, the head.

CAP, a covering for the head.
CAP'ITAL†, chief ; principal.
CAPITA'TION, counting by heads.
CAPIT'ULATE, to surrender on conditions.
CAP'TAIN, a chief commander.
CHAP'TER, a division of a book.
DECAP'ITATE, to behead.
PREC'IPICE, a headlong steep.
PRECIP'ITANCE, rash, haste.
RECAPIT'ULATE, to repeat.

Carbo, carbon-is, a coal.

CARBON'IC, containing carbon.
CAR'BUNCLE,°a gem ; a tumor.

Carcer, a prison. INCAR'CERATE, to imprison.

Cardo, cardin-is, a hinge. CAR'DINAL,°chief ; principal.

Caro, carn-is, flesh.

CAR'NAGE, slaughter.
CAR'NAL, fleshly ; lustful.
CARNIV'OROUS, flesh-eating.
CHAR'NEL, holding dead bodies.
INCAR'NATE, clothed with flesh.

Car-us, dear, kind.

CARESS', to fondle.
CHER'ISH, to support ; to nurse.

Castig-o, to chastise, to punish.

CAS'TIGATE, to chastise ; to whip.
CHAS'TEN, to correct ; to punish.
CHAS'TISEMENT, punishment.

Cast-us, pure, chaste.

CHASTE, pure ; uncorrupt.
CHAS'TITY, purity.

Caten-a, a chain.

CATENA'RIAN, relating to a chain.
CONCAT'ENATE, to link together.

---

* This is the imperative mood of the Latin verb, *recipio*. In medical prescriptions written in Latin, it is the first word used—"*Recipe*" ("take"), &c.
† *Capital* crimes or punishments are those involving a loss of the *head*.

Cavall-o (Ital.), a horse.

CAV'ALCADE, a procession on horseback.
CAVALIER,' an armed horseman.
CAV'ALRY, mounted troops.

Cav-us, hollow.

CAV'ITY, a hollow place.
CAV'ERN, a cave; a den.
CON'CAVE, hollow.
EX'CAVATE, to hollow out.

Caus-a, a cause.

ACCUSE',°to charge with a crime.
CAUSE, reason; motive.
EXCUSE', to pardon; to remit.
INEXCU'SABLE, not to be excused.

Cautio, caution-is, caution.

CAU'TION, foresight; warning.
INCAU'TIOUS, unwary.
PRECAU'TION, previous care.

Ced-o, cess-um, to go, to yield.

ACCEDE',°to assent; to agree.
ACCESS', approach; admission.
AN'CESTOR, a forefather.
ANCES'TRAL, relating to ancestors.
AN'CESTRY, lineage; a series of ancestors.
ANTECE'DENT, going before.
CEASE, to leave off; to stop.
CEDE, to yield; to resign.
CES'SION, the act of yielding.
CONCEDE', to yield; to grant.
CONCES'SION, the act of granting.
DECEASE', death.
EXCEED', to go beyond; to excel.
EXCESS', superfluity.
INCES'SANT, unceasing.
INACCES'SIBLE, not to be approached.
INTERCEDE', to mediate.
INTERCES'SION, mediation.
PRECEDE', to go before.
PREDECES'SOR, one going before.
PROCEED', to go on; to advance.
PROC'ESS, a progress; a method.
RECEDE,' to retreat.
RECESS', a place of retreat.
SECEDE', to withdraw from.
SECESSI'ON, the act of seceding.
SUCCEED', to follow; to prosper.
SUCCESS', fortune; prosperity.
SUCCES'SIVE, following in order.
SUCCES'SOR, one that follows another.

Celebr-is, renowned.

CEL'EBRATE,°to praise; to extol.
CELEB'RITY, fame; renown.

Celer, swift.

ACCEL'ERATE, to hasten; to quicken.
CELER'ITY, rapidity; speed.

Cœleb-s, single, unmarried. CEL'IBACY, single life.

Cell-a, a cellar.

CELL, a small, close room.
CEL'LAR, a room under a house.
CEL'LULAR, consisting of little cells or cavities.

Cels-us, high.

EXCEL', to outdo; to surpass.
EX'CELLENCE, purity; goodness

Cel-o, to hide.

CONCEAL', to hide ; to secrete.
INCONCEA'LABLE, not to be hid.

Cens-eo, censum, to judge, to value, to blame.

CENSO'RIOUS, apt to censure.
CEN'SURE, to blame; to condemn.
CEN'SUS, an enumeration of the people.

Cent-um, a hundred.

CENT, a coin 100 of which = $1.
CEN'TURY, a hundred years.
CENTEN'NIAL, occurring every hundred years.
CEN'TIPEDE, an insect with many feet.
CENTU'RION, a Roman military officer, commanding 100 men.

Cer-a, wax.

CERE, to cover with wax.
CE'RATE, an ointment of wax, oil, &c.
INSINCERE', not hearty ; false.
SINCER'ITY,° honesty ; purity.

Ceremoni-a, a rite, a form.

CER'EMONY, outward rite.
CEREMO'NIOUS, civil ; formal.

Cern-o, cret-um, to sift, to distinguish.

CONCERN', business ; care.
DECREE', an edict ; a law.
DECRE'TAL, a book of decrees.
DISCERN',° to descry ; to judge.
DISCRETI'ON,° prudence.
DISCRIM'INATE, to distinguish.
INDISCER'NIBLE, not perceptible.
INDISCREET', imprudent.
INDISCRIM'INATE, not making any distinction.
SE'CRET,° concealed ; private.
SECRETE', to hide ; to conceal.
SEC'RETARY, one who writes for another.

Cert-o, to contend.

CONCERT',° to settle ; to contrive.
DISCONCERT', to disturb.
PRECONCERT'ED, contrived beforehand.

Cert-us, certain, sure.

ASCERTAIN', to make certain.
CER'TAIN, sure ; undoubted.
CER'TIFY, to assure.
CERTIF'ICATE, a testimony in writing.
UNCER'TAIN, doubtful.

Cerule-us, blue. CERU'LEAN, sky-colored ; blue.

Cet-us, a whale. CETA'CEOUS, of the whale kind.

Cheval (Fr.), a horse.

CHEVALIER', a knight ; a gallant man.
CHIV'ALRY, knighthood ; valor.

Chor-us, a company of singers.

CHOIR, a band of singers.
CHO'RAL, belonging to a choir.
CHOR'ISTER, a singer.
CHO'RUS, a number of singers.

Cing-o, cinct-um, to bind.

CINC'TURE, a belt; a sash.
PRECINCT', a boundary.
SUCCINCT', concise; brought into small compass.

Circul-us, a ring.

CIR'CLE, a round plane space.
CIR'CULAR, round like a circle.
ENCIR'CLE, to surround.
CIR'CULATE, to spread; to diffuse.
SEMICIR'CLE, a half circle.

Cit-o, to call, to stir up.

CITE, to summon; to quote.
EXCITE', to rouse; to animate.
INCITE', to stir up; to urge on.
RECITE', to rehearse; to repeat.
RESUS'CITATE, to revive; to bring back to life.

Civ-is, a citizen.

CIT'Y, a large corporate town.
CIT'IZEN, an inhabitant of a city or state.
UNCIV'IL, impolite; rude.
CIV'IC, relating to civil affairs or honors.
CIV'IL, relating to the community; well-bred.

Clam-o, clamat-um, to cry, to shout.

ACCLAIM', to give applause.
ACCLAMA'TION, a shout of applause.
CLAIM, to demand of right.
CLAM'OR, outcry; noise.
DECLAIM', to harangue.
DISCLAIM', to disown; to deny.
EXCLAIM', to cry out.
EXCLAMA'TION, vehement outcry.
PROCLAIM', to publish.
PROCLAMA'TION, a public notice.
RECLAIM', to reform, to recall.

Clar-us, clear.

CLAR'IFY, to purify.
CLARIFICA'TION, the act of making clear.
CLAR'ION, a kind of trumpet.
CLEAR, bright; serene.
DECLARE', to make known.

Class-is, a fleet.

CLASS, a rank; a division.
CLAS'SIC, relating to authors of the first rank; elegant.
CLAS'SIFY, to arrange in classes.
CLASSIFICA'TION, a ranging into classes.

Claud-o, claus-um, to shut.

LAUSE, a part of a sentence; a stipulation.
CLOSE, end; cessation.
CLO'SET, a small, private room.
CONCLUDE', to determine; to finish.
CONCLU'SION, determination; close.
DISCLOSE', to reveal; to tell.
DISCLO'SURE, discovery.
ENCLOSE', to shut in; to surround.
EXCLUDE', to shut out; to debar.
EXCLU'SION, a shutting out.
INCLO'SURE, a space enclosed.
INCLUDE', to admit; to comprise.
INCONCLU'SIVE, not decisive.
PRECLUDE', to hinder or prevent.
RECLUSE', a solitary person.
SECLUDE', to shut up apart.

Clemens, clement-is, mild.

CLEM'ENCY, mercy; mildness.
INCLEM'ENT, severe; rough.

Clin-o, to bend; to lean.

DECLEN'SION, fall; degeneracy.
DECLINE', to fail; to refuse.
INCLINE', to bend; to lean.
RECLINE', to lean back.

Cliv-us, a slope, an ascent.

ACCLIV'ITY, steepness upwards.
CLIFF, a steep rock.
DECLIV'ITY, gradual descent.

Colo, cult-um, to till; to inhabit.

AG'RICULTURE, the art of cultivating the ground.
COL'ONY,° a settlement.
CUL'TIVATE, to till; to improve.
CUL'TURE, cultivation; tillage.

Color, color, hue.

COL'OR, hue; tint.
DISCOL'OR, to stain.

Comes, comit-is, a companion.

CONCOM'ITANT, going with.
COUNT, a title of nobility.
COUN'TY, a shire; a district.

Concili-o, to make friends.

CONCIL'IATE, to win; to reconcile.
REC'ONCILE, to adjust.

Contra, against, opposite to.

CON'TRARY, opposite; adverse.
CONTRAST', to place in opposition.
COUN'TER, contrary to.
COUNTERACT', to act contrary to.

Copi-a, plenty.

CO'PIOUS, plentiful; abundant.
CORNUCO'PIÆ, the horn of plenty.

Copula, a band.

COP'ULA, a connective.
COP'ULATE, to unite; to conjoin.
COU'PLE, two; a pair.
COUP'LET, two verses.

Coqu-o, coct-um, to boil; to digest.

COOK, one who prepares victuals.
CONCOCT', to digest; to ripen.
DECOC'TION, a preparation made by boiling.

Cor, cord-is, the heart.

ACCORD',° to agree; to harmonize.
CON'CORD,° agreement; union.
COR'DIAL, warm; hearty.
CORE, the heart; the inner part.
COUR'AGE, bravery; valor.
DIS'CORD,° disagreement.
DISCOUR'AGE, to depress; to deter.
ENCOUR'AGE, to animate.
RECORD', to register.

Cori-um, a skin or hide.

CORIA'CEOUS, consisting of leather.
CUR'RIER, one who dresses leather.

Corn-u, a horn.

CORʹNEA, the horny coat of the eye.
CORʹNET, a musical instrument.
CORNU-COʹPIÆ, the horn of plenty.
UNICORNʹ, a beast with one horn.

Coron-a, a crown.

CORONAʹTION, the act of crowning.
CORʹONET, a little crown.
CROWN, an ornament for a king's head.
UNCROWNʹ, to deprive of a crown.

Corpus, corpor-is, a body.

CORʹPORAL, relating to the body.
CORPOʹREAL, having a body; not spiritual.
CORPS, a body of soldiers.
CORPʹULENCE, fulness of body.
INCORʹPORATE, to embody.

Cost-a, a rib or side.

COSʹTAL, belonging to the ribs.
INTERCOSʹTAL, placed between the ribs.

Couvr-ir (Fr.), to cover, to hide.

COVʹER, to overspread.
COVʹERLET, the upper covering of a bed.
COVʹERT, a shelter; a defence.
DISCOVʹER, to reveal; make known.

Cras, to-morrow. PROCRASʹTINATE, to put off.

Cred-o, credit-um, to believe.

CREʹDENCE, belief; credit.
CREDʹIBLE, worthy of credit.
CREDʹITOR, he to whom money is owed.
CREDUʹLITY, inclination to believe.
CREDʹIT, belief; reputation.
CREDʹULOUS, apt to believe.
CREED, religious belief.
DISCREDʹIT, to disgrace.
INCREDʹIBLE, surpassing belief.

Cre-o, creat-um, to create.

CREATE,ʹ to form; to cause.
CREAʹTURE, a being created.
MISCREAʹTED, deformed.
RECʹREANT, cowardly; false.
RECREAʹTION, amusement; diversion.

Crep-o, crepit-um, to crackle.

CREVʹICE, a crack; a cleft.
DECREPʹIT, broken down by age.
DISCREPʹANCY, difference; contrariety.

Cresc-o, cret-um, to grow.

ACCRUEʹ, to arise from.
CONCRETEʹ, grown together into one mass.
CRESʹCENT, the shape of the new moon.
DECREASEʹ, to grow less.
EXCRESʹCENCE, a fleshy protuberance; a tumor.
INCREASEʹ, to make greater.
RECRUITʹ, to repair; to supply

Crimen, crimin-is, a crime, an accusation.

CRIME, an offence; a great fault.
CRIM'INAL, faulty; guilty.
RECRIM'INATE, to retort a charge.

Crux, cruc-is, the cross.

CROSS, one straight body laid at right angles over another.
CRO'SIER, a bishop's staff.
CRU'CIBLE, a chemist's melting pot.
CRU'CIFY, to nail to a cross.
CRU'CIFIX, a cross bearing an image of our Saviour.
EXCRU'CIATE, to torture.

Crust-a, a crust.

CRUST, an outer coat; a case.
INCRUST', to cover with a crust.

Cub-o, to lie down.

CUB, the young of a beast.
ENCUM'BER, to burden.
INCUM'BENT, resting upon.
PROCUM'BENT, lying down.
RECUM'BENCE, rest; repose.
SUCCUMB', to yield; to submit.

Culc-o, to tread upon. INCUL'CATE, to impress by admonitions.

Culin-a, a kitchen. CU'LINARY, relating to cookery.

Culp-a, a fault, blame.

CUL'PABLE, guilty; blamable.
EXCUL'PATE, to excuse.

Cumul-o, to heap up.

ACCU'MULATE, to heap up.
CU'MULATIVE, heaped up.

Cune-us, a wedge.

CU'NEAL, relating to a wedge.
CU'NEIFORM, wedge-shaped.

Cupio, cupit-um, to desire. ***Cupid-us,*** eager.

CUPID'ITY, eager desire.
COV'ET, to wish for.

Cur-a, care.

AC'CURATE, exact; correct.
AC'CURACY, exactness.
CARE, solicitude; anxiety.
CURE, to heal; to restore health.
CU'RACY, the office of a curate.
CU'RATE,°a parish priest.
CU'RIOUS, inquisitive; rare.
INAC'CURATE, not exact.
INSECURE', not safe.
PROCURE', to obtain; to acquire.
PROX'Y,°a substitute.
SECU'RITY, safety.
SI'NECURE, an office of profit without employment.

Curr-o, curs-um, to run.

CAREER', a course; a race.
CAR'RY, to convey; to transport.
CON'COURSE,°a gathering.
CONCUR', to agree.
COU'RIER, a messenger sent in haste.
COURSE, career; progress.
CUR'RENT, common; popular
CUR'SORY, hasty; slight.
DISCOURSE', conversation; speech.
EXCUR'SION, a ramble; a journey.
INCUR', to become liable to.

IN'TERCOURSE, communication.
OCCUR', to happen.
OCCUR'RENCE, an accidental event.
PRECUR'SOR, a forerunner.
RECOURSE', appeal to for help.
RECUR',° to rehappen; to return.
SUC'COR,° to help; to relieve.

Curv-us, crooked, bent.

CUR'VATURE, crookedness.
CURVE, a bent line.
CURVILIN'EAR, composed of curved lines.

Cut-is, the skin.

CU'TICLE, the thin outer skin.
CUTA'NEOUS, affecting the skin.

Cuti-o, cuss-um, to shake.

CONCUSSI'ON, a striking together.
DISCUSS',° to debate.

Coutume (Fr.), habit.

ACCUS'TOM, to habituate.
CUS'TOM, habit; usage.

Damn-um, loss, hurt.

CONDEMN', to find guilty; to blame.
DAMN, to curse; to condemn.
INDEM'NIFY, to secure against loss.
INDEM'NITY, security from loss.

Debil-is, weak.

DEBIL'ITY, weakness; languor.
DEBIL'ITATE, to weaken.

Debit-is, a due.

DEBT, a sum due.
DEB'IT, to charge with debt.
DEBT'OR, one who is in debt.
INDEBT', to bind by debt.

Decens, becoming.

DE'CENT, becoming; fit.
INDE'CENCY, want of modesty.

Decor, grace, comeliness.

DECORA'TION, ornament.
DECO'RUM, propriety of conduct

De-us, a god.

DE'IST, one who believes in God but denies revelation.
DE'ITY, the Divine Being.
DIRE, dreadful; dismal.

Delici-æ, niceties.

DELICI'OUS, sweet; agreeable.
DEL'ICACY, softness; politeness.
DEL'ICATE, nice; soft.
INDEL'ICATE, wanting delicacy.

Dens-us, thick, close.

CONDENSE', to compress.
DENSE', compact; thick.

Dens, dent-is, a tooth.

DEN'TAL, belonging to the teeth.
DENTIC'ULATED, set with small teeth.
INDENT', to notch.
INDEN'TURE,* a covenant.
TRI'DENT, an instrument having three prongs.

* So called from the notches in the edge of the paper or parchment on which it is written.

Deterior, worse.

DETE'RIORATE, to impair; to grow worse.

DETERIORA'TION, the act of making worse.

Dexter, right-handed. DEXTER'ITY, readiness.

Di-es, a day.

DI'ARY, a daily account.
DIS'MAL, sorrowful; gloomy.
DIUR'NAL, daily.
MERID'IAN, noon; mid-day.

Dic-o, dicat-um, to set apart, to show.

AB'DICATE, to resign.
DED'ICATE, to devote.
IN'DEX, a pointer.
IN'DICATE, to point out.
PREDIC'AMENT, condition; class.
PRED'ICATE, to affirm.

Dic-o, dict-um, to speak.

ADDICT', to devote.
BENEDIC'TION,° a blessing.
DIC'TATE, to give commands.
DIC'TION, style; language.
DIC'TIONARY, a book defining the words of a language.
ENDITE', to compose.
INDICT', to impeach; to accuse.
INTERDICT', to prohibit.
JURISDIC'TION, legal authority extent of power.
MALEDIC'TION, a curse.
CONTRADICT', to gainsay.
PREDICT', to foretell; to foreshow.
VER'DICT, the decision of a jury.

Dign-us, worthy.

CONDIGN', merited.
DEIGN, to condescend.
DIG'NIFY, to exalt; to honor.
DIG'NITY, true honor; rank.
DISDAIN', to scorn.
INDIG'NANT, enraged.

Diluvi-um, the deluge.

ANTEDILU'VIAN, one that lived before the flood.
DEL'UGE, a flood.
POSTDILU'VIAN, after the flood.

Discipul-us, a disciple.

DISCI'PLE, a follower.
DIS'CIPLINE, instruction; rule.

Div-us, a god.

DIVINE', godlike; heavenly.
DIVIN'ITY, the Deity; theology.

Do, dat-um, to give.

ABSCOND', to hide one's self.
ADD, to join to.
ADDITI'ON, the act of adding.
COMMAND', to govern; to order.
CONDITI'ON, quality; state.
DATE, a particular time.
ED'IT, to superintend a publication.
MAN'DATE, a command.
PERDITI'ON, ruin; death.
SUBDUE', to crush; to conquer.

Doc-eo, doct-um, to teach.

DOC'ILE, easily taught.
DOCIL'ITY, aptness to be taught.
DOC'TOR,° the title of a learned man.
DOC'TRINE, a principle; a precept.
DOC'UMENT, a record.
INDOC'TRINATE, to instruct.

Dogma, dogmat-is, a tenet, an opinion.

DOG'MA, a settled principle.
DOGMAT'IC, positive; arrogant.
DOG'MATIST, one who teaches with an air of authority.

Dole-o, to grieve.

CONDOLE', to lament with others.
DOLE'FUL, sorrowful.
DO'LOR, grief; complaint.
IN'DOLENCE, idleness.

Domin-us, a master.

DOMAIN', empire; estate.
DOMINEER', to rule with insolence.
DOMIN'ION, power; territory.
DON, a Spanish title.
PREDOM'INANCE, superiority.
PREDOM'INATE, to prevail over the rest.

Dom-o, domit-um, to tame. INDOM'ITABLE, untamable.

Dom-us, a house.

DOMES'TIC, private; belonging to the house or family.
DOM'ICILE, a mansion; a residence.

Don-um, a gift.

DO'NOR, a giver; a bestower.
DONA'TION, a gift.
DON'ATIVE, a present.
DONEE', one who receives a gift

Dorm-io, dormit-um, to sleep.

DOR'MANT, sleeping; concealed.
DOR'MITORY, a place to sleep in

Dors-um, the back.

DOR'SAL, relating to the back.
ENDORSE', to write on the back.

Dos, dot-is, a dowry.

DO'TAL, relating to a dowry.
ENDOW', to furnish; to enrich.

Dubi-us, doubtful.

DOUBT uncertainty of mind.
DU'BIOUS, doubtful.

Duc-o, duct-um, to lead, to bring.

ADDUCE', to bring forward.
AQ'UEDUCT, a conveyance for water.
CONDUCE', to tend; to contribute.
CONDUCT', to lead; to manage.
CON'DUIT, a water-pipe.
DEDUCE', to draw from; to infer.
DEDUC'TION, an inference.
DU'CAL, pertaining to a duke.
DUC'AT,* a European coin.
DUCT, a canal; a passage.
DUC'TILE, flexile; pliable.
DUKE, a leader; a noble.
ED'UCATE, to bring up.
EDUCE', to bring out.
INDUCE', to lead; to persuade.
INDUCT', to bring in.
INTRODUCE', to usher in.
INTRODUC'TORY, serving to introduce.
MISCON'DUCT, ill behavior.
PRODUCE', to bring forth; to bear.

* This coin is struck by dukes. In silver it is valued at $1.00; in gold at $2.11.

PRODUC'TIVE, capable of producing.
PROD'UCT, a thing produced.
REDUCE', to diminish; to subdue.
SEDUCE', to entice; to corrupt.
SEDUC'TIVE, fitted to entice.
VEN'TIDUCT, a passage for the air.

Dulc-is, sweet to the taste.

DUL'CET, sweet; luscious.
DUL'CIFY, to sweeten.

Dur-us, hard, solid.

DU'RABLE, lasting.
DURA'TION, continuance.
ENDURE', to bear; to last.
OB'DURATE, stubborn; harsh.

Ebri-us, drunk.

INE'BRIATE, to intoxicate.
SOBRI'ETY, soberness.

Ed-es, *for* ***Ædes,*** a house.

ED'IFY,° to instruct; to improve.
ED'IFICE, a building.

Ed-o, to eat. ED'IBLE, fit to be eaten.

Eg-eo, to need.

IN'DIGENCE, want; penury.
IN'DIGENT, poor; needy.

Ego, I. E'GOTIST, one who talks much of himself.

Electr-um, amber.

ELEC'TRIC, relating to electricity.
ELEC'TRIFY, to communicate electricity to.
ELECTRI'CITY,° a subtile fluid diffused through most bodies and evolved by friction:—first observed in amber.

Em-o, empt-um, to buy.

EXEMPT', to free from.
PER'EMPTORY, absolute; positive.
PROMPT, quick; ready.
PRE-EMP'TION, a right of buying before others.
REDEEM', to ransom; to rescue.

Emul-us, *for* ***Æmulus,*** vying with.

EM'ULATE, to rival.
EM'ULOUS, rivalling.

Ens-is, a sword. EN'SIFORM, sword-shaped.

Ens, ent-is, being. ***Esse,*** to be.

AB'SENT,°not present.
ABSENTEE', one who is absent.
AB'SENCE, state of being away.
ES'SENCE, the nature of any thing.
DISIN'TERESTED, without interest or partiality.
IN'TEREST, to concern; to affect.
MISREPRESENT', to represent falsely.
OMNIPRES'ENCE,°presence everywhere.
PRES'ENT, within sight; near.
REPRESENT', to describe.
UNESSEN'TIAL, not necessary

Eo, it-um, to go.

AMBITI'ON,* desire of honor.
CIR'CUIT, extent round about.
IMPER'ISHABLE, not liable to perish.
INTRAN'SITIVE, not passing over upon an object.
OBIT'UARY, relating to the decease of a person.
PER'ISH,° to die; to decay.
SEDITI'ON,° a popular outbreak.
TRAN'SIENT,° short; momentary
TRAN'SIT, a passing over.

Eques, equit-is, a horseman.

EQUES'TRIAN, relating to horsemanship.
E'QUERY, a stable for horses.
EQUIP', to furnish; to dress.

Equ-us, for Æquus, equal, just.

AD'EQUATE, equal to.
COE'QUAL, of the same rank.
E'QUALIZE, to make equal.
EQUANIM'ITY, composure.
EQUA'TOR, a line dividing the earth into two equal parts.
EQUIDIS'TANT, being at the same distance.
EQUILAT'ERAL, having all sides equal.
EQ'UITY, justice; right.
EQUILIB'RIUM, equality of weight.
E'QUINOX, the time of equal day and night.
EQUIV'ALENT, equal in value.
EQUIV'OCAL, ambiguous.
EQUIV'OCATE, to use doubtful expressions.
INAD'EQUACY, insufficiency.
INEQUAL'ITY, unevenness.
INIQ'UITY, injustice; sin.

Erc-eo,° for Arceo, to drive.

COERCE',° to restrain.
COER'CIVE, forcible.

Err-o, to wander.

ABERRA'TION, a wandering away.
AR'RANT, bad in a high degree.
ERR, to stray; to mistake.
ERRO'NEOUS, incorrect.
ER'ROR, a mistake.

Etern-us, for Æternus, without beginning or end.

CO-ETER'NAL, equally eternal with another.
ETER'NIZE, to make eternal.

Ether, for Æther, the sky.

E'THER, a volatile fluid.
ETHE'REAL, celestial.

Ev-um, for Ævum, life, time.

COE'VAL, of the same period, or age.
LONGEV'ITY, length of life.
PRIME'VAL, original; first.

Exempl-um, a copy.

EXAM'PLE, pattern; instance.
EXEM'PLAR, a model; a copy.
EXEM'PLIFY, to illustrate by example.

---

* Those who sought honor or preferment among the Romans, endeavored to gain the favor of the people by every popular art, viz., by *going round* their houses, (*ambiendo*, ab *am* et *eo*,) by shaking hands, by addressing and naming them, &c.: hence *ambitio, ambition.*

Exter-us, outward, foreign.

EXTE'RIOR, outward.
EXTER'NAL, exterior; visible.
EXTRA'NEOUS, not belonging to.
EXTREME', utmost; last.
EXTRIN'SIC, outward.
STRANGE, foreign; unusual.

Fabric-o, to make.

FAB'RIC, a building; an edifice.
FAB'RICATE, to form; to forge

Fabul-a, a feigned story.

FA'BLE, a feigned story.
FAB'ULOUS, feigned; forged.

Faci-es, the face.

DEFACE', to disfigure.
EF'FACE, to blot out; to destroy.
FACE, the visage; the front.
FASH'ION, form; custom.
FEA'TURE, cast of the face.
SUPERFIC'IAL, shallow; being on the surface.
SUR'FACE, the outside.

Facil-is, easy.

DIF'FICULT, hard to be done; laborious.
FACIL'ITY, ease; readiness.
FACIL'ITATE, to make easy.

Faci-o, fact-um, to make; to do.

AFFECT', to act upon; to move.
AFFEC'TION, love; kindness.
AM'PLIFY, to enlarge; to extend.
AR'TIFICE, a trick; a fraud.
BEATIF'IC, blissful.
BENEFAC'TION, the act of conferring a benefit.
BEN'EFICE, a church living.
BEN'EFIT, advantage.
CER'TIFY,° to give evidence.
CERTIF'ICATE, a testimony in writing.
CLAR'IFY, to make clear.
CLAS'SIFY, to arrange in classes.
CONFEC'TION, a sweetmeat.
COUN'TERFEIT, forged; fictitious.
CRU'CIFY, to nail to a cross.
DEFEAT', an overthrow.
DEFECT', a fault; a blemish.
DEFICI'ENT, wanting.
DEFIC'IT, want; deficiency.
DIG'NIFY, to exalt; to honor.
DISAFFEC'TION, dislike.
DISQUAL'IFY, to make unfit.
DISQUALIFICA'TION, incapacity.
DIVER'SIFY, to make different.
ED'IFICE, a fabric; a building.
EFFECT',° result; consequence.
EFFICI'ENT, active; able.
EXEM'PLIFY, to illustrate by example.
FACT, a reality; a thing done.
FAC'TION, a party; a division.
FAC'TORY, a building where any article is manufactured.
FAL'SIFY, to make false.
FEAT, an action; an exploit.
FOR'FEIT, a fine for an offence.
FOR'TIFY,° to strengthen.
GRAT'IFY, to indulge; to please.
GRATIFICA'TION, pleasure.
IMPER'FECT, defective; frail.
INARTIFICI'AL, plain; artless.
INEF'FICACY, want of power.
INFEC'TIOUS, pestilential.
INFECT', to impart disease.
INOFFICI'OUS, not meddling.
INSIGNIF'ICANCE, want of meaning; unimportance.
INSUFFICI'ENT, inadequate.
MAG'NIFY, to make great.
MALEFAC'TOR,° a criminal.
MANUFAC'TURE,° any thing made by art.

MOL'IFY, to soften; to assuage.
MUNIF'ICENT, liberal; generous.
NO'TIFY, to declare.
NOTIFICA'TION, the act of notifying.
OF'FICE, a place of business.
OFFICI'AL, pertaining to office.
OR'IFICE, an opening to a cavity.
PAC'IFY, to appease; to quiet.
PER'FECT, to finish; to complete.
PETRIFAC'TION, the act of turning to stone.
PROFICI'ENT, one skilled in a study or business.
PROF'IT, gain; advantage.
PROLIF'IC, productive.
PUR'IFY, to cleanse.
RAMIFICA'TION, a branching.
REC'TIFY, to make right.
REFEC'TORY, an eating room.
REFIT', to repair.
SAC'RIFICE, to destroy; to devote.
SANC'TIFY, to make holy.
SAT'ISFY, to content; to please.
SIG'NIFY, to declare; to mean.
SIGNIF'ICANCE, meaning; force
SIM'PLIFY, to render simple.
SUDORIF'IC, causing sweat.
SUFFICE', to supply; to satisfy
TER'RIFY, to frighten.
TES'TIFY, to bear witness.
VER'IFY, to prove true.

Fall-o, fals-um, to deceive.

FALSE, not true; not real.
FAL'LIBLE, liable to error.
FAL'SITY, an untruth.
FAL'LACY, deceitful argument.

Fam-a,* fame.

DEFAME', to slander.
FAME, celebrity; renown.
FA'MOUS, known; celebrated.
IN'FAMY, disgrace.

Fam-es, hunger.

FAM'ISH, to starve.
FAM'INE, scarcity of food.

Famili-a, a family.

FAMIL'IAR, easy in conversation; affable; well known.
FAM'ILY, the persons living in a house; a class.

Fan-um, a temple.

FANAT'IC,† an enthusiast.
FANE, a temple.
PROFANE',‡ without respect for sacred things; secular.

Fa-ri (*ab* ***For***), to speak.

AF'FABLE, easy to be spoken to.
INEF'FABLE, unspeakable.
IN'FANT, a young child.
IN'FANCY, the first stage of life.
INFAN'TICIDE, the murder of an infant.
NEFA'RIOUS, wicked.
PREF'ACE, an introductory speech or writing.

---

* A heathen goddess, celebrated by the poets, who represented her, as having her palace in the air, and as possessing a vast number of eyes, ears, and tongues.

† *Fanatics*, those who passed their time in temples (*fana*), and being often seized with a kind of enthusiasm, as if inspired by the Divinity, showed wild and antic gestures: such as cutting and slashing their arms with knives, shaking their heads, &c.

‡ *The profane*, those who were not initiated into the mysteries of *religion*, and therefore made to stand before or on the outside of the *temple*.

Fatig-o, to tire, to weary.

FATIGUE', to tire; to weary.

INDEFAT'IGABLE, not to be wearied; persevering.

Fedus, *for* **Fœdus, feder-is,** a league.

CONFED'ERACY, a number of persons or states united by a league.

CONFED'ERATE, one joined in a league.

FED'ERAL, relating to a league.

Felix, felic-is, happy.

FELIC'ITATE, to congratulate.

FELIC'ITY, happiness.

Femin-a, a woman, a female.

FEM'ININE, of the female sex.

EFFEM'INATE, womanish; soft.

Fend-o, fens-um, to keep off, to strike.

DEFEND',° to protect.

DEFENCE', guard; security.

INOFFEN'SIVE, harmless.

OFFEND', to displease.

FEN'CING, practice in using a sword for defence.

FEN'DER, a utensil placed before the fire.

OFFENCE', crime; injury.

Fer-a, a wild beast.

FEROC'ITY, cruelty; fierceness.

FIERCE, savage; furious.

Feri-o, to strike. INTERFERE', to interpose; to intermeddle.

Fer-o, to carry, to bear.

CIRCUM'FERENCE, the measure around the outside.

CONFER', to converse; to consult.

DEFER', to put off; to delay.

DEF'ERENCE, regard; respect.

DIF'FER, to vary; to disagree.

FER'RY, the passage over which ferry boats pass.

FER'TILE, fruitful; abundant.

FLORIF'EROUS, bearing flowers.

INDIF'FERENCE, impartiality; neglect; unconcern.

INFER', to deduce.

IN'FERENCE, a conclusion.

INSUF'FERABLE, not to be borne.

MISINFER', to infer wrong.

OF'FER, to present for acceptance.

PREFER', to regard more.

PROF'FER, to propose; to offer.

REFER', to submit.

SUF'FER, to undergo; to permit.

TRANSFER', to convey; to remove.

VOCIF'ERATE, to make outcries.

Ferv-eo, to grow hot.

FER'VOR, heat; zeal.

FER'VENT, hot; ardent.

FER'VID, eager; zealous.

Fess-um, to own, to declare.

CONFESS',° to acknowledge.

PROFESS', to declare openly.

Fest-um, a feast.

FES'TAL, befitting a feast.

FESTIV'ITY, gayety.

Fibr-a, a thread.

FI'BRE, a small thread.

FI'BROUS, composed of fibres.

Fid-es, faith.

AFFI'ANCE, a marriage contract.
CONFIDE', to trust in.
DEFY', to challenge; to dare.
DIF'FIDENT, distrustful.
FIDEL'ITY, faithfulness.
IN'FIDEL, a disbeliever.
PER'FIDY,° breach of faith.

Figur-a, a figure.

DISFIG'URE, to deform; to deface.
EF'FIGY, image; likeness.
FIG'URE, shape; semblance.

Fili-us, a son. FIL'IAL, relating to a son.

Fil-um, a thread.

FIL'AMENT, a slender thread.
FIL'TER, to strain.

Finance (Fr.), revenue.

FINANCE', income; revenue.
FINAN'CIAL, respecting finance.

Fing-o, fict-um, to feign.

FEIGN, to invent; to pretend.
FICTITI'OUS, false; not real.
FIC'TION, a tale; an invention.

Fin-is, the end.

AFFIN'ITY,° relation by marriage.
CON'FINE, border; edge.
DEFINE', to explain; to describe.
DEF'INITE, certain; limited.
FI'NAL, ultimate; conclusive.
FIN'ISH, to perfect; to end.
INDEF'INITE, not limited.
IN'FINITE, boundless.
REFINE', to improve; to polish.
SUPERFINE', eminently fine.

Firm-us, strong.

AFFIRM',° to declare positively.
CONFIRM', to establish; to strengthen.
FIR'MAMENT, the sky.
INFIRM', weak; feeble.
INFIRM'ARY, an hospital.

Fisc-us, a bag.

CONFIS'CATE,* to seize as a forfeit.
FIS'CAL, belonging to a public treasury.

Fix-us, fixed.

AFFIX',° to subjoin.
CRU'CIFIX, a cross bearing an image of our Saviour.
FIX'TURE, any thing fixed to a place or house.
INFIX', to drive in; to set.
POST'FIX,° a syllable added.
PRE'FIX,° to fix at the beginning.
TRANSFIX', to pierce through.

* The *Fiscus* was originally a *hamper* or *bag*, in which the emperor's treasure was kept: hence, to confiscate a person's property is to put it into the *Fiscus* or treasury of the king.

Flag-ro, to burn.

CONFLAGRA'TION, a general fire.
FLA'GRANT, burning; notorious.

Flamm-a, a flame.

FLAM'BEAU, a lighted torch.
INFLAME', to set on fire.
INFLAMMA'TION, a swelling and redness of an animal body.

Flat-us, a puff, a blast.

FLAT'ULENT, windy; vain.
INFLATE', to puff up.

Flect-o, flex-um, to bend.

CIR'CUMFLEX, an accent denoting a long syllable. L. (^) Gr. (~).
FLEXIBLE', ductile; pliant.
FLEX'URE, a bending; a joint.
REFLECT', to cast back; to think.

Fligo, flict-um, to beat, to strike.

AFFLICT', to pain; to grieve.
CON'FLICT, contest; struggle.
INFLICT', to lay on; to apply.

Flos, flor-is, a flower.

FLO'RA, the goddess of flowers.
FLO'RAL, relating to flowers.
FLOR'ID, flushed; brilliant.
FLO'RIST, a cultivator of flowers.

Fluctu-o, to rise in waves.

FLUC'TUATE, to move as waves.
FLUCTUA'TION, uncertainty.

Flu-o, flux-um, to flow.

AF'FLUENCE, riches; plenty.
AF'FLUX, a flowing to.
CON'FLUENCE, a junction of streams.
EF'FLUX, a flowing out.
FLU'ENCY, smoothness of speech.
FLU'ID, any thing that flows.
IN'FLUENCE, to bias; to modify.
INFLUEN'TIAL, exerting influence.
IN'FLUX, the act of flowing in.
SUPER'FLUOUS, unnecessary.

Foc-us, a point.

FO'CUS, the point where rays of light meet.
FO'CAL, belonging to the focus.

Foli-um, a leaf.

FOIL, leaf-metal.
FOLIA'CEOUS, consisting of leaves.
FO'LIO, a large book in which the paper is only once folded.
FO'LIAGE, a growth of leaves.
PORTFO'LIO, a case for loose leaves.

Fons, font-is, a source.

FONT, a baptismal vessel.
FOUN'TAIN, a well; a spring.

For-is, a door; abroad.

FOR'AGE, food for cattle.
FOR'EIGN, alien; remote.
FOR'FEIT, a fine for an offence.

Form-a, a form.

CONFORM', to make like.
DEFORM', to disfigure.
FORM, shape; figure.
INFORM', to instruct; to acquaint.
PERFORM', to execute; to do.
REFORMA'TION, a growing better.
RET'IFORM, having the form of a net.
TRANSFORM', to change the form.
VER'MIFORM, having the shape of a worm.
U'NIFORM, even; regular.

Formid-o, fear, dread. FOR'MIDABLE, dreadful.

For-o, to bore. PER'FORATE, to pierce; to bore.

Fors, fort-is, chance, luck.

FOR'TUNE, chance; wealth.
MISFOR'TUNE, calamity.
UNFOR'TUNATE, unlucky; unhappy.

Fort-is, strong, valiant.

COM'FORT,° support; consolation.
EF'FORT, exertion.
FORCE, to compel; to press.
FORT, a castle.
FOR'TIFY, to strengthen.
FOR'TITUDE, courage; bravery.
FOR'TRESS, a strong-hold.
ENFORCE', to put in execution.

For-um,° a public place in Rome.

FOREN'SIC, belonging to courts of judicature.
FAIR, a stated market.

Franc, Franche (Fr.), free.

ENFRAN'CHISE, to liberate.
FRAN'CHISE, privilege; right.
FRANK, liberal; open.
FRANK'LIN,° a freeholder.

Frang-o, fract-um, to break.

FRAC'TION, a part.
FRAC'TURE, a breach; a rupture.
FRAG'ILE, brittle; frail.
FRAIL, weak; infirm.
FRAIL'TY, weakness; infirmity
INFRAC'TION, violation.
INFRINGE', to violate; to break.
REFRACT', to break the course of rays of light.

Frater, fratr-is, a brother.

CONFRATER'NITY, a brotherhood.
FRATER'NAL, brotherly.
FRAT'RICIDE, the murder of a brother.

Fraus, fraud-is, fraud.

FRAUD, deceit.
DEFRAUD', to cheat.
FRAU'DULENCE, deceitfulness.

Frequens, frequent-is, frequent.

FREQUENT', to visit often.
INFRE'QUENCY, rareness.

Fric-o, frict-um, to rub.

DEN'TIFRICE, a powder for the teeth.
FRIC'TION, the act of rubbing.

Frig-us, frigor-is, cold.

FRIG'ID, cold; dull. | REFRIG'ERATE, to cool.

Frivol-us, trifling.

FRIV'OLOUS, light; trifling. | FRIVOL'ITY, triflingness.

Frons, front-is, the forehead.

AFFRONT', to insult; to offend.
CONFRONT',° to face; to oppose.
EFFRON'TERY, impudence.
FRONT, the face; the forepart.
FRONT'AL, relating to the forehead.

Frug-es, fruit, (figuratively *thrifty.*)

FRU'GAL, thrifty; sparing. | FRUGIF'EROUS, bearing fruit.

Frument-um, corn.

FRUMENTA'CEOUS, made of grain.
FRUMENTA'TION, a general distribution of corn.

Fruor, fruit-us, to enjoy. ***Fruct-us,*** fruit.

FRUC'TIFY, to make fruitful.
FRUITI'ON, enjoyment; use.
FRUIT, the produce of a tree or plant; profit.

Frustr-a, in vain. FRUS'TRATE, to make void; to defeat.

Fugi-o, fugit-um, to flee.

FU'GITIVE, unstable; fleeting.
SUB'TERFUGE, a shift; an evasion.
REF'UGE, shelter; protection.
VER'MIFUGE, medicine that expels worms.

Fulge-o, to shine.

EFFUL'GENCE, lustre; brightness.
REFUL'GENCE, brightness.
REFUL'GENT, shining.

Fum-us, smoke, fume.

FUME, to smoke; to be in a rage. | PERFUME', to scent.

Fund-o, fus-um, to pour, to melt.

CONFOUND',° to mingle; to perplex.
CONFUSE', to confound; to mix.
DIFFUSE', to pour out; to spread.
EFFU'SION, a pouring out.
INFUSE', to pour into; to inspire.
PROFUSE', lavish; prodigal.
REFUND',° to repay; to restore.
REFUSE', to deny; to decline.
REFU'SAL, a denial.

Fund-us, the bottom.

FOUND,° to raise; to establish.
FOUN'DERY, a casting-house.
FOUNDA'TION, basis; origin.
FOUN'DLING, a child deserted.
FUNDAMEN'TAL, lying at the foundation.
PROFOUND',° deep; thorough.
PROFUND'ITY, depth

Fun-is, a rope.

FUNIC'ULAR, consisting of cord.
FUNAM'BULIST, a rope-dancer.

Funus, funer-is, a burial.

FU'NERAL, burial; interment.
FUNE'REAL, suiting a funeral.

Fur, a thief. FUR'TIVE, stolen.

Furi-a, a madness.

FU'RIOUS, mad; raging.
FU'RY, rage; frenzy.
INFU'RIATE, to make furious.

Futil-is, trifling.

FU'TILE, trifling; worthless.
FUTIL'ITY, unimportance.

Fut-o, to blame, to disprove.

IRREFU'TABLE, not to be overthrown by argument.
REFUTE', to prove false.

Gala (Sp.), fine dress.

GA'LA, a festival.
GAL'LANT, brave; gay.

Galli-a, ancient France.

GAL'LIC, French.
GAL'LICISM, a French idiom.

Garr-io, to prattle.

GAR'RULOUS, talkative.
GARRUL'ITY, talkativeness.

Gel-u, frost, ice.

CONGEAL', to freeze.
CONGELA'TION, a freezing.
GEL'ATINE, an animal substance resembling jelly.
GEL'ID, extremely cold.
JEL'LY, a kind of sweetmeat.
INCONGEAL'ABLE, that cannot be frozen.

Genus, gener-is, a race, a family.

CONGE'NIAL, kindred.
DEGEN'ERATE,°fallen; base.
DEGEN'ERACY, a growing worse.
ENGEN'DER, to beget; to produce.
GEN'DER, sex.
GEN'ERAL,°public; extensive.
GEN'ERATE, to beget; to cause.
GEN'EROUS,°liberal; munificent.
GENEROS'ITY, liberality.
GE'NIAL,°cheerful; gay.
GE'NIUS, mental power.
GENTEEL', polite; elegant.
GENTIL'ITY, dignity of birth.
GEN'TILE, a pagan; a heathen.
GEN'TLE, soft; bland.
GEN'TRY, people of education and good breeding.
GEN'UINE,°not spurious; real.
INGE'NIOUS,°witty; skilful.
INGEN'UOUS,°open; frank.
INGENU'ITY, wit; acuteness.
PRIMOGEN'ITURE, state of being first born.
PROG'ENY, offspring; race.
PROGEN'ITOR, a forefather.
REGEN'ERATED, born anew.

Ger-o, gest-um, to bear, to carry.

BELLIG'ERENT, waging war.
CORNIG'EROUS, horned.
CONGES'TION, a collection of matter.
DIGEST',° to arrange; to dissolve.
GESTIC'ULATE, to use gestures.
GES'TURE, action; posture.
INDIGEST'IBLE, not digestible.
SUGGEST',° to hint; to intimate.
VICEGE'RENT,° a vicar; a substitute.

Gigas, gigant-is, a giant.

GI'ANT, a man of extraordinary size.
GIGAN'TIC, like a giant.

Glaci-es, ice. GLA'CIERS, fields of ice and snow.

Gladi-us, a sword.

GLADIA'TOR, a sword-player.
GLADIATO'RIAL, relating to sword-playing.

Glans, gland-is, a gland.

GLAND, a secretory organ of the human body.
GLANDIF'EROUS, bearing acorns.
GLAN'DULE, a small gland.

Glob-us, a globe, a round body.

GLOBE, a sphere; a ball.
GLOB'ULE, a little globe.

Glori-a, honor.

GLO'RIFY, to honor; to exalt.
GLO'RY, praise; renown.
INGLO'RIOUS, shameful.

Gluten, glutin-is, glue.

AGGLU'TINATE, to join; to glue to.
GLU'TINOUS, gluey; viscous.

Gnor-us, *for* ***Gnarus,*** knowing.

IG'NORANCE, want of knowledge.
IGNORA'MUS, a foolish fellow.

Gradi-or, gress-us, to go step by step.

AGGRESSI'ON, an attack.
CON'GRESS, a meeting of legislators.
DEGRADE',° to lower; to sink.
DEGRADA'TION, meanness of condition.
DEGREE', a rank; a step.
DIGRESS', to turn aside.
E'GRESS, a going out.
GRADE, rank; degree.
GRADA'TION, regular progress.
GRAD'UAL, advancing by steps.
GRAD'UATE,° to receive a degree.
INGRE'DIENT, a component part.
IN'GRESS, entrance.
PROGRESS', to proceed; to advance.
PROGRES'SIVE,° advancing.
RET'ROGRADE, going backwards.
TRANSGRESS',° to violate; to break.

Gramen, gramin-is, grass. GRAMINIV'OROUS, eating grass.

Grand-is, grand.

AG'GRANDIZE, to make great; to enlarge.
GRAND, great; illustrious.
GRANDEE', a man of high rank.
GRAN'DEUR, state; splendor.

Gran-um, a grain of corn.

GRAIN, all kinds of corn; a minute particle.
GRAN'ARY, a storehouse for grain.
GRAN'ITE,° a hard stone.
GRAN'ULE, a small grain.
GRAN'ULATE, to break into grains.
GRENADIER', a tall foot soldier, formerly a thrower of grenades.°

Grati-a, favor, gratitude.

AGREE', to concur; to assent.
AGREE'MENT, concord; compact.
CONGRAT'ULATE, to wish joy to.
DISAGREE'ABLE, unpleasing.
DISGRACE', to bring to shame.
GRACE, favor; kindness.
GRA'CIOUS, merciful; kind.
GRATE'FUL, thankful; pleasing.
GRAT'IFY, to indulge; to please
GRA'TIS, for nothing.
GRAT'ITUDE, thankfulness.
GRATU'ITOUS, bestowed freely.
GRATU'ITY, a present.
IN'GRATE, ungrateful.
INGRA'TIATE, to put in favor.

Grav-is, heavy.

AG'GRAVATE, to make worse.
AGGRIEVE', to vex; to trouble.
GRAVE, solemn; serious.
GRAV'ITY, weight; heaviness.
GRIEF, sorrow; trouble.
GRIE'VANCE, an injury.

Grex, greg-is, a flock.

AG'GREGATE, the sum of many collected parts.
CONG'REGATE, to assemble.
CONGREGA'TION, an assembly.
EGRE'GIOUS,° remarkably bad.
GREGA'RIOUS, flocking together.

Grus, gru-is, a crane.

CONGRU'ITY,° consistency; fitness.
INCONG'RUOUS, unsuitable.

Guarant-ir, for Garantir (Fr.), to guard, to secure.

GUARANTEE', to secure performance.
WAR'RANT, to authorize.
WAR'RANTY, authority; security.

Guard-er, for Garder (Fr.), to keep, to watch.

GUARD, to protect; to defend.
GUAR'DIAN, a protector.
WARD, one who is under the care of a guardian.

Guhern-o, to govern.

GOV'ERN, to rule; to manage.
GUBERNATO'RIAL, relating to a governor.
MISGOV'ERNMENT, bad government.

Gust-us, a taste, a relish.

DISGUST', aversion; dislike.
GUS'TO, relish; liking.

Guttur, the throat. GUT'TURAL, belonging to the throat.

Hab-eo, habit-um, to have, to hold.

A'BLE, having strength.
ABIL'ITY, power; capacity.
DISA'BLE, to deprive of force.
ENA'BLE, to empower.
EXHIB'IT,° to show; to display.
HABIL'IMENT, dress; garment.
HAB'IT, custom; use.
HABITA'TION, a dwelling.
HABIT'UATE, to accustom.
INHAB'ITANT, a resident.
PROHIB'IT,° to forbid; to restrain.

Hær-eo, hæs-um, to stick.

ADHERE', to stick to.
COHE'SIVE, sticking.
HES'ITANCY, uncertainty; delay.
HES'ITATE, to delay; to pause.
INCOHE'RENT, unconnected.
INHE'RENT, existing in; innate.

Hæres, hæred-is, an heir.

COHEIR', a joint heir.
DISINHER'IT, to deprive of an inheritance.
HEIR, one who inherits.
HER'ITABLE, capable of being inherited.
HER'ITAGE, the thing inherited.
HERED'ITARY, descending from father to son.
INHER'IT, to receive by descent.

/ ***Hal-o***, to breathe.

EXHALE', to send out vapors.
EXHALA'TION, vapor; effluvia.
INHALE', to draw in with the breath.

Haust-um (ab ***haurio***), to draw.

EXHAUST', to drain.
INEXHAUS'TIBLE, not to be drained.

Herb-a, an herb. HER'BAGE, herbs; pasture.

Hilar-is, cheerful.

EXHIL'ARATE, to enliven.
HILAR'ITY, mirth; merriment.

Homo, homin-is, a man.

HOM'ICIDE, manslaughter.
HU'MAN, belonging to mankind.
HU'MANIZE, to soften.
INHUMAN'ITY, brutality.

Honor, honor.

DISHON'EST, wicked; fraudulent.
DISHON'OR, disgrace; shame.
HON'ESTY, justice; truth.
HON'ORARY, conferring honor.

Horre-o, to be dreadful.

ABHOR', to detest; to loathe.
HOR'RIBLE, dreadful; shocking.
HOR'RID, hideous; frightful.
HORRIF'IC, causing horror.
HOR'ROR, dread; terror.

Hort-us, a garden.

HOR'TICULTURE, the art of cultivating gardens.

Hospes, hospit-is, a host or guest.

HOS'PITABLE, kind to strangers.
HOS'PITAL, a building for the sick.
HOST, one who entertains another.
HOTEL, an inn.
OST'LER, a man who takes care of horses.
INHOSPITAL'ITY, unkindness to strangers.

Host-is, an enemy.

HOST, an army; multitude.
HOSTIL'ITY, open war.

Hum-eo, to be moist.

HU'MID, wet; moist.
HU'MOR, moisture of the body

Hum-us, the ground. ***Humil-is,*** low, poor.

HUMIL'IATE, to depress.
HUM'BLE, to crush; to subdue.
HUMIL'ITY, freedom from pride.
INHUME', to bury.
POST'HUMOUS, published after one's death.

Idem, the same.

IDEN'TITY, sameness.
IDEN'TICAL, the same.
IDEN'TIFY, to prove the same.

Ign-is, fire.

IG'NEOUS, containing fire.
IGNITE', to set on fire.

Imag-o, an image.

IM'AGE, a picture; an idol.
IMAG'INE, to fancy; to conceive.

Imbecill-is, weak.

IM'BECILE, weak; feeble.
IMBECIL'ITY, weakness.

Imit-or, to copy or resemble.

IM'ITATE, to follow; to copy.
INIM'ITABLE, that cannot be imitated.

Imper-o, imperat-um, to command.

EM'PEROR, a monarch.
EM'PIRE, the dominion of an emperor.
IMPER'ATIVE, commanding.
IMPE'RIAL, royal; regal.
IMPE'RIOUS, overbearing.

Infer-us, below.

INFE'RIOR, lower in place.
INFER'NAL, hellish.

Insul-a, an island.

IN'SULAR, belonging to an island.
IN'SULATE, to detach.
PENIN'SULA, a piece of land almost surrounded by water.

Integer, entire.

IN'TEGER, a whole number.
IN'TEGRAL, whole; complete.
INTEG'RITY, honesty.
IN'TEGRATE, to make entire.

9*

Intestin-a, the bowels.

INTES'TINAL, belonging to the intestines.
INTES'TINE, internal; inward.
INTES'TINES, the entrails.

Int-us, within.

INTE'RIOR, inner; inland.
INTER'NAL, inward.
IN'TIMATE, inmost; familiar.
IN'TIMACY, close familiarity.
INTIMA'TION, a hint.
INTRIN'SIC, internal; real.

Invit-o, invitat-um, to invite.

INVITE', to bid; to ask.
INVITA'TION, the act of inviting.

Ir-a, anger.

DIRE,° dreadful; dismal.
IRE, anger; rage.
IR'RITABLE, easily provoked.
IR'RITATE, to tease; to fret.

Itali-a, Italy.

ITAL'IAN, a native of Italy.
ITAL'ICISE, to mark in italics.
ITAL'ICS, leaning letters, first used in Italy.

Iter-um, again. REIT'ERATE, to repeat again and again.

Iter, itiner-is, a journey. ITIN'ERANT, travelling.

Jac-eo, to lie.

ADJA'CENT, lying near.
INTERJA'CENT, lying between.

Jac-io, jact-um, to throw.

AB'JECT, mean; vile.
AD'JECTIVE, a describing word.
CONJEC'TURE, a guess.
DEJEC'TION, lowness of spirits.
EJECT', to throw out; to expel.
EJAC'ULATE,° to utter abruptly.
INJECT', to throw in.
INTERJEC'TION, an exclamation.
MISCONJEC'TURE, a wrong guess.
OBJEC'TIVE, relating to the object.
PRO'JECT, scheme; contrivance.
REJECT', to cast off; to discard.
SUB'JECT, placed under.

Janu-a, a gate, a door. JAN'ITOR, a door-keeper.

Joc-us, a joke.

JOCOSE',° merry; waggish.
JOC'ULAR, sportive; merry.
JOC'UND, gay; lively.
JOKE, to jest; to frolic.

Jour (Fr.), a day.

ADJOURN', to put off; to defer.
JOURN'AL, a diary.
JOUR'NEY,° travel by land.
SOJOURN', a temporary stay.

Judic-o, judicat-um, to judge

ADJUDGE', to pass a sentence.
ADJU'DICATE, to try and decide.
INJUDICI'OUS, unwise.
JUDGE, to discern; to decide.
JU'DICATURE, power of distributing justice.
JUDICI'AL, pertaining to courts of law.
JUDICI'ARY, the system of courts of justice.
MISJUDGE', to mistake.
PREJ'UDICE,° bias; injury.

Jug-um, a yoke.

CON'JUGAL, matrimonial.
CON'JUGATE, to inflect a verb.
SUBJUGA'TION, the act of subduing.

Jung-o, junct-um, to join.

ADJOIN', to join to.
AD'JUNCT,°something joined.
CONJOIN', to unite; to associate.
DISJOIN', to separate.
ENJOIN', to direct; to order.
INJUNC'TION, order; precept.
JOIN, to combine; to unite.
JUNC'TURE, union.
JUN'TO,°a cabal; a faction.
MISJOIN', to join unfitly.
SUBJOIN', to add to the end.
SUBJUNC'TIVE,°conditional.

Jur-o, to swear.

ABJURE', to renounce upon oath.
CONJURE', to enjoin solemnly.
JU'ROR, one that serves on a jury.
JU'RY, twelve men sworn to render a true verdict.
PER'JURY, false swearing.

Jus, juris, law, right.

IN'JURE, to hurt; to wrong.
INJU'RIOUS, unjust; hurtful.
JURISDIC'TION, extent of power.
JURISPRU'DENCE, the science of law.
JU'RIST, one versed in the civil law.

Just-us, just.

ADJUST', to regulate.
INJUST'ICE, iniquity; wrong.
JUST, upright; honest.
JUSTIC'IARY, an administrator of justice.
JUS'TIFY, to free from fault.

Juven-is, young.

JU'VENILE, youthful.
JU'NIOR, one younger.

Juvo, jut-um, to help.

AD'JUTANT, a major's aid.
COADJU'TOR, a fellow-helper.

Labor, laps-us, to fall or glide.

COLLAPSE', to fall together.
ELAPSE', to pass away.
LAPSE, flow; fall.
RELAPSE', to slide back.

Labor, labor.

ELAB'ORATE, finished with care.
LAB'ORATORY, a chemist's work room.

Lac, lact-is, milk.

LAC'TEAL, pertaining to milk.
LACTIF'EROUS, bearing milk.

Lacer, torn. LAC'ERATE, to tear; to rend.

Laconi-a,°the country of the Spartans. LACON'IC, concise; brief.

Lan-a, wool.

LAN'IFICE, woollen manufacture.
LANIG'EROUS, bearing wool.

Langu-eo, to droop.

LAN'GUID, faint; weak.
LAN'GUISH, to grow feeble.
LANG'UOR, faintness; weakness.

Lapis, lapid-is, a stone.

DILAPIDA'TION,°ruin; decay.
LAP'IDARY, a dealer in gems.

Larg-us, big, liberal.

ENLARGE', to increase; to expand.
LARGESS', a gift; a bounty.

Lass-us, weary. LAS'SITUDE, weariness.

Late-o, to hide. LA'TENT, hidden.

Latin-us, Latin.

LAT'INIST, one skilled in Latin.
LATIN'ITY, purity of Latin style

Lat-um (*ab* ***Fero***), to carry, to bring.

DIL'ATORY,°tardy; slow.
ELA'TED, flushed with success.
LEG'ISLATE,°to enact laws.
MISRELATE', to relate falsely.
OBLA'TION, an offering.
PREL'ACY, the office of a prelate.
PREL'ATE,°a church dignitary.
RELATE', to tell; to recite.
REL'ATIVE, having relation.
SUPER'LATIVE, highest.
TRANSLA'TION, the act of interpreting into another language.

Latus, later-is, the side.

COLLAT'ERAL, from the side; not direct.
EQUILAT'ERAL, of equal sides.
LAT'ERAL, belonging to the side.

Lat-us, broad.

DILATE', to extend; to widen.
DILATA'TION, expansion.
LAT'ITUDE, breadth; extent.

Laus, laud-is, praise.

ALLOW', to permit.
LAUD, to praise.
LAU'DABLE, praise-worthy.
LAU'DATORY, bestowing praise

Lav-o, lot-um, to wash.

LA'VA, liquid and vitrified matter discharged by volcanoes.
LAVE, to wash; to bathe.
LO'TION, a medicinal wash

Lax-us, loose.

LAX, loose; vague.
PROLIX'ITY, tediousness.
RELAX', to slacken; to remit.
RELAXA'TION, ease; remission.

Leg-o, legat-um, to send as an ambassador, to bequeath.

ALLEGE',°to affirm; to plead.
ALLEGA'TION, declaration; plea.
COL'LEAGUE, a partner.
ALLE'GIANCE, the duty of a subject.
COL'LEGE, a seminary of learning.

DEL'EGATE, to send on an embassy.
LEG'ACY, a gift made by will.
LEGATEE', one who has a legacy.
LEG'ATE, the Pope's ambassador.

Leg-o, lect-um, to gather, to read, to choose.

COL'LECT, to gather together.
DI'ALECT,° manner of expression.
DIL'IGENT, industrious; active.
ELEC'TION, choice.
ELEC'TORATE, the office of an elector.
EL'EGANCE, beauty; grace.
EL'IGIBLE, fit to be chosen.
INEL'EGANT, not beautiful.
IN'TELLECT, understanding.
INTEL'LIGENCE, information.
INTEL'LIGIBLE, that may be understood.
LEC'TURE,° a discourse.
LE'GEND,° a chronicle; a wild narrative.
LEG'IBLE, that may be read.
LE'GION,° a body of soldiers.
LEX'ICON,° a dictionary.
NEGLECT',° inattention; slight.
NEG'LIGENT, careless; heedless.
PREDILEC'TION, a liking beforehand.
RECOLLECT', to bring to mind.
RE-ELEC'TION, election a second time.
SELEC'TION, choice.

Len-is, gentle, soft, mild.

LE'NIENT, mild; soothing.
LEN'ITY, mildness.

Le-o, *or* ***Lin-o,*** to besmear, to blot

DELETE'RIOUS, destructive.
INDEL'IBLE, not to be blotted out

Lev-o, levat-um, to lift up, to raise: ***Levis,*** light.

ALLE'VIATE, to ease; to soften.
EL'EVATE, to raise up.
LEAV'EN, a fermenting mixture.
LEV'EE,° a concourse; a crowd.
LE'VER,° a mechanical power.
LEV'Y, to raise; to collect.
LEV'ITY, lightness; vanity.
REL'EVANT,° pertinent; suitable
RELIEVE', to ease; to succor.
RELIEF', ease; assistance.

Lex, leg-is, a law or rule.

ILLE'GAL, contrary to law.
ILLEGIT'IMATE, contrary to law.
LEGAL'ITY, lawfulness.
LE'GALIZE, to authorize.
LEGISLA'TURE, the power that makes laws.
LEG'ISLATE, to make laws
LEGIT'IMACY, lawfulness of birth.
PRIV'ILEGE,° a peculiar advantage.
SAC'RILEGE,° a violation of things sacred.

Liber, libr-i, a book. LI'BRARY, an apartment for books.

Libr-a, a pound, a balance. EQUILIB'RIUM, equality of weight

Lice-o, licit-um, to be lawful. ***Licenti-a,*** license.

ILLIC'IT, unlawful.
LI'CENSE, permission; excess.
LICEN'TIOUS, unrestrained.

Lici-o, licit-um, to draw, to allure. ELIC'IT, to draw out.

Lido, lis-um, to hurt, to strike.

COLLISI'ON, a striking together.
ELISI'ON, a striking out.

Lieu (Fr.), place, stead.

LIEU, place ; room.
LIEUTEN'ANCY, the office of a lieutenant.
LIEUTEN'ANT, a deputy.
PUR'LIEU,° border ; district.

Lign-um, wood. LIG'NEOUS, made of wood.

Lig-o, ligat-um, to bind, to tie.

DISOBLIGE', to give offence to.
IRRELIGI'ON, impiety.
LEAGUE, a confederacy.
LI'ABLE, subject.
LIEGE, a sovereign.
LIG'AMENT,°a tie ; a ligature.
LIG'ATURE, a band ; a cord.
OB'LIGATE, to bind by contract.
OB'LIGATORY, binding.
OBLIGE', to gratify ; to compel.
RELIGI'ON, duty to God ; piety

Limen, limin-is, a threshold.

ELIM'INATE, to expel.
PRELIM'INARY, introductory.

Limes, limit-is, a path, a limit.

ILLIM'ITABLE, that cannot be limited.
LIM'IT, to confine ; to restrain.
LIMITA'TION, a restriction.

Line-a, a line.

CURVILIN'EAR, composed of curved lines.
DELIN'EATE,° to describe ; to sketch.
INTERLINE', to write between lines.
LINE, a rank ; a row.
LIN'EAL, descending in a line.
LIN'EAMENT, feature ; outline.
LIN'EAGE,°race ; progeny.
RECTILIN'EAR, right-lined.

Lingu-a, the tongue, a language.

LIN'GO, language ; speech.
LAN'GUAGE, human speech.
LIN'GUIST, one skilled in languages.

Linqu-o, lict-um, to leave, to forsake.

DELINQ'UENT,°an offender.
DERELIC'TION, a forsaking.
REL'IC, something left.
REL'ICT, a widow.
RELIN'QUISH, to forsake ; to quit.

Lique-o, to melt, to be liquid.

LIQ'UEFY, to become liquid.
LIQ'UOR, any liquid.
LIQ'UIDATE, to clear away ; to pay.

Lis, lit-is, strife ; a lawsuit.

LIT'IGATE, to contest in law.
LITIGI'OUS, given to litigation.

Liter-a, a letter.

ILLIT'ERATE, unlearned.
LET'TER, an alphabetical character.
LIT'ERAL, according to the letter.
LIT'ERARY, relating to letters.
LITERA'TI, men of learning.
LIT'ERATURE,° learning.
OBLIT'ERATE,° to rub out.

Livr-er (Fr.), to give or deliver up.

DELIV'ER, to set free.
LIV'ERY,° a particular dress.

Loc-us, a place.

COL'LOCATE, to place together.
DISLOCA'TION, the act of displacing; a putting out of joint.
LO'CAL, relating to place.
LO'CATE, to place; to fix.
LOCOMO'TION, the power of changing place.

Long-us, long.

ELON'GATE, to lengthen.
LONGEV'ITY, length of life.
LON'GITUDE, distance east or west.
OB'LONG, longer than broad.
PROLONGA'TION, the act of lengthening.

Loqu-or, locut-us, to speak.

CIRCUMLOCU'TION, a circuit of words.
COL'LOQUY, conversation.
COLLO'QUIAL, relating to common conversation.
EL'OQUENT, having the power of oratory.
ELOCU'TION, utterance; delivery.
LOQUAC'ITY, talkativeness.
OB'LOQUY, blame; slander.
SOLIL'OQUY, a speech to one's self.
VENTRIL'OQUISM,* the act of speaking from the stomach.

Loy, or ***Loi*** (Fr.), law.

DISLOY'ALTY, want of fidelity.
LOY'AL,° true; faithful.

Luc-eo, to shine.

ELU'CIDATE,° to explain.
LU'CIFER,° the morning star.
PELLU'CID, clear; not opaque.
TRANSLU'CENT, transparent; clear.

Lucr-um, gain, profit.

LU'CRE, gain; profit.
LU'CRATIVE, profitable.

Luct-or, to struggle. RELUC'TANCE,° unwillingness

Ludo, lus-um, to play, to deceive.

ALLUDE',° to refer to.
ALLU'SION, a reference; a hint.
COLLU'SION,° deceitful agreement.
DELUDE', to beguile.
DELU'SIVE, deceptive.
ELUDE', to evade.
ILLU'SION, false show; error.
LU'DICROUS, comical; sportive.
PRE'LUDE, something introductory.

* The art of speaking, so that the voice does not seem to come from the speaker, but from some one at a distance.

Lumen, lumin-is, light.

ILLUMINA'TION, a lighting up.
LU'MINOUS, shining; bright.
LU'MINARY, any body which gives light.

Lun-a, the moon

LU'NACY,* madness.
LU'NATIC, a madman.
LU'NAR, relating to the moon.
SUB'LUNARY,° of this world.

Lu-o, lut-um, to wash away, or purge.

ABLU'TION,° the act of cleansing.
ALLU'VIAL,° added to land by the wash of water.
DILUTE',° to make thin or weak.
DIL'UENT, that which dilutes.
POLLUTE',° to defile; to taint.

Lustr-um, ° a survey made every four years.

ILLUS'TRATE,° to explain.
ILLUS'TRIOUS, noble; eminent.
LUS'TRE, splendor; renown.

Luxuri-a, luxury.

LUS'CIOUS, sweet; delicious.
LUX'URY, delicious fare.
LUXU'RIANT, very abundant.
LUXU'RIOUS, voluptuous.

Mace-o, to be lean or thin.

EMA'CIATE, to grow lean; to waste.

Macul-a, a stain or spot; a fault.

IMMAC'ULATE, spotless; pure.

Magister, magistr-i, a master.

MAG'ISTRACY, the office of a magistrate.
MAG'ISTRATE, a civil officer.
MAS'TER, one who controls.

Magnes, magnet-is, the loadstone.

MAG'NET,° the loadstone.
MAGNET'ICAL, attractive.
MAG'NETISM, the power of attraction.

Magn-us, great.

MAGNANIM'ITY, greatness of mind.
MAGNAN'IMOUS,° noble; brave.
MAGNIF'ICO, a grandee of Venice.
MAG'NIFY, to make greater.
MAGNIF'ICENT, grand; splendid.
MAG'NITUDE, size; greatness.
MAJ'ESTY, dignity; grandeur.
MAJES'TICAL, august; grand.
MA'JOR, greater; senior.
MAJOR'ITY, the greater number.

Mag-us, a diviner or enchanter.

MA'GI, wise men; eastern philosophers.
MAG'IC, enchantment.
MAGICI'AN, one skilled in magic.

---

* So called from a superstitious belief that the moon exerted an influence upon those who were insane.

Male, evil, ill.

DIS'MAL,°sorrowful; gloomy.
MALEDIC'TION, a curse.
MALEFAC'TOR, a criminal.
MALEV'OLENCE, ill-will.

Malign-us, envious, fatal to life.

MALIG'NANT, pernicious; evil.
MALIG'NITY, violent hatred.

Maliti-a, deliberate mischief.

MAL'ICE, desire to injure.
MALICI'OUS, ill-disposed.

Malle-us, a hammer.

MAL'LEABLE, that may be spread by beating.
MAL'LET, a wooden hammer.

Mand-o, mandat-um, to commit, to command.

COMMAND', to order; to lead.
COMMEND', to praise.
COMMENDA'TION, praise.
COUNTERMAND', to revoke a command.
DEMAND', a claim; a question.
MAN'DATE, a command.
REMAND', to send back.
RECOMMEND', to commend to another.

Mane-o, mans-um, to stay, to abide.

MAN'SION, a house; a residence.
PER'MANENCE, duration.
REMAIN', to continue; to endure.
REM'NANT, that which is left.

Manifest-us, clear, evident.

MAN'IFEST, plain; open.
MANIFES'TO, a declaration.

Mano, manat-um, to flow. EM'ANATE, to issue from.

Man-us, the hand.

AMANUEN'SIS, a person who writes what another dictates.
EMAN'CIPATE,°to set free.
MAINTAIN', to preserve.
MAIN'TENANCE,°sustenance.
MAN'ACLE,°to shackle.
MAN'AGE,°to conduct.
MANIPULA'TION,°a handling.
MANŒU'VRE,° skilful management.
MAN'UAL,°performed by hand.
MANUFAC'TURE, any thing made by art.
MANUMISS'ION,°the act of giving liberty to slaves.
MANUMIT', to release from slavery.
MANURE',°to fertilize.
MAN'USCRIPT, a writing.
MISMAN'AGE, to manage ill.
PORTMAN'TEAU, a bag for clothes

Mar-e, the sea.

MARINE', belonging to the sea.
MAR'INER, a seaman.
MAR'ITIME, near to the sea.
SUBMARINE', under the sea.

Margo, margin-is, a brink or edge.

MAR'GIN, the border; the edge.
MAR'GINAL, on the margin.

Mars, mart-is, the god of war. MAR'TIAL, warlike.

Mascul-us, a male. MAS'CULINE, male; manly.

Mater, matr-is, a mother.

MATER'NAL, motherly.
MAT'RICIDE, the murder of a mother.
MA'TRON, an elderly woman.
MA'TRIMONY, marriage.

Matur-us, ripe.

IMMATURE', not ripe.
MATU'RITY, ripeness.
PREMATURE', ripe too soon.

Medi-us, middle.

IMME'DIATE, instant; direct.
INTERME'DIATE, coming between.
MEDIA'TION, interposition.
MEDIA'TOR, an intercessor.
MEDIOC'RITY, middle rate.
MEDITERRA'NEAN, encircled with land.
ME'DIUM, the middle state.

Mede-or, to cure, to heal.

MED'ICAL, relating to medicine.
REME'DIAL, affording remedy.

Medit-or, to muse, or think upon.

MEDITA'TION, deep thought.
PREMED'ITATE, to think beforehand.

Melior, better.

AME'LIORATE, to improve.
MELIORA'TION, improvement.

Memor, mindful.

COMMEM'ORATE, to hold in memory.
COMMEM'ORABLE, worthy of remembrance.
IMMEMO'RIAL, beyond memory.
MEMEN'TO,° a memorial.
MEMOIR', an account written from memory.
MEMORAN'DUM, a note to help the memory.
MEM'ORY, the faculty of recollecting.
MEMO'RIAL, something to keep in memory.
MEN'TION, to speak of.
REMEM'BER, to bear in mind.
REMINIS'CENCE, recollection.

Menage (Fr.), household, a collection of animals.

MENAG'ERY, a collection of animals.
ME'NIAL, a domestic servant.

Mend-a, a blemish, a mistake.

AMEND', to correct; to reform.
MEND, to repair; to improve.

Mendic-us, a beggar. MEN'DICANT, a beggar.

Mens, ment-is, the mind.

COM'MENTARY, a writing to explain another.
COMMENTA'TOR, a writer of commentaries.
COM'MENT, note; explanation.
MEN'TAL, relating to the mind
VEHE'MENCE, force; ardor.

Mensur-a, a measure. ***Meti-or***, to measure.

COMMEN'SURATE, proportionate.
DIMEN'SION, bulk; extent.
IMMENSE', unbounded; vast.
IMMEN'SITY, infinity; vastness.
METE, to measure.
MEAS'URE, to compute quantity by a rule.
ME'TER, a measurer.
MENSURA'TION, the art of measuring.

Me-o, meat-um, to glide, to flow.

MEAN'DER,° to run with a winding course.
PER'MEATE, to pass through.

Merc-or, to buy, to traffic.

COM'MERCE, trade; intercourse.
COMMER'CIAL, relating to commerce.
MER'CANTILE, trading.
MER'CENARY, a hireling.
MER'CER, one who sells silks.
MAR'KET, a place of sale.
MER'CHANDISE, things bought and sold.
MER'CHANT, a trader.
MER'CURY*, an ancient heathen deity.

Merg-o, mers-um, to plunge, to overwhelm.

EMERGE', to rise out of.
EMER'GENCY,°sudden occasion.
IMMERSE', to put under water.
MERGE, to sink.
SUBMERGE', to put under water.
SUBMER'SION, a drowning.

Meridi-es, mid-day, noon; the south.

ANTEMERID'IAN, before noon.
MERID'IAN, noon; mid-day.
MERID'IONAL, southern.
POSTMERID'IAN, afternoon.

Merit-um, (ab ***mereo***), to earn, to deserve.

DEMER'IT, ill desert; fault.
MER'IT, to deserve.
MERITO'RIOUS, deserving of reward.

Migr-o, migrat-um, to remove from one place to another.

EM'IGRANT, one who emigrates.
EM'IGRATE, to remove from a place.
IM'MIGRANT, one who immigrates.
IMMIGRA'TION, the act of coming into a new country.
MI'GRATE, to remove to another country.

Miles, milit-is, a soldier.

MIL'ITANT, fighting.
MIL'ITARY, relating to soldiers.
MIL'ITATE, to oppose.
MILIT'IA,°the enrolled soldiers.

Mille, a thousand.

MILLEN'NIUM,°a thousand years.
MIL'LEPED, an insect having many feet.

* He was the god of eloquence, the patron of merchants, the inventor of the lyre and harp, the protector of poets or men of genius, of musicians, wrestlers &c., the conductor of departed ghosts to their proper mansions, and conveyed the messages of Jupiter and all the other gods.

Min-æ, threats. MEN'ACE, to threaten.

Min-eo, to jut out, to hang over.

EM'INENT, high ; exalted.
IM'MINENT, threatening ; near.
PRE-EM'INENCE, superiority.
PROM'INENCE, distinction.
PROM'INENT, standing out.

Mineral (Fr.), a mineral. MINERAL'OGY, the science of minerals.

Minister, ministr-i, a servant, a helper.

ADMIN'ISTER, to supply.
ADMINISTRA'TION, act of administering; dispensation.
MIN'ISTER,° a clergyman.
MIN'ISTRY, the body of ministers
MINISTRA'TION, agency ; service.

Minu-o, minut-um, to lessen.

DIMIN'ISH, to impair ; to lessen.
DIMINU'TION, act of making less.
DIMIN'UTIVE, small.
MIN'IATURE, a picture less than the reality.
MIN'IMUM, the smallest quantity.
MIN'ION, a favorite ; a small type.
MI'NOR,° one under age.
MINOR'ITY, the less number.
MIN'UEND, the number to be diminished.
MI'NUS, diminished by.
MINUTE', very small.

Mir-us, strange, wonderful.

ADMIRE', to regard with wonder or esteem.
ADMIRA'TION, wonder; esteem.
MIR'ACLE,° a supernatural event.
MIRAC'ULOUS, supernatural.
MIR'ROR, a looking-glass.

Misc-eo, mixt-um, to mix.

ADMIX'TURE, the substance mingled.
COMMIX', to mingle ; to blend.
INTERMIX', to mingle together.
MIS'CELLANY, a collection of various things.
MIN'GLE, to mix ; to join.
MIX, to put together.
MIX'TURE, a mixed mass.
PROMIS'CUOUS, mingled ; confused.

Miser, wretched, pitiful.

COMMIS'ERATE, to compassionate, to pity.
MIS'ERABLE, wretched ; helpless.
MI'SER, a person covetous to excess.
MIS'ERY, calamity ; distress.

Mitt-o, miss-um, to send.

ADMISSI'ON, the act of admitting.
ADMIT', to receive ; to allow.
ADMIT'TANCE, entrance.
COMMISSI'ON, a trust ; a warrant.
COM'MISSARY—a delegate ; a deputy.
COMMIT'MENT, the act of committing.
COMMIT'TEE,° persons selected to examine or manage any matter.
COM'PROMISE,° to adjust by concession.
DEMISE', death ; decease.
DISMISSI'ON, discharge.
EM'ISSARY,° one sent on a mission.
EMISSI'ON, a sending out.
EMIT', to send forth.
INADMIS'SIBLE, not to be allowed.
INTERMISSI'ON,° cessation ; pause.
INTERMIT'TENT, ceasing at intervals.
MANUMISSI'ON, the act of giving liberty to slaves.

MANUMIT', to release from slavery.
MIS'SILE, that may be thrown.
MISSI'ON, a being sent.
MISSI'ONARY, one sent to propagate religion.
MIS'SIVE,°a letter sent.
OMIT', to leave out.
OMISS'ION, neglect; failure.
PER'MIT,°a written permission.
PERMIS'SIVE, granting leave.
PREMISE', to state beforehand.
PROM'ISE,°a binding declaration.
PROM'ISSORY, containing a promise.
RE-ADMIT', to let in again.
RE-COMMIT', to commit anew.
REMISS',°slack; careless.
REMISSI'ON, abatement; pardon.
REMIT'TANCE, a sum sent back.
SUBMIS'SIVE, humble.
SUBMIT',°to resign; to yield.
SURMISE', a suspicion.
TRANSMISSI'ON, a sending over.
TRANSMIT', to send over.
UNREMIT'TED, not abated; incessant.

Mod-us, a measure, a manner.

ACCOM'MODATE, to fit; to adjust.
COMMO'DIOUS, convenient.
COMMOD'ITY, interest; merchandise.
DISCOMMODE', to put to trouble.
IMMOD'ERATE,°excessive.
IMMOD'EST, wanting modesty.
MODE, method; form.
MOD'EL, a mould; a pattern.
MOD'ERATE, temperate; not violent.
MOD'ERN, late; recent.
MOD'ESTY, decency; diffidence.
MOD'IFY, to shape; to soften.
MODIFICA'TION, the act of modifying.
MOOD, temper; disposition.
MOD'ULATE,°to vary sound.
REMOD'EL, to model anew.

Moli-or, to rear, to build.

DEMOL'ISH, to destroy.
DEMOLITION, destruction.

Moll-is, soft.

EMOL'LIENT, softening.
MOL'LIFY, to assuage; to quiet.

Moment-um, motion, force.

MO'MENT, importance; an instant.
MOMEN'TOUS, weighty.
MOMEN'TUM,°force; impetus.
MO'MENTARY, lasting for a moment.

Mone-o, monit-um, to put in mind, to warn.

ADMON'ISH, to warn; to reprove.
ADMONITI'ON, gentle reproof.
MON'ITOR, one who warns.
MON'UMENT, a memorial; a tomb.
PREMON'ITORY, giving warning beforehand.
SUM'MON, to call; to cite.
SUM'MONS, a call of authority.

Mons, mont-is, a high hill.

DISMOUNT', to alight from a horse.
MOUND, a heap or bank of earth.
MOUN'TAIN, a very large hill.
MOUN'TEBANK,°a quack.
PROM'ONTORY, a high land jutting into the sea.
REMOUNT', to mount again.
SURMOUNT', to rise above.

Monstr-o, to show, to declare.

DEM'ONSTRATE, to show plainly.
MON'STER, something unnatural.
MON'STROUS, strange; shocking.
REMON'STRATE, to exhibit reasons against.
REMON'STRANCE, expostulation.

Morb-us, a disease. MOR'BID, diseased; sickly.

Mord-eo, mors-um, to bite.

MOR'SEL, a mouthful.
REMORSE', sorrow for a fault.

Mors, mort-is, death.

IMMOR'TAL, exempt from death.
IMMOR'TALIZE, to make immortal.
MORTAL'ITY, death.
MOR'TIFY, to subdue; to humble.
MUR'DER, to destroy.

Mos, mor-is, a custom, or manner.

DEMOR'ALIZE, to destroy the morals of.
IMMOR'AL, vicious.
MORAL'ITY, correctness of life.

Move-o, mot-um, to move.

COMMO'TION, tumult; sedition.
EMO'TION, passion; excitement.
IMMOV'ABLE, fixed; firm.
LOCOMO'TION, the power of changing place.
MOB, a tumultuous crowd.
MOBIL'ITY, fickleness.
MO'TION, the act of changing place.
MO'TIVE, causing motion.
MOVE, to put in motion.
PROMOTE', to forward; to raise.
REMOTE', distant.
REMOVE', to put from its place.

Mult-us, many.

MULTANG'ULAR, many-cornered.
MULTIFA'RIOUS, having great variety.
MUL'TIPLE, a number which exactly contains another several times.
MUL'TIPLEX, manifold.
MULTIPLICAND', the number to be multiplied.
MULTIPLICA'TION, the act of multiplying.
MUL'TIPLY, to increase in number.
MUL'TITUDE, a crowd or throng.

Mund-us, the world.

MUN'DANE, belonging to this world.
SUPRAMUN'DANE, situated above the world.

Munio, munit-um, to fortify.

AMMUNITI'ON, military stores.

Mun-us, muner-is, a gift, or present; an office.

COM'MON, an open, public ground.
COM'MONALTY, the common people.
COMMU'NION, intercourse.
COMMU'NITY, the commonwealth.
COMMUNE', to talk together.
COMMUNICA'TION, conference.
EXCOMMU'NICATE, to eject from church membership.
IMMU'NITY, privilege.
MUNIF'ICENT, liberal.
REMU'NERATE, to reward.

Mur-us, a wall. IMMURE', to inclose; to confine.

Mut-o, mutat-um, to change.

COMMUTE', to exchange.
IMMU'TABLE, unchangeable.
MUTA'TION, change.
MU'TINY, to rise against authority.
MU'TINEER, one guilty of mutiny.
MU'TINOUS, seditious.
PERMUTA'TION, exchange.
TRANSMUTE', to change to another nature.

Nasc-or, to be born: **Nat-us,** born.

IN'NATE, inborn.
NA'TAL, relating to one's birth.
NA'TION, a distinct people.
NA'TIVE, natural; original.
NATIV'ITY, birth.
NA'TURE, the universe.
NAT'URAL, produced by nature.
NAT'URALIST, one versed in the study of nature.
NAT'URALIZE, to invest with the privileges of a native citizen.
SUPERNAT'URAL, above nature.

Nas-us, the nose. NA'SAL, belonging to the nose.

Naut-a, a sailor, a mariner.

NAU'TICAL, relating to ships.
NAU'TILUS, a shell-fish.

Ne, not.

NEC'ESSARY, needful.
NEFA'RIOUS, wicked.

Necess-e (*ab* **Ne,** not, and **Cesso,** to give up), needful.

NEC'ESSARIES, things needful.
NECES'SITY, compulsion; want.
NECES'SITOUS, needy.
UNNEC'ESSARY, not needed.

Nect-o, nex-um, to tie or bind, to knit.

ANNEX', to join to.
CONNECT', to join; to link.
CONNEC'TION, union; relation.
UNCONNECT'ED, not coherent.

Neg, *for* **Nec,** neither, not.

NEGLECT', inattention; slight.
NEG'LIGENT, careless; heedless.
NEGO'TIATE, to transact business; to treat with.

Neg-o, negat-um, to deny, to refuse.

DENY', to contradict; to refuse.
NEGA'TION, a denial.
NEG'ATIVE, implying denial.
REN'EGADE, a deserter.

Neuter, neutr-um, neither.

NEU'TER, of neither party.
NEUTRAL'ITY, a neutral state.
NEU'TRALIZE, to render indifferent.

Nihil, nothing. ANNI'HILATE, to destroy.

Noc-eo, to hurt. **Noxi-us,** hurtful.

IN'NOCENCE, purity; simplicity.
NOX'IOUS, hurtful.
NU'ISANCE, something offensive.
OBNOX'IOUS, subject; exposed

No-men, nomin-is, a name.

DENOMINA'TION, a name; a class.
IG'NOMINY,°disgrace; shame.
NAME, the term by which we call or distinguish things.
NO'MENCLATURE, a system of names.
NOM'INAL, not real; in name only.
NOM'INATE, to name; to propose.
PRO'NOUN, a word used instead of a noun.
TRINO'MINAL, containing three terms.

Non, not.

NON'AGE, minority in age.
NONDESCRIPT', not yet described.
NON'PLUS, a great difficulty.
NON'SENSE, unmeaning words.

Nox, noct-is, night.

E'QUINOX, the time of equal day and night.
NOCTUR'NAL, nightly.
EQUINOC'TIAL, pertaining to the equinox.
NIGHT, the time of darkness.

Norm-a, a rule or square.

ENOR'MOUS, excessive.
NOR'MAL, according to rule.

Nosc-o, not-um, to know. ***Nobil-is,*** noble.

IGNO'BLE, of low birth.
KNOWL'EDGE, learning; information.
NOBIL'ITY, dignity; rank.
NOTE, a mark; notice.
NO'TICE, to note; to heed.
NO'TIFY, to make known.
NO'TION, thought; idea.
NOTO'RIOUS,°publicly known.
REC'OGNIZE, to know again.
RECOGNITI'ON, the art of recognizing.
RECONNOI'TER, to examine; to survey.

Not-a, a mark.

NO'TARY,°an officer who attests contracts and writings.
DENOTE', to betoken.
NO'TICE, observation.

Nov-us, new.

IN'NOVATE, to introduce novelties or change.
NOV'EL, new; unusual.
NOV'ELTY, newness; freshness.
NOV'ICE, one unskilled.
NOVI'TIATE, state of a novice.
RENEW', to make again.
RENOVA'TION, renewal.

Nub-o, nupt-um, to veil, to marry.

CONNU'BIAL, nuptial; matrimonial.
NUP'TIAL, relating to marriage.

Nud-us, naked, bare.

DENUDE', to strip; to make bare.
NU'DITY, nakedness.

Null-us, none, no one.

ANNUL', to abolish.
NULL, void; of no force.
NUL'LIFY, to make void.
NUL'LITY, nothingness.

Numer-us, a number.

ENU'MERATE, to reckon up singly.
INNU'MERABLE, that cannot be numbered.
NUM'BER, to count; to reckon.
NU'MERAL, relating to number.
NUMERA'TION, art of numbering.
NUMER'ICAL, denoting number.
NU'MEROUS, many; not few.

Nuncio, nunciat-um, to bring news, to tell.

ANNOUNCE', to publish.
ANNUNCIA'TION, the act of announcing.
DENOUNCE', to declare against.
DENUNCIA'TION, public threat.
ENUN'CIATE, to declare; to express.
MISPRONOUNCE', to pronounce improperly.
PRONOUNCE', to speak; to utter.
PRONUNCIA'TION, mode of utterance.
RENOUNCE', to disown; to disclaim.
RENUNCIA'TION, a disowning.

Nutri-o, nutrit-um, to nourish, to suckle.

NOUR'ISH, to support by food.
NURSE, a person who has the care of infants or sick persons.
NU'TRIMENT, nourishment; food.
NUTRITI'ON, the act or process of nourishing.

Occult-us, hidden, secret. OCCULT',° secret; hidden.

Ocul-us, the eye.

BINOC'ULAR, having two eyes.
OC'ULIST, an eye-doctor.
INOC'ULATE, to insert the eye or bud of one tree in another.

Odi, I hate, or have hated.

O'DIOUS, hateful.
O'DIUM, hatred.

Odor, a scent or smell.

INO'DOROUS, wanting scent.
O'DOR, scent; fragrance.

Ol-eo, to emit odor, to grow.

ABOL'ISH,° to annul; to repeal.
ABOLITI'ON, the act of abolishing.
ADULT', one full grown.
OB'SOLETE, out of use.
OLFAC'TORY, having the sense of smelling.
RED'OLENT, diffusing odor.

Omen, omin-is, an omen.

ABOM'INATE,° to abhor; to detest.
ABOM'INABLE, hateful.
O'MEN, a sign; a prognostic.
OM'INOUS, foreboding.

Omn-is, all, every.

OMNIPRES'ENT, present everywhere.
OMNIP'OTENT, almighty.
OMNIS'CIENCE, infinite wisdom.

Onus, oner-is, a burden, or load.

EXON'ERATE, to disburden.
O'NEROUS, burdensome.

Oper-a, work, labor.

CO-OP'ERATE, to labor jointly for the same end.
MANŒU'VRE,° a skillful movement.
OP'ERA, a dramatic composition set to music.
OPERA'TION, agency; influence

Opin-or, to think, to imagine.

OP'INE, to think.
OPIN'ION, judgment; notion.

Opt-o, to wish, to choose.

ADOPT',° to receive as one's own.
OP'TION, choice; preference.

Opulent-us, wealthy, rich. OP'ULENCE, wealth; affluence.

Orb-is, a circle or globe.

EXOR'BITANT,° enormous; excessive.
ORB, a sphere; a wheel.
OR'BIT, a line described by a revolving planet.

Ord-o, ordin-is, order, arrangement, rank.

CO-OR'DINATE, holding the same rank.
DISOR'DER, to ruffle; to confuse.
EXTRAOR'DINARY,° remarkable.
INOR'DINATE,° immoderate.
INSUBORDINA'TION, disobedience; revolt.
ORDAIN',° to appoint; to decree.
OR'DINAL, noting order.
OR'DINANCE, a public law.
OR'DINARY, common; usual.
PREORDAIN', to ordain beforehand.
SUBOR'DINATE, inferior; subject.

Ori-or, ort-us, to rise, to spring. **Orig-o**, the beginning.

ABOR'TION, failure.
O'RIENTAL, eastern.
OR'IGIN, beginning; source.
ORIGINAL'ITY, the state of being original.
ORIG'INATE, to bring into being.

Orn-o, ornat-um, to deck, or dress.

ADORN', to dress; to decorate.
OR'NAMENT, an embellishment.
SUBORN',° to procure to take a false oath.

Or-o, orat-um, to speak, to beg.

ADORE', to worship.
INEX'ORABLE, not to be moved by entreaty.
OR'ACLE,* one famed for wisdom.
ORAC'ULAR, uttering oracles.
OR'ISON, a supplication.
O'RAL, delivered by mouth.
OR'ATOR, an eloquent speaker.
OR'IFICE, an opening to a cavity.

Os, oss-is, a bone.

OS'SEOUS, bony.
OS'SIFY, to change to bone.
OSSIFICA'TION, the act of ossifying.

Oti-um, ease, retirement from business.

DISEASE', distemper; malady.
NEGO'TIATE, to transact business.
EASE, quiet; facility.
NEGOTIA'TION, a treaty of business.

---

* *Oracle*, among *Pagans*, the *answer* of a god or some person reputed to be a god, to an inquiry made respecting some affair of importance, usually some future event, as the success of an enterprise or battle. The *deity* who gave, or was supposed to give an answer to inquiries, as the *Delphic oracle.*

Ov-um, an egg.

O'VAL, shaped like an egg.
O'VARY, the seat of eggs.
O'VOID, egg-shaped.
OVIP'AROUS, producing eggs.

Pall-eo, to be pale.

PAL'LID, pale; not bright.
PAL'LOR, paleness.

Palli-um, a cloak.

PALL, a covering for the dead.
PAL'LIATE,°to soften; to ease.

Palm-a, the palm of the hand; the palm tree.

PALMET'TO, a species of the palm tree.
PALMIF'EROUS, bearing palms.
PA'LMY, flourishing.
PAL'MISTRY, fortune-telling by the palm of the hand.

Palp-o, palpat-um, to touch gently or softly.

PAL'PABLE, that may be felt.
PAL'PITATE, to beat; to flutter.

Pand-o, pans-um, to open, to spread.

EXPAND', to spread; to open.
EXPAN'SION, a spreading out.

Pan-is, bread.

PANA'DA, bread boiled in water and sweetened.
PAN'TRY, an apartment for provisions.

Pann-us, cloth.

ACCOM'PANY, to go along with.
COM'PANY,°a band; a society.
COMPAN'ION, an associate.
IMPAN'NEL,°to enroll jurors.

Par, equal, like.

COMPARE', to set side by side; to examine together.
COMPAR'ATIVE, estimated by comparison.
COMPEER', an equal.
DISPAR'AGE,°to cause disgrace.
DISPAR'ITY, inequality.
PAIR, a couple.
PEER'AGE, the rank of a peer.
PEER'LESS, without an equal.

Par-eo, parit-um, to appear.

APPEAR', to become visible.
APPA'RENT, visible; evident.
APPARITI'ON, a spectre; a ghost.
DISAPPEAR'ANCE, removal from sight.
TRANSPA'RENT, that can be seen through.

Par-io, part-um, to bring forth.

O'VERT, open to view; public.
O'VERTURE, opening; proposal.
OVIP'AROUS, producing eggs.
PA'RENT, a father or mother

Parl-er (Fr.), to speak.

PAR'LEY, a conference.
PAR'LIAMENT,°a supreme legislative council.
PAR'LOR, a room for the reception of company.
PAROLE', a word of mouth.

Par-o, parat-um, to prepare.

APPARA'TUS, necessary instruments for any trade or art.
APPAR'EL, dress; clothing.
DISSEV'ER, to part in two.
EM'PEROR, a monarch.
EM'PIRE, the dominion of an emperor.
IMPER'ATIVE, commanding.
IMPE'RIAL, royal.
IMPE'RIOUS, haughty.
INSEP'ARABLE, not to be parted.
IRREP'ARABLE, not to be repaired.
PARADE', show; ostentation.
PREPAR'ATORY, introductory.
REPAIR', to restore; to amend.
REPARA'TION, amends.
SEP'ARABLE, that may be parted.
SEP'ARATE, to divide; to part.
SEV'ER, to force asunder.
SEV'ERAL, many; distinct.

Pars, part-is, a part, a portion.

APART', at a distance.
APPOR'TION, to divide into just parts.
COPART'NER, a joint partner.
DEPART', to go away; to leave.
DEPAR'TURE, a going away.
IMPART', to give; to make known.
IMPAR'TIAL, equitable; just.
MISPROPOR'TION, to join without symmetry.
PAR'CEL,°a small bundle.
PARSE, to resolve by grammatical rules.
PART, a portion; a share.
PAR'TIAL, biased to one party.
PARTIC'IPATE, to partake.
PAR'TICIPLE, one of the parts of speech.
PAR'TICLE, a minute part.
PARTIC'ULAR, not general; distinct from others.
PAR'TISAN, an adherent.
PARTITI'ON, a division.
PART'NER, an associate.
PAR'TY, a faction.
POR'TION, a part; an allotment.
PROPOR'TION,°symmetry; size.
PROPOR'TIONATE, in proportion.
REPARTEE', a witty reply.

Pasc-o, past-um, to feed.

PAS'TOR,°a clergyman.
PAS'TORAL, relating to shepherds.
PAS'TURE, land on which cattle graze.
REPAST', a meal.

Pass-us, a pace, a step.

COM'PASS, grasp; space.
ENCOM'PASS, to surround.
PACE, to measure by steps.
PAS'SAGE, the act of passing; a journey.
PAS'SENGER, a traveller.
PASS'PORT, a permission of passage.
PAS'TIME, sport; amusement.
SURPASS', to excel; to exceed.
TRES'PASS,°an offence.

Pater, patr-is, a father.

COMPA'TRIOT, one of the same country.
EXPA'TRIATE, to banish from one's country.
PAR'RICIDE, the murder of a parent.
PATER'NAL, fatherly; kind.
PATRICI'AN,°a nobleman.
PA'TRIARCH, the father and ruler of a family.
PAT'RIMONY, an inherited estate.
PA'TRIOT, a lover of his country.
PA'TRON,°a supporter.
PAT'RONIZE, to protect; to support.

Pati-or, pass-us, to suffer, to endure.

COMPASSI'ON,° pity; sympathy.
IMPASSI'ONED, strongly affected.
IMPA'TIENT, hasty; eager.
PASSI'ON,° anger; zeal.
PAS'SIVE,° unresisting.
PA'TIENCE, calm endurance.

Pauper, poor.

IMPOV'ERISH, to make poor.
PAU'PER, a poor person.
POOR, indigent; lean.
POV'ERTY, indigence; want.

Pax, pac-is, peace.

APPEASE', to quiet; to still.
PAC'IFY, to appease; to quiet.
PACIFICA'TION, the act of making peace.
PEACE, quiet; rest.

Pecc-o, to do wrong, to sin.

PECCADIL'LO, a petty fault.
PEC'CANT, sinning; guilty.

Pect-us, pector-is, the breast.

EXPEC'TORATE, to eject from the breast.
PEC'TORAL, belonging to the breast.

Pecuni-a, money. PECU'NIARY, relating to money.

Pell-o, pellat-um, to call, to name.

APPEAL', to refer to another tribunal.
APPELLA'TION, a name; a title.
REPEAL', to recall; to revoke.

Pell-o, puls-um, to drive, to strike.

COMPEL',° to force; to oblige.
COMPUL'SORY, forcing.
DISPEL', to drive away.
EXPEL', to drive out.
EXPUL'SION, act of driving out.
IMPEL', to urge forward.
IM'PULSE, force given.
IMPUL'SIVE, causing to move.
PROPEL', to drive forward.
PULSE,° the throbbing of the arteries.
PULSA'TION, a beating; a throbbing.
REPEL', to drive back.
REPULSE', a rejection.
REPUL'SIVE, driving off; forbidding.

Pend-eo, pens-um, to hang.

APPEND', to hang or join to.
APPEND'IX, something appended.
DEPEND', to hang from; to rely.
DEPEND'ENCE, trust; reliance.
IMPEND', to hang over.
INDEPEND'ENT, free; not controlled.
PEND'ULUM, a vibrating body.
PERPENDIC'ULAR, directly downwards.
PROPENS'ITY,° inclination.
SUSPEND', to hang; to interrupt.
SUSPENSE', uncertainty.
SUSPEN'SION, a hanging up.

Pend-o, pens-um, to weigh, to lay out.

COMPEND'IUM, an abridgment.
COM'PENSATE,° to requite.
DISPENSA'TION,° distribution.
DISPENS'ARY, the place where medicines are given to the poor.

DISPENSE', to deal out.
EXPEND', to spend; to lay out.
EXPEND'ITURE, amount expended.
EXPENSE', cost; charges.
EXPEN'SIVE, lavish; costly.
PEN'SIVE, serious.
INDISPENS'ABLE, not to be omitted or spared.
PEN'SION, an annual allowance.
PEN'SIONARY, one who receives a pension.
REC'OMPENSE, a reward.
STI'PEND, wages; stated pay.

Pen-e, almost.

PENIN'SULA, a piece of land almost surrounded by water.
PENULT', the last syllable of a word but one.

Penit-eo, *for* ***Pœniteo,*** to repent. ***Pœna,*** punishment.

IMPEN'ITENT,°obdurate.
PAIN, uneasy sensation.
PE'NAL, enacting punishment.
PEN'ITENT, contrite for sin.
PEN'ANCE, voluntary suffering on account of sin.
PENITEN'TIARY, a prison.
REPENT', to sorrow for sin.

Penn-a, a feather, a wing.

PEN, an instrument of writing.
PEN'NATE, winged.

Peri-or, perit-us, to try, to prove.

EXPER'IMENT, trial.
EXPE'RIENCE, to know by trial.
EXPERT',°skilful; prompt.
UNEXPERT', wanting skill.

Perpes, perpet-is, entire, never-ceasing.

PERPET'UAL, never-ceasing.
PERPET'UATE, to make perpetual.
PERPETU'ITY, duration to all futurity.

Person-a, a mask used by players; a person.

IMPER'SONAL, not varied by persons. (in grammar.)
PER'SONATE, to represent.
PER'SON, a human being.
PERSON'IFY, to change from a thing to a person.

Pes, ped-is, the foot, a foot.

BI'PED, a two-footed animal.
EXPE'DIENT, device; means.
EX'PEDITE,°to facilitate.
EXPEDITI'OUS, quick.
IMPEDE',°to hinder.
IMPED'IMENT, hinderance.
PED'ESTAL, the base of a pillar or statue.
PEDES'TRIAN, going on foot.
PED'IGREE,°lineage; descent.
QUAD'RUPED, a four-footed animal.

Pest-is, a plague, an infection.

PEST, a plague; an annoyance
PES'TILENCE, a contagious distemper.

Petit, (Fr.), little, small.

PET'TIFOGGER, a petty lawyer.
PET'TY, small; little.

Pet-o, petit-um, to seek, to ask.

AP'PETITE,° desire; hunger.
COMPAT'IBLE,° consistent.
COMPETE', to rival.
COM'PETENCE, sufficiency.
COMPET'ITOR, a rival.
IMPE'TUS,° force from motion.
IMPET'UOUS, violent; fierce.
INCOM'PETENT, not adequate.
PETITI'ON, entreaty.
REPEAT', to do again; to recite.

Pil-o, pilat-um, to pillage, to rob.

COMPILE', to collect from various authors.
PIL'FER, to steal.
PIL'LAGE, plunder; spoil.

Ping-o, pict-um, to paint.

DEPICT', to paint; to describe.
PAINT, to describe; to color.
PICTO'RIAL, containing pictures.
PIC'TURE, a painting.
PICTURESQUE', like a picture.
PIG'MENT, paint; color.

Pi-o, piat-um, to atone for.

EX'PIATE, to atone for.
EX'PIATORY, for atonement.

Pisc-is, a fish. PIS'CATORY, relating to fishes.

Plac-eo, to please.

COMPLA'CENCY, calm satisfaction.
COM'PLAISANT, pleasing in manners.
DISPLEASE', to make angry.
PLAC'ID, gentle; quiet.
PLEASE, to delight; to gratify.
PLEAS'ANT, gay; agreeable.
PLEAS'ANTRY, gayety; mirth.
PLEAS'URE, delight; choice.

Plac-o, to appease; to pacify.

IMPLA'CABLE, not to be appeased.

Plang-o, planct-um, to beat, to bemoan.

COMPLAIN', to murmur; to lament.
COMPLAINT', PLAINT, a lamentation; a murmuring.
PLAGUE, to infest; to tease.
PLAIN'TIFF,° he that commences a lawsuit.
PLAIN'TIVE, lamenting.

Plant-a, the sole of the foot; a plant.

DISPLANT', to pluck up.
IMPLANT', to insert; to engraft.
PLANTA'TION, a farm; a colony.
SUPPLANT',° to displace.
TRANSPLANT', to move and plant in another place.

Plan-us, plain, smooth; evident.

EXPLAIN', to expound; to make clear.
EXPLANA'TION, act of explaining.
PLAIN, flat; clear.

Plaud-o, plaus-um, to praise by clapping hands.

APPLAUD', to praise; to extol.
APPLAUSE', approbation.
EXPLODE', to drive out; to burst.
EXPLO'SION, a sudden bursting.
PLAU'DIT, loud praise.
PLAU'SIBLE,° specious; seemingly right.

Plebs, pleb-is, the common people. PLEBE'IAN, vulgar; low.

Plen-us, full.

PLE'NARY, full; complete.
PLEN'ITUDE, fulness; repletion.
PLEN'TY, abundance.
REPLEN'ISH, to stock; to fill.

Ple-o, plet-um, to fill.

ACCOM'PLISH, to execute; to finish.
COM'PLEMENT, full quantity.
COMPLETE', perfect; full.
EX'PLETIVE, a word used to fill a vacancy.
COM'PLIMENT,°an act of civility.
IM'PLEMENT,°a tool; a utensil.
INCOMPLETE', not finished.
REPLETE', full.
SUP'PLEMENT, an addition.
SUPPLY', to fill up; to furnish.

Plic-o, plicat-um, to fold, to knit.

ACCOM'PLICE,° an associate in crime.
APPLY',°to put to; to suit to.
AP'PLICABLE, suitable.
AP'PLICANT, he who applies.
APPLICA'TION, great industry.
COM'PLEX, intricate; entangled.
COMPLEX'ION, the color of the skin and features.
COM'PLICATE,°to entangle.
COMPLY', to yield to.
COMPLI'ANCE, submission.
DISPLAY', to exhibit.
DOUB'LE, to make twice as great.
DUPLIC'ITY, deceit.
EXPLIC'IT,°plain; clear.
IMPLY',°to express indirectly.
IMPLIC'IT, resting on; trusting.
INAP'PLICABLE, unfit.
INEX'PLICABLE, incapable of being explained.
MISAPPLY', to apply to wrong purposes.
MUL'TIPLE, a number which exactly contains another several times.
MUL'TIPLY, to make many fold.
MULTIPLIC'ITY, great variety.
PERPLEX',°to entangle; to vex.
PERPLEX'ITY, distraction of mind.
PLI'ABLE, flexible; pliant.
PLI'ANT, yielding; easily bent.
PLY, to work on closely.
PLI'ERS, small pincers.
QUAD'RUPLE, four-fold.
REPLY', to answer.
SIM'PLE, plain; artless.
SIM'PLETON, a silly person.
SIMPLIC'ITY, plainness; singleness.
SIM'PLIFY, to render easy.
SUP'PLIANT,°a petitioner.
SUP'PLICATE, to implore.
TRIP'LE, three-fold.
TREB'LE, to multiply by three.

Plor-o, plorat-um, to cry out, to wail.

DEPLORE', to bewail; to mourn.
DEPLO'RABLE, lamentable; sad.
EXPLORE', to search into.
IMPLORE', to entreat; to beg.

Plum-a, a feather

PLUME, a feather.
PLU'MAGE, feathers.

Plumb-um, lead, a leaden bullet.

PLUMB, a plummet.
PLUMBA'GO, black lead.
PLUM'MET, a weight of lead attached to a string.

Plus, plur-is, more.

NON'PLUS, to bring to a stand.
PLU'RAL, implying more than one.
PLUS, increased by ; added to.
SUR'PLUS, that which remains over a certain quantity.

Pol-us, the pole.

CIRCUMPO'LAR, round the pole.
POLAR'ITY, tendency to the pole.
POLE, the end of the earth's axis.

Pom-um, an apple.

POMACE', the substance of apples or similar fruit ground.
POMEGRAN'ATE,° a kind of fruit.
POM'MEL,° a knob or ball.

Pondus, ponder-is, weight.

IMPON'DERABLE, that cannot be weighed.
POISE, to weigh ; to balance.
PON'DER,° to consider.
PON'DEROUS, heavy.
PREPON'DERATE, to outweigh.

Pon-o, posit-um, to put, or place.

COMPOSE', to put together ; to settle.
COMPOS'ITOR, one who sets types.
COM'POST,° manure ; any mixture.
COMPO'SURE, tranquillity.
DECOMPOSE', to take apart.
DEPO'NENT,° a witness on oath.
DEPOSE', to put down; to divest.
DEPOS'IT, to lodge ; to place.
DE'POT, a place of deposit.
DISCOMPOSE', to disorder ; to vex.
DISPO'SAL, regulation ; control.
DISPOSITI'ON, temper of mind.
EXPOSE', to lay open.
EXPOS'ITOR, an explainer.
EXPO'SURE, act of exposing.
EXPOUND', to explain ; to clear.
IMPOSE', to lay on.
IMPOSITI'ON, constraint ; cheat.
IM'POST,° a tax ; a toll.
IMPOS'TOR,° a deceiver.
INDISPOSE , to make unfit.
INTERPOSE', to place between.
OPPO'NENT, an adversary.
OP'POSITE, adverse.
POSITI'ON, situation ; place.
POS'ITIVE,° absolute ; certain.
POST,° station ; office.
POSTPONE', to put off; to delay.
POS'TURE, state ; attitude.
PREPOSITI'ON, a part of speech.
PROPO'SAL, an offer.
PROPOSITI'ON, a thing proposed
PROV'OST, a chief officer.
PUR'POSE, intention ; design.
RECOMPOSE', to form anew.
REPOSE', to rest ; to place.
REPOS'ITORY, a place for laying up things.
SUPPOSE', to imagine ; to think
TRANSPOSE', to put out of place

Pons, pont-is, a bridge.

PONT'IFF,° a high-priest ; the pope.
PONTOON',° a boat used for making floating bridges.

Popul-us, the people. **Public-us,** public.

DEPOP'ULATE, to deprive of inhabitants ; to lay waste.
PE'OPLE, a nation ; persons.
POP'ULACE, the common people.
POP'ULAR, pleasing to the people.
POPULAR'ITY, the favor of the people.
POP'ULOUS, full of inhabitants.

POPULA'TION, the whole people of a country or place.
PUB'LIC,°common; open.
PUB'LISH, to make known.
REPE'OPLE, to people anew.
REPUB'LIC, a free state.

Porr-o, forth, farther.

PORTEND', to foretoken.
PORTENT', an omen of ill.

Port-o, portat-um, to carry, to import.

COMPORT', to suit; to bear.
DEPORT'MENT, conduct; bearing.
EXPORT', to carry out.
IMPORT'ANT,°weighty; forcible.
IMPORT'ER, one who brings in goods from abroad.
IMPORTUNE',°to solicit earnestly.
OPPORTU'NITY, a fit place; occasion.
PORT, a harbor.
PORT'ABLE, that may be carried.
PORT'LY, bulky; swelling.
POR'TAL, a gate; a door.
PORT'FO'LIO, a case for loose papers.
PORT'ICO, a covered walk.
PORTMAN'TEAU, a portable bag for clothes.
REPORT', a rumor.
SUPPORT,' to bear; to uphold.
TRANSPORTA'TION, conveyance.

Poss-e, pot-ui, to be able.

DISPOSSESS', to put out of possession.
IMPOS'SIBLE, that cannot be.
IM'POTENCE, want of power.
OMNIP'OTENCE, almighty power.
POS'SE, an armed power.
PO'TENT, powerful; strong.
POSSESSI'ON, property.
PO'TENTATE, a monarch; a prince.
PREPOSSES'SED, biassed.

Poster-us, after, that comes after.

POSTE'RIOR, later.
POSTER'ITY, succeeding generations.
POST'ERN,°a small gate; a door.
PREPOS'TEROUS,°absurd; foolish.

Pot-o, to drink. PO'TION, a draught.

Prav-us, crooked; wicked.

DEPRAVE', to corrupt to debase.
DEPRAV'ITY, corruption.

Preci-um, *for* ***Pretium***, a price; worth.

APPRAISE', to set a price upon.
DEPRECIA'TION, a falling in value.
PRE'CIOUS, of great value.
PRICE, value; rate.
PRIZE, to value highly.

Prec-or, precat-us, to pray; to entreat.

DEP'RECATE, to pray against.
IMPRECA'TION, a curse.
PREACH,°to proclaim; to teach.
PRECA'RIOUS, uncertain.

Pred-a, *for* ***Præda***, prey; plunder.

DEP'REDATE, to rob; to pillage.
PRED'ATORY, rapacious.

Prehend-o, prehens-um, to take hold of, to seize.

APPREHEND', to seize; to fear.
APPREHEN'SION seizure; fear.
APPREN'TICE, one bound to learn an art or trade.

APPRISE', to give notice.
COMPREHEND',° to include; to understand.
COMPREHEN'SIVE, capacious; full.
COMPRISE', to include.
EN'TERPRISE, an undertaking.
IMPRIS'ON, to confine.
INCOMPREHEN'SIBLE, not to be understood.
MISAPPREHEND', to misunderstand.
PRIS'ON, a place of confinement
PRIZE,°reward; plunder.
REPREHEND',°to reprove.
REPRI'SAL, a seizure in retaliation.
REPRIEVE', to respite.
SURPRISE',°to astonish.

Prem-o, press-um, to press.

COMPRESS', to press together.
DEPRESSI'ON, dejection.
EXPRESS', to utter; to press out.
EXPRESS'IVE, serving to express.
IMPRESS', to stamp; to fix deep.
IMPRESSI'ON, a stamp; influence.
IMPRINT', to press on.
OPPRESS', to crush by severity.
PRESS, to squeeze; to urge.
PRINT, a mark made by types.
REPRESS', to subdue; to quell.
SUPPRESS', to put down.

Prim-us, first. ***Princeps, princip-is,*** a prince.

PRE'MIER, a prime minister.
PRIM, formal; precise.
PRI'MACY, the office of primate.
PRI'MARY, first; chief.
PRI'MATE, the chief ecclesiastic in a church.
PRIME, best; principal.
PRIM'ER, a child's first book.
PRIM'ITIVE, original.
PRIN'CIPLE, fundamental truth; motive
PRINCE, a king's son.
PRIN'CIPAL, chief; essential.
PRINCIP'IA, first principles.
PRI'OR, former; anterior.
PRI'ORY, a convent.
PRIS'TINE, first; original.

Priv-us, single; one's own.

DEPRIVE', to take from.
PRI'VACY, secrecy; retirement.
PRI'VATE, secret; secluded.
PRIVA'TION, loss; absence.
PRIVATEER', a private ship of war.
PRIV'ILEGE,°a peculiar benefit
PRIV'Y, secret; private.

Prob-o, probat-um, to prove, to try.

APPROVE', to commend.
APPROBA'TION, act of approving.
DISAPPROVE', to censure.
DISPROVE', to prove false.
IMPROVE'MENT, a growing better.
PROB'ABLE, likely.
PROBA'TIONER, one upon trial.
PROBE,°to search; to pierce.
PROB'ITY, honesty.
PROOF, evidence; test.
PROVE, to evince; to test.
REP'ROBATE,°lost to virtue.
REPROVE', to blame; to chide
REPROOF', open censure.

Prop-e, near: ***Proxim-us,*** nearest; next.

APPROX'IMATE, to draw near.
APPROACH', to go or come near to.
PROPIT'IATE,°to conciliate.
PROPITI'OUS, favourable.
PROXIM'ITY, nearness
REPROACH', to censure.

Propri-us, peculiar, one's own, fit.

Appro'priate, peculiar; fit.
Improp'er, unbecoming.
Impropri'ety, unfitness.
Prop'er, natural; fit.
Prop'erty, an estate; goods.
Propri'ety, fitness; justness.

Pros-a, prose. Prosa'ic, belonging to prose.

Prosper, successful.

Pros'per, to thrive.
Prosper'ity, success; welfare

Pud-eo, to be ashamed.

Im'pudent, saucy; shameless.
Repu'diate, to put away; to reject.

Puer, a boy.

Pu'erile, childish; trifling.
Pueril'ity, childishness.

Pugn-a, a fight, a battle.

Impugn', to attack; to oppose.
Oppugn', to oppose; to assault.
Pu'gilism, boxing.
Repug'nance, opposition of mind.

Pung-o, punct-um, to point, or prick.

Compunc'tion,° remorse.
Expunge',° to rub out.
Poig'nant, keen; severe.
Point, to aim; to direct.
Pon'iard, a dagger.*
Pounce, to fall on and seize.
Punch, to perforate; to push.
Punctil'io, a nice point of exactness.
Punc'tual, exact; precise.
Punc'tuate, to point off.
Punc'ture, a small prick; a point.
Pun'gent, pricking; sharp.

Puni-o, punit-um, to punish.

Impu'nity, exemption from punishment.
Pun'ish, to chastise.
Pu'nitive, inflicting punishment.

Purg-o, purgat-um, to make clean.

Expurga'tion, act of cleansing.
Purge, to clear; to cleanse.
Purg'ative, a purging medicine.
Purg'atory, a place in which Papists suppose souls are purged from impurities.

Pur-us, pure, clean.

Impure', not pure; unholy.
Pure, chaste; clear; holy.
Pu'rify, to make pure.
Pu'ritan, one of a sect professing to follow the pure word of God.
Pu'rity, innocence; chastity

Pus, pur-is, the corrupt matter of sores.

Pus'tule, a pimple.
Sup'purate, to form matter.

Pusill-us, weak, little. Pusillan'imous, cowardly.

Put-o, putat-um, to prune, to adjust accounts, to think.

ACCOUNT' reckoning.
AM'PUTATE, to cut off.
COMPUTE', to reckon; to calculate.
COUNT, to number.
DEPUTE', to send; to empower to act.
DEP'UTY, one that transacts business for another.
DIS'COUNT,* a deduction.
DISPUTE', contest; controversy
DISREP'UTABLE, dishonorable.
IMPUTE', to attribute.
RECOUNT', to relate.
REPUTA'TION, credit; honor

Putr-is, rotten, fetid.

PUTRID'ITY, rottenness.
PU'TREFY, to make rotten; to rot.
PUTRES'CENT, growing rotten.
PUTREFAC'TIVE, making rotten.

Quadr-a, a square. ***Quatuor,*** four.

QUAD'RANGLE, a square.
QUAD'RANT,° a quarter of a circle.
QUADRILLE', a game at cards; a kind of dance, in sets of four.
QUADROON', a person quarter-blooded.
QUAD'RUPED, a four-footed animal.
QUAD'RUPLE, fourfold.
QUADRU'PLICATE, to double twice.
QUAR'ANTINE,° the time that ships, suspected of infection, are prohibited from intercourse with the shore.
QUART, one-fourth of a gallon.
QUART'ER, to divide into four parts.
SQUAD'RON,° part of a fleet.
SQUARE, a figure of four equal sides and four right angles.

Quær-o, quæsit-um, to ask, to obtain, to seek.

ACQUIRE',° to gain; to procure.
ACQUISITI'ON, the thing acquired.
CON'QUER, to gain by force.
CON'QUEST, victory; a subduing.
EX'QUISITE,° excellent; fine.
IN'QUEST, a judicial inquiry.
INQUIRE', to seek out.
INQUISITI'ON, search; trial.
INQUIS'ITIVE, curious.
PER'QUISITE, a fee or gift of office.
QUE'RIST, one who asks questions.
QUE'RY, an inquiry; a doubt.
QUEST, a search.
QUES'TION, to examine by questions.
REQUEST', to ask; to solicit.
REQUIRE', to demand; to claim.
REQ'UISITE, necessary.

Qual-is, of what kind or sort.

DISQUAL'IFY, to make unfit.
QUALIFICA'TION, fitness.
QUAL'IFY, to render fit.
QUAL'ITY, nature; property.

Quer-or, to complain, to bewail.

QUAR'REL, a brawl; a dispute.
QUERIMO'NIOUS, complaining.

Quies, quiet-is, rest, ease.

ACQUIESCE', to quietly assent.
DISQUI'ET, to make uneasy.
QUI'ETUDE, rest; repose.
RE'QUIEM,° a hymn for the dead

---

* *Discount,* literally a *counting* back or from; a sum deducted from the principal for prompt or advanced payment.

Quinque, five. **Quint-us**, fifth.

QUINTES'SENCE, the best part.
QUINTU'PLE, fivefold.

Quot, how many, so many.

AL'IQUOT,° exactly measuring.
QUO'RUM,° a competent number to transact business.
QUO'TA, a share.
QUO'TIENT, that which results on dividing one number by another.
QUOTID'IAN, a fever which returns daily.

Radi-us, the spoke of a wheel; a beam or ray.

IRRA'DIATE, to illumine.
RA'DIANCE, sparkling lustre.
RA'DIUS, the semi-diameter of a circle.

Radix, radic-is, a root.

ERAD'ICATE, to root out.
RAD'ICAL, primitive; thorough.

Rad-o, ras-um, to shave, to scrape.

ABRADE', to rub off.
ERASE', to rub out.
RAZE, to utterly overthrow.
RA'ZOR, a tool for shaving.

Ram-us, a bough or branch.

RAMIFICA'TION, a branch; a division into branches.
RAM'IFY, to separate into branches.

Ranc-eo, to be stale, or strong scented.

RAN'CID, having a rank smell.
RAN'COR,° malice; enmity.
RANK, strong to the taste.
RAN'KLE,° to fester.

Rang (Fr.), a row, order.

ARRANGE', to put in order.
DERANGE', to disorder.
RANGE, to place in a row.
RANK, a row; a class.

Rap-io, rapt-um, to snatch, to seize.

ENRAP'TURE,° to delight highly.
ENRAV'ISHED, enraptured.
RAP, a quick smart blow.
RAPA'CIOUS, given to plunder.
RAP'ID, quick; swift.
RA'PIER, a thrusting sword.
RAP'TURE, ecstasy; transport.
RAV'AGE, to lay waste; to sack.
RAV'ISH, to delight; to transport.

Rar-us, scarce, thin.

RAR'EFY, to make thin.
RAR'ITY, thinness; infrequency.

Rat-us, thinking, established.

IRRA'TIONAL, contrary to reason.
RAT'IFY, to confirm; to settle.
RA'TIO, proportion.
RA'TION, a fixed allowance.
RATIONAL'ITY, reasonableness.
REA'SON, to argue rationally.

Reg-o, to govern. **Regul-a**, a rule. **Rect-us**, straight.

CORRECT', right, accurate.
DIRECT',° to aim; to regulate.
DIREC'TION, aim; order.
ERECT',° to raise; to build.
INCOR'RIGIBLE, that cannot be corrected.

INCORRECT', not exact; wrong.
INDIRECT', not direct; not fair.
IRREG'ULAR, not regular.
RECT'ANGLE, a right-angled parallelogram.
REC'TIFY, to make right.
REC'TITUDE, uprightness.
REC'TOR,° a minister of a parish.
RE'GAL, royal; kingly.
REGA'LIA, ensigns of royalty.
RE'GENT, a governor.
REG'ICIDE, murder of a king.
REG'IMEN, regulation of diet.
REG'IMENT,° a body of soldiers.
RE'GION,° a country; a tract.
REGULAR'ITY, conformity to rule.
REGULA'TION, method; rule.
REIGN, to rule as a king.
RIGHT, equity; justice.
RULE, to govern; to control.

Rend-re (Fr.), to give back, to restore.

REN'DER, to return; to make.
SURREN'DER, to deliver up.

Rept-um (ab ***repo***), to creep. REP'TILE, an animal that creeps.

Res, a thing.

RE'AL, true; relating to things.
REAL'ITY, actual existence.
RE'ALIZE, to bring into being; to conceive of.

Ret-e, a net.

RET'ICULE, a small bag.
RETI'FORM, having the form of a net.
RET'INA,° one of the coats of the eye, like a net.

Ride-o, ris-um, to laugh, to mock.

DERIDE', to laugh at; to mock.
DERISI'ON, contempt; scorn.
RID'ICULE, to expose to laughter
RIS'IBLE, exciting laughter.

Rig-eo, to be cold or stiff.

RIG'ID, stiff; strict.
RIG'OR, severity.

Riv-us, a river.

ARRIVE',° to come to; to reach.
DERIVE', to deduce; to draw.
RI'VALRY, emulation.
RIV'ULET, a small river.

Robur, robor-is, an oak, strength.

CORROB'ORATE, to confirm.
ROBUST', strong; vigorous.

Rod-o, ros-um, to gnaw, to eat away.

CORRODE', to eat away slowly.
CORRO'SION, the act of corroding

Rog-o, rogat-um, to ask, to request.

AB'ROGATE,° to repeal; to annul.
AR'ROGANT, assuming.
DER'OGATE, to disparage.
INTER'ROGATE, to question.
INTERROG'ATIVE, denoting a question.
PREROG'ATIVE,° an exclusive privilege.
PROROGUE',° to protract.

Ros-a, a rose.

RO'SEATE, rosy; fragrant.
RO'SY, blooming; red.

Rot-a, a wheel. **Rotund-us**, round.

ROTA'TION, a turning round.
ROTE, a mere repetition of words.
ROTUND', round; circular.
ROUTINE', a round of business.

Roy, *for* **Roi** (Fr.), a king.

POM'EROY, a royal apple.
ROY'AL, kingly; regal.
VICE'ROY, a king's deputy governor.

Rub-er, red, ruddy.

RUBICUND', inclining to redness.
RU'BY, a precious red stone.

Rud-is, unwrought, rude.

ERUDITI'ON, learning.
RU'DIMENT, a first principle.

Rupt-um (*ab* **Rumpo**), to break, to burst.

ABRUPT', broken off; sudden.
BANK'RUPT,° unable to pay.
CORRUPT',° to deprave; to debase.
CORRUP'TION, wickedness; depravity.
ERUPT'IVE, bursting forth.
INCORRUPT'IBLE, incapable of corruption.
INTERRUPT',° to stop; to hinder.
RUP'TURE, a breach.

Rus, rur-is, the country.

RU'RAL, relating to the country.
RUS'TIC, rude; plain; rural.

Sacer, sacri, sacred, devoted.

CON'SECRATE, to make sacred.
DESECRA'TION, a profaning.
EX'ECRATE, to curse.
EX'ECRABLE, accursed.
SACERDO'TAL, belonging to the priesthood.
SAC'RAMENT,° the Lord's supper.
SA'CRED, holy; inviolable.
SAC'RIFICE, to destroy; to devote.
SAC'RILEGE, a violation of things sacred.
SAC'RISTY, the vestry room of a church.

Sagax, sagac-is, knowing, foreseeing.

PRE'SAGE, to forebode.
SAGA'CIOUS, discerning; acute.
SAGAC'ITY, acuteness.
SAGE, wise; grave.

Sal, salt, wit.

SAL'AD, food composed of raw herbs.
SAL'ARY, a periodical payment for services.
SALINE', briny.
SAUCE, something to give relish to food.

Sali-o, salt-um, to leap, to jump.

ASSAIL', to fall upon; to attack.
ASSAULT', an attack.
CON'SUL, a Roman magistrate.
CON'SULATE, the office of consul.
CONSULT',° to ask advice of.
COUN'SEL, to advise.
DES'ULTORY,° roving; unconnected.
EXULT',° to triumph.
IN'SULT,° a gross abuse.
RESULT',° consequence; effect.
SAL'LY,° to issue out.

Saliv-a, spittle. SAL'IVARY, relating to spittle.

Salus, salut-is, safety, health. ***Salv-us***, unhurt.

SAFE, free from danger.
SALU'BRITY, wholesomeness.
SAL'UTARY, healthful; safe.
SALUTE', to greet; to hail.
SALUTA'TION, a greeting.
SALV'AGE, a recompense for saving goods from a wreck.
SALVA'TION, a deliverance from injury.
SALVE, an ointment.
SAL'VO,° a reservation; excuse.

Sanct-us, holy, sacred.

SANC'TIFY, to make holy.
SAINT, a person eminent for piety.
SANC'TIMONY, holiness.
SANC'TION, confirmation.
SANC'TITY, godliness.
SANC'TUARY, a temple.

Sanguis, sanguin-is, blood.

CONSANGUIN'ITY, relation by blood.
SAN'GUINARY, cruel; bloody.
SAN'GUINE,° warm; ardent.

San-us, sound, whole.

INSANE', mad; distracted.
SAN'ITY, soundness of mind.

Sapi-o, to savor, to know.

INSIP'ID, tasteless; flat.
SA'VOR, odor; taste.

Satis, enough, sufficient.

INSA'TIABLE, not to be satisfied.
INSAT'URABLE, not to be saturated.
SATE, to glut; to pall.
SAT'ISFY, to content; to please.
SAT'URATE, to impregnate fully

Scal-a, a ladder, a stair.

ESCALADE', the act of scaling walls.
SCALE, to climb; to mount.

Scand-o, scans-um, to go, to mount.

ASCEND', to move upwards.
ASCENT', an eminence.
CONDESCEND', to stoop; to submit.
CONDESCEN'SION, a voluntary stooping from dignity.
ASCEN'SION, the act of ascending.
DESCEND', to go down.
DESCENT', declivity; progress downward.
SCAN,° to examine nicely.
TRANSCEND'ENT, pre-eminent.

Scind-o, sciss-um, to cut.

RESCIND', to revoke.
SCIS'SORS, small shears.

Scintill-a, a spark of fire.

SCIN'TILLATE, to emit sparks.
SCINTILLA'TION, the act of throwing off sparks.

Sci-o, to know. ***Sciens, scient-is***, knowing.

CON'SCIENCE, the knowledge of right and wrong.
CON'SCIOUS, knowing; perceiving.
OMNISC'IENT, all-knowing.
CONSCIEN'TIOUS, regulated by conscience.
SCI'ENCE,° knowledge.
SCIENTIF'IC, relating to science.

Scrib-o, script-um, to write.

ASCRIBE',° to attribute.
ASCRIP'TION, the act of ascribing.
CIRCUMSCRIBE', to bound, to limit.
CON'SCRIPT, one enrolled for the army.
DESCRIBE', to give an account of.
INSCRIBE', to write on.
INSCRIP'TION, a title; an address.
MAN'USCRIPT, a book or paper written, not printed.
PRESCRIBE',° to set down; to order.
PRESCRIP'TION, a medical receipt.
PROSCRIBE',* to condemn; to denounce.
PROSCRIP'TIVE, denouncing.
SCRIB'BLE, to write carelessly.
SCRIBE,° a writer; a notary.
SCRIP,° a small writing.
SCRIP'TURE, a writing; the Bible.
SUBSCRIBE',° to sign; to attest.
SUBSCRIP'TION, the act of subscribing.
SUPERSCRIBE', to write on the outside.
SUPERSCRIP'TION, a writing on the outside.
TRANSCRIBE', to copy; to write from.
TRAN'SCRIPT, a copy.

Scrut-or, to seek, to trace out.

SCRU'TINIZE, to search.
SCRU'TINY, examination; search

Sculpo, sculpt-um, to carve.

SCULP'TOR, a carver of stone or wood.
SCULP'TURE, the art of carving.

Scurr-a, a scoffer, a buffoon.

SCURRIL'ITY,° abusive language.
SCUR'RILOUS, abusive; vulgar

Scut-um, a shield, a defence.

SCUTCH'EON, the shield on which a coat of arms is represented.

Sec-o, sect-um, to cut.

DISSECT', to cut in pieces.
DISSEC'TION, act of dissecting.
IN'SECT,° a small creeping animal.
INTERSECT', to cut mutually.
SECT, a division; a party.
SEC'TARY, one of a sect.
SEC'TION, a part; a division.
SEG'MENT, a part cut off.
VENESEC'TION, blood-letting.

Sedat-us, calm, peaceful.

SEDATE', calm; quiet.
SED'ATIVE, assuaging.

---

* The sense of this word originated in the Roman practice of *writing* the names of persons doomed to death, and posting the list in public.

Sed-eo, sess-um, to sit.

ASSESS',° to value.
ASSID'UOUS,° constant in application.
BESIEGE', to hem in; to beset.
CONSID'ER,° to study; to ponder.
CONSID'ERATE, thoughtful.
DISPOSSESS', to put out of possession.
INSID'IOUS,° treacherous.
POSSESS',° to enjoy; to own.
PREPOSSESSI'ON, preconceived opinion.
PRESIDE', to be set over; to direct.
PRES'IDENCY, the office of president.
RESIDE',° to live in a place.
RES'IDENT, one who resides.
RES'IDUE, that which is left.
SEDAN',° a portable chair.
SED'ENTARY, sitting; inactive.
SED'IMENT, that which settles at the bottom.
SED'ULOUS,° diligent.
SESSI'ON, a sitting.
SIEGE, the act of besetting a fortified place.
SUBSIDE',° to sink away.
SUBSID'IARY, assisting.
SUB'SIDIZE, to furnish with money and arms.
SUPERSEDE',° to set aside.

Semen, semin-is, seed.

DISSEMINA'TION,° a scattering.
SEM'INARY,° a nursery; a school

Senex, sen-is, an old man.

SEI'GNIOR, a lord; a title.
SEN'ATE,* a body of senators.

Sent-io, sens-um, to feel, to think.

ASSENT',° the act of agreeing to.
CONSENT', to yield; to agree.
DISSENT', to differ in opinion.
DISSEN'SION, strife; quarrel.
NON'SENSE, unmeaning language.
PRESENT'IMENT, apprehension of something future.
RESENT', to take as an affront.
SCENT, smell; odor.
SENSA'TION, perception by the senses.
SENSE, perception; meaning.
SENS'UAL, pleasing the senses
SEN'TENCE, to judge; to condemn.
SENT'IMENT,° thought; opinion.
SENT'INEL, a soldier on guard.

Septem, seven.

SEPTEM'BER, the ninth month, (see note p. 165.)
SEV'EN, one more than six.
SEPTEN'NIAL, lasting seven years

Sequ-or, secut-us, to follow.

CONSEC'UTIVE, following in regular order.
CON'SEQUENT, following as an effect.
CONSEQUEN'TIAL, conclusive; pompous.
ENSUE', to follow.
EX'ECUTE,° to carry into effect.

---

* This was so called, because it originally consisted of the *oldest* members of the state.

OBSE'QUIOUS, servilely obedient.
PER'SECUTE, to pursue with malignity.
PROS'ECUTE,° to carry on; to continue.
PURSUE', to chase; to follow.
PURSUIT', act of pursuing.
SE'QUEL, what follows.
SUB'SEQUENT, coming after.
SUE, to prosecute by law.
SUIT, a petition, a set.
SUITE, retinue; company.

Seren-us, clear, fair, calm.

SERENADE',°music performed at night in the open air.
SERENE', calm; placid.
SEREN'ITY, calmness; peace.

Serp-o, to creep.

SER'PENTINE, winding like a serpent.
SER'PENT, a creeping animal.

Sert-um (*ab* ***Sero***), to knit, to join in discourse.

ASSERT', to maintain; to affirm.
DESERT', to abandon.
DISSERTA'TION, a discourse; a treatise.
INSERT', to set in or among.
REINSERT', to insert again.
SE'RIES, a succession of things
SER'MON, a religious discourse

Serv-io, servit-um, to serve, to obey.

DESERVE', to be worthy; to merit.
SER'GEANT, an officer in the army.
SERVE, to assist; to wait on.
SERV'ILE, slavish; dependent.
SERV'ITUDE, slavery.
SUBSERVE', to serve as an instrument.

Serv-o, servat-um, to keep, to save.

CON'SERVE,°a sweet-meat.
CONSERV'ATIVE, opposing injury.
OBSERVE', to watch; to keep.
OBSERVA'TION, the act of observing.
PRESERVE', to keep; to save.
RESERVE',°to hold back.
RESERVOIR', a place where any thing is stored; a cistern.
SERV'ANT, a menial; a dependant.

Sever-us, severe.

SEVERE', sharp; harsh.
SEVER'ITY, cruelty; harshness.

Sex, six.

SEN'ARY, containing six.
SEXANG'ULAR, having six angles.
SEX'TUPLE, six-fold.
SIX, twice three.

Sex-us, sex. SEX'UAL, belonging to sex.

Sidus, sider-is, a star.

CONSID'ER, to deliberate; to think of.
DESIRE', a request; a wish.
DESIDERA'TUM, something needed.
SIDE'REAL, relating to the stars.

Sign-um, a mark or sign.

ASSIGN', to mark out; to appoint.
ASSIGN'MENT, a making over.
CONSIGN', to transfer; to commit.
DESIGN', a scheme; a purpose.
DES'IGNATE, to point out.
INSIG'NIA, marks of office or honor.
RESIGN', to give up; to yield.
INSIGNIF'ICANT, wanting meaning; unimportant.
SIGN, a mark; a token.
SIG'NAL, a sign, to give notice.
SIG'NALIZE, to render memorable.
SIG'NATURE, a stamp; a mark.
SIGNIFICA'TION, meaning.
UNDESIGN'ED, not intended.

Silv-a, a wood, a grove.

SAV'AGE, wild; uncivilized.
SILV'AN, woody.
PENNSYLVA'NIA, the groves of Penn; one of the U. S. of N.A.

Simil-is, like, resembling.

ASSIM'ILATE, to make like to.
DISSEM'BLE, to hide under false appearance.
DISSIM'ILAR, unlike.
DISSIMULA'TION, hypocrisy.
SIM'ILAR, like; uniform.
SIM'ILE,° a comparison.
SIMIL'ITUDE, resemblance.

Simul, together. SIMULTA'NEOUS, at the same time.

Sinister, on the left hand. SIN'ISTER, unfair; corrupt.

Sinus, the bosom, a bend.

INSIN'UATE,° to hint; to introduce slowly and artfully.

Sist-o, to stand, to stop.

ASSIST',° to help.
CONSIST',° to be composed of.
DESIST', to cease from; to stop.
EXIST',° to have being.
INCONSIST'ENT, incompatible.
INSIST', to stand upon; to urge.
IRRESIST'IBLE, superior to opposition.
PERSIST',° to persevere.
RESIST',° to make opposition.

Situs, place.

SITE, local position.
SITUA'TION, place; state.

Soci-o, to join.

ASSO'CIATE, a partner; a companion.
SO'CIABLE,° familiar; friendly.
SO'CIAL, relating to society.
SOCI'ETY, a collection of persons.

Sol, the sun.

SO'LAR, belonging to the sun.
SOL'STICE,° the tropical point.

Sol-eo, to be accustomed.

IN'SOLENCE, haughtiness; impudence.
IN'SOLENT,° haughty; contemptuous.

Solicit-us, anxious, uneasy.

SOLIC'IT,° to importune; to intreat
SOLICITA'TION, entreaty.
SOLIC'ITOUS, anxious; concerned.
SOLIC'ITUDE, anxiety; concern.

Solid-us, firm, hard.

CONSOL'IDATE, to unite into a solid mass.
SOL'DIER,°a warrior.
SOL'DER, to unite with metallic cement.
SOLID'ITY, hardness; firmness.

Sol-or, to cheer, to comfort.

CONSOLE', to comfort; to cheer.
DISCON'SOLATE, hopeless; sorrowful.
INCONSO'LABLE, not to be comforted.
SOL'ACE, ease; comfort.

Sol-us, alone.

DES'OLATE, without inhabitants; laid waste.
SOLE, single; alone.
SOLIL'OQUY, a speech to one's self.
SOL'ITARY, retired; alone.
SOL'ITUDE, loneliness.

Solv-o, solut-um, to loose, to free, to melt.

ABSOLVE', to clear; to acquit.
AB'SOLUTE, complete; positive.
ABSOLU'TION, acquittal; remission.
DISSOLVE', to melt; to loose.
DIS'SOLUTE, loose; debauched.
INSOL'VENT, unable to pay.
INDIS'SOLUBLE, that cannot be separated.
IRRES'OLUTE, wavering; not determined.
RESOLVE',°to determine.
RESOLU'TION, firmness.
SOLVE,°to explain.
SOLV'ENCY, ability to pay.

Somn-us, sleep. SOMNAM'BULIST, one who walks in his sleep.

Son-us, a sound.

ALTIS'ONANT, high-sounding.
CON'SONANCE, agreement.
DIS'SONANT, harsh; discordant.
RESOUND', to send back sound.
SON'NET, a small poem.
SONO'ROUS, loud sounding.

Sopor, sleep. SOPORIF'IC, causing sleep.

Sorb-eo, sorpt-um, to suck up.

ABSORB', to suck up.
ABSORP'TION, a sucking up.

Sors, sort-is, lot, kind.

ASSORT', to arrange; to select.
CON'SORT, a companion; a wife or husband.
RESORT', to betake; to turn to.
SORT, a kind; a species.
SORTIE', an issuing out; a sally.

Sparg-o, spars-um, to scatter.

ASPERSE', to bespatter with calumnies.
DISPERSE', to scatter.
INTERSPERSE', to scatter between.
SPARSE, thinly scattered.

Spati-um, space.

EXPA'TIATE, to enlarge upon; to move at large.
SPACE, room; extension.
SPA'CIOUS, wide; roomy.

Speci-o, spect-um, to look. *Speci-es*, a sort.

AS'PECT, look; appearance.
AUSPICI'OUS, favorable.
CIR'CUMSPECT,° watchful; cautious.
CONSPIC'UOUS,°in full view.
DES'PICABLE, contemptible; worthless.
DESPISE',°to scorn; to contemn.
DISRESPECT', want of regard; rudeness.
ESPECI'AL, special; particular.
EXPECT', to look for.
INSPECT', to look into; to examine.
PERSPECT'IVE,°the art of representing scenes on a plain surface.
PERSPICU'ITY,°clearness.
PROS'PECT, sight; appearance.
RESPECT',°regard; honor.
RETROSPECT'IVE, looking backwards.
SPECIF'IC, limited; peculiar.
SPEC'IMEN, a sample.
SPE'CIOUS, plausible; showy.
SPECT'ACLE, a show; a sight.
SPECTA'TOR, a looker-on.
SPEC'TRE, an apparition.
SPEC'ULUM, a mirror.
SPEC'ULATE,° to meditate; to theorize.
SUSPECT',°to mistrust; to doubt.
SUSPICI'ON, act of suspecting.

Sper-o, to hope.

DESPAIR', to be without hope.
DESPERA'DO, a reckless villain.
DES'PERATE, hopeless.
PROSPER'ITY, success; fortune.
PROS'PER,°to succeed; to flourish.

Spin-a, a thorn; the spine.

SPINE, the back-bone.
SPINIF'EROUS, bearing thorns.
SPI'NOUS, thorny; relating to the back-bone.

Spir-o, spirat-um, to breathe.

ASPIRE', to desire ardently.
AS'PIRATE, to pronounce with full breath.
CONSPIRE', to concert; to plot.
CONSPIR'ACY, a plot; treason.
CONSPI'RATOR, one who plots.
DISPIR'IT, to discourage.
EXPIRE',°to die.
INSPIRE', to breathe into.
PERSPIRE', to emit by the pores.
RESPIRE',°to breathe.
SPIR'IT, the soul; the life.
SPIR'ITUAL, belonging to the spirit.
SPIR'ITUALIZE, to refine.
SPRITE, a spirit.
TRANSPIRE', to pass out; to become known.

Splend-eo, to shine.

RESPLEN'DENT, bright; shining.
SPLEN'DID, showy; magnificent.
SPLEN'DOR, lustre; pomp.
TRANSPLEN'DENCY, great splendor.

Spoli-um, booty.

DESPOIL', to rob; to strip.
SPOIL, plunder; pillage.

Spond-eo, spons-um, to promise.

CORRESPOND', to suit; to answer.
DESPOND',° to despair.
DESPOND'ENT, despairing.
ESPOUSE', to wed; to betroth.
RESPOND', to answer; to reply.
RESPONSE', answer.
RESPONS'IBLE, accountable.
SPOUSE, a husband or wife.

Stell-a, a star.

CONSTELLA'TION, a cluster of stars.
STEL'LATE, like a star.
STELLIF'EROUS, having stars.

Steril-is, barren.

STER'ILE, barren; unfruitful.
STERIL'ITY, barrenness.

Stern-o, strat-um, to cast down, to lay flat.

CONSTERNA'TION, great terror; amazement.
PROS'TRATE, lying flat.
STRA'TIFY, to arrange in layers

Stig-o, to prick, to spur.

IN'STIGATE, to provoke; to set on.
INSTIGA'TOR, one who instigates.

Still-a, a drop.

DISTILL, to drop; to extract spirit.
DISTILL'ERY, a place for distilling.
INSTILL', to infuse by drops; to teach slowly.
STILL, a vessel for distillation.

Stimul-us, a spur. STIM'ULATE, to urge; to animate.

Stingu-o, stinct-um, to mark, to thrust.

DISTING'UISH,° to mark difference; to make eminent.
DISTINCT', different; clear.
EXTIN'GUISH, to quench; to destroy.
EXTINCT', put out; destroyed.
INDISTINCT', not plain; confused.
INEXTING'UISHABLE, unquenchable.
INSTINCT'IVE,° natural; intuitive.

Stin-o (obs.), to fix.

DES'TINE, to doom; to appoint.
DESTINA'TION, purpose; end.
OB'STINATE, stubborn.
PREDES'TINE, to foredoom.
PREDESTINA'TION, the act of ordaining beforehand.

Stipendi-um, wages.

STI'PEND, settled pay; pension.
STIPEN'DIARY, a pensioner.

Stirps, stirp-is, a root or stem.

EX'TIRPATE, to root out; to destroy.
EXTIRPA'TION, a rooting out; total destruction.

St-o, stat-um, to stand, to set.

AR'MISTICE, a short truce.
ARREST', to stop; to seize.
CIR'CUMSTANCE,° event; condition.
CIRCUMSTAN'TIAL, incidental; particular.
CON'STABLE,° a police officer.
CON'STANT, fixed; unvaried

CON'STITUTE, to establish ; to form

CONSTITU'TION, the fundamental laws of a nation or society.

CONTRAST',° to place in opposition.

DESTITU'TION, want; poverty.

DIS'TANT,° remote ; not near.

ESTAB'LISH, to settle firmly.

EX'TANT,° in being; not suppressed.

IN'STANCE,° example ; urgency.

IN'STANT, pressing ; urgent.

INSTANTA'NEOUS, immediate.

IN'STITUTE, to establish.

IN'TERSTICE,° narrow space between things.

OB'STACLE, a hinderance.

PROS'TITUTE, to debase.

REINSTATE', to put again in possession.

REST,° repose ; quiet.

RESTITU'TION, a giving back.

STAM'EN, the fixed, firm part of a body which gives it strength.

STAND, to be erect ; to remain fixed.

STAN'DARD,° an ensign of war ; a test.

STATE,° rank ; condition.

STA'TION, situation ; position.

STA'TIONARY, fixed.

STATIS'TICS,° statement of the strength and resources of nations.

STAT'UE, a standing image.

SUB'STANCE, being ; body.

SUBSTAN'TIAL, real ; material.

SUB'STITUTE, to put in place of another.

SUPERSTITI'ON,° false religion.

String-o, strict-um, to bind, to contract.

ASTRING'ENT, binding; contracting.

CONSTRIC'TION, a contraction.

CONSTRAIN', to compel.

RESTRAINT', hinderance of the will.

RESTRICT', to limit ; to confine.

STRAIN, to make violent efforts.

STRICT, exact ; severe.

UNCONSTRAIN'ED, voluntary.

Stru-o, struct-um, to build.

CON'STRUE,° to interpret ; to explain.

CONSTRUCT', to build ; to form.

DESTROY', to ruin ; to pull down.

DESTRUC'TION, the act of destroying.

INSTRUCT', to teach ; to inform.

IN'STRUMENT, a tool ; a means.

MISCONSTRUE', to interpret wrong.

OBSTRUCT', to oppose ; to hinder.

SUPERSTRUC'TURE, that part of the building above the foundation.

UNINSTRUCT'IVE, not imparting knowledge.

Stud-eo, to study.

STU'DENT, a scholar.

STU'DIOUS, given to study.

STUD'Y, to learn ; to consider attentively.

Stup-eo, to be dull, to astonish.

STUPEN'DOUS, amazing ; wonderful.

STU'PEFY, to make stupid.

STUPEFAC'TION, insensibility ; dullness.

STU'PID, dull ; senseless.

Suad-eo, suas-um, to advise.

ASSUAGE', to appease ; to ease.

ASSUA'SIVE, mitigating.

DISSUADE', to advise from.

DISSUA'SION, the act of dissuading.

PERSUADE', to influence by argument or entreaty.

PERSUA'SIVE, having power to persuade.

Suav-is, sweet.

SUAV'ITY, sweetness; softness.
SWEET, not sour; agreeable.

Sublim-is, high; exalted.

SUBLIME', lofty; grand.
SUBLIM'ITY, grandeur.

Subtil-is, fine, cunning.

SUB'TILE, acute; artful.
SUBT'LETY, artifice; slyness.

Sud-o, to sweat.

EXUDE', to sweat out.
SUDORIF'IC, causing sweat.
SWEAT, moisture from the skin.
TRANSUDE', to sweat through.

Sug-o, suct-um, to suck or draw in.

SUCK, to draw into the mouth.
SUCK'LE, to nurse at the breast.
SUC'TION, the act of sucking.
SUC'CULENT, juicy; moist.

Sui, of one's self.

SU'ICIDE, self-murder.
SUICI'DAL, self-destroying.

Summ-a, the whole.

CON'SUMMATE, complete; finished.
SUM, the amount.
SUM'MARY, an abridgment.
SUM'MIT, the top; the utmost height.

Sum-o, sumpt-um, to take.

ASSUME', to arrogate; to take to.
CONSUME', to waste slowly.
CONSUMP'TION, a disease; waste.
PRESUMP'TUOUS, arrogant; confident
PRESUME',°to suppose.
RESUME', to take back; to recommence.
SUMP'TUARY, relating to expense.
SUMP'TUOUS, expensive.

Super, above; high.

INSU'PERABLE, invincible; insurmountable.
SUPERCIL'IOUS,° haughty; overbearing.
SUPERB', grand; magnificent.
SUPER'LATIVE, highest.
SUPREME', highest in authority.

Surg-o, surrect-um, to rise.

INSURG'ENT,°a rebel.
INSURREC'TION,°a rebellion.
SOURCE, origin; first cause.
SURGE, a large wave.

Tabern-a, a tent. TAB'ERNACLE,°a temporary dwelling.

Tabul-a, a board; a table.

TA'BLE, an article of furniture.
TAB'ULAR, in the form of a table.
TA'BLET, a flat surface for writing.

Taceo, tacit-um, to be silent.

TAC'IT, silent; implied.
TACITURN'ITY, habitual silence.

Taill-er (Fr.), to cut, to deal.

DETAIL', a minute account.
ENTAIL', to settle the descent of an estate.
RETAIL', sale by small quantities.
TAI'LOR, one who cuts out men's clothes.

Tal-is, such; like for like.

RETAL'IATE, to return like for like.
TA'LION, the law of retaliation.
TAL'LY, to fit; to suit.

Tang-o, tact-um, to touch.

ATTAIN',°to gain; to reach to.
CON'TACT, touch; close union.
CONTA'GION, propagation of disease by touch; infection.
CONTIGU'ITY, actual contact.
CONTIN'GENT, accidental; casual.
ENTIRE', whole; unbroken.
IN'TEGER,°a whole number.
IN'TEGRAL, whole; not fractional.
INTEG'RITY, honesty; purity.
TACT', touch; peculiar skill.
TANG'IBLE, that can be touched or taken hold of.

Tard-us, slow.

RETARD', to delay; to hinder.
TAR'DY, slow; not swift.

Teg-o, tect-um, to cover.

DETECT', to discover.
PROTECT'ORATE, government by a protector.
INTEG'UMENT,°a covering.
PROTECT', to defend; to cover.

Temn-o, tempt-um, to scorn.

CONTEMN', to despise; to slight.
CONTEMPT', disregard; scorn.

Temper-o, to temper, to regulate.

DISTEM'PER,° disease.
TEM'PER, disposition.
TEM'PERANCE, moderation.
TEM'PERATE, moderate.
TEM'PERATURE, state as regards heat or cold.

Tempus, tempor-is, time.

CONTEM'PORARY, one who lives in the same age with another.
CONTEMPORA'NEOUS, existing at the same time.
EXTEM'PORE,° without premeditation.
TEM'PORAL,°relating to time.
TEM'PORARY, lasting for a time
TEM'PORIZE, to yield to circumstances.
TIME, the measure of duration.

Tend-o, tens-um, to stretch.

ATTEND',°to regard; to wait on.
ATTEN'TION,° regard; care.
CONTEND', to strive; to struggle.
CONTEN'TION, strife; emulation.
DISTEND', to stretch; to expand.
EXTEND', to reach; to spread.
EXTEN'SIVE, large; wide-spread.
EXTENT', size; compass.
INTEND',° to mean; to design.
INTENSE',° strained; ardent.
INTENS'ITY, ardor; violence.
INTENT', purpose.
OSTENS'IBLE, plausible; seeming
OSTENTA'TION, vain display.

PORTEND', to foretoken.
PORTENT', an omen ; a prodigy.
PRETEND',°to feign.
PRETENSE', a feigning.
SUPERINTEND', to direct ; to overlook.
TEND, to aim at ; to contribute.
TEND'ENCY,°direction ; course.
TEND'ON, a sinew ; a cord.
TEND'RIL, a spiral shoot of a plant.
TENSE, stiff ; stretched.
TEN'SION, tightness.
TENT,°a portable dwelling.

Ten-eo, tent-um, to hold.

ABSTAIN', to keep from.
ABSTE'MIOUS, temperate ; sober.
AB'STINENT, refraining.
APPERTAIN', to belong ; to relate.
CONTAIN', to hold ; to comprise.
CONTENT',°satisfied.
CONTIN'UE, to remain ; to last.
CONTIN'UAL, incessant.
CONTINU'ITY, unbroken connection.
COUN'TENANCE,°features ; look.
DETAIN', to keep back.
DETENT'ION, confinement ; restraint.
DISCONTENT'ED, uneasy ; dissatisfied.
DISCONTIN'UANCE, cessation.
ENTERTAIN', to harbor ; to amuse.
IMPER'TINENCE, rudeness ; insolence.
LIEUTEN'ANT, an officer who acts in the absence of a superior.
MAINTAIN',° to support ; to persist in.
OBTAIN', to gain ; to acquire.
PERTAIN', to belong to.
PERTINA'CIOUS,°obstinate ; stubborn.
PER'TINENT, to the purpose.
RETAIN', to keep ; to reserve.
RETENT'IVE, having the power to retain.
RET'INUE, a train of attendants.
SUSTAIN', to support ; to prop.
SUS'TENANCE, support.
TENA'CIOUS, holding fast.
TEN'ANT, an occupier of a house or lands.
TEN'EMENT,°a house ; an abode.
TEN'ET,°an opinion ; a principle.
TEN'URE, a holding.

Tent-o, tentat-um, to try.

ATTEMPT', a trial ; an effort.
TEMPT', to solicit ; to entice.
TENT'ATIVE, trying ; essaying.

Tenu-is, thin.

ATTEN'UATE, to make thin.
TENU'ITY, thinness.
EXTEN'UATE,°to lessen ; to palliate.

Tepe-o, to be warm.

TEP'EFY, to make warm.
TEP'ID, lukewarm.

Termin-us, a limit, end.

DETERM'INE, to resolve ; to fix.
EXTERM'INATE, to destroy.
INTER'MINABLE, having no end.
TERM, boundary ; condition ; a word or expression.
TERM'INATE, to close ; to end.

Tern-us, threefold : ***Terti-us,*** three.

TERN'ARY, consisting of three.
THIRD, the ordinal of three.
TER'TIAN, occurring every other day.

Tero, trit-um, to rub, to wear by rubbing.

CON'TRITE,° sorrowful; penitent.
DET'RIMENT,° loss; damage.
DET'RITUS, matter worn off.
TRITE, worn out; common.
TRIT'URATE, to rub or grind to a fine powder.

Terr-a, the earth.

DISINTER', to take out of the earth.
FRONTIER', the border of a country.
INTER', to bury in the earth.
MEDITERRA'NEAN, encircled with land.
TERRES'TRIAL, earthly.
TER'RACE, a raised bank of earth; a flat roof.
TERRA'QUEOUS, composed of land and water.
TER'RIER, a small dog that hunts under ground.
TER'RITORY, a tract of land.

Terr-eo, to make afraid.

DETER',° to hinder; to discourage.
TER'ROR, extreme fear.
TER'RIFY, to frighten.
TERRIF'IC, causing fear.

Test-is, a witness.

ATTEST', to bear witness.
CON'TEST, dispute; struggle.
DETESTA'TION, abhorrence.
INCONTEST'ABLE, not to be disputed.
INTES'TATE, dying without having made a will.
PROTEST',° to declare against.
PROT'ESTANT, one who protests
TEST'AMENT, a will.
TESTA'TOR, one who makes a will.
TESTIMO'NIAL, a certificate.
TEST'IFY, to witness; to give evidence.
TEST'IMONY,° a declaration; evidence.

Text-us, woven.

CON'TEXT,° the connected passages.
PRE'TEXT, pretence; feigned motive.
TEXT, a passage upon which a discourse is made.
TEXT'URE, the thing woven; the quality of that which is woven.

Tim-eo, to fear.

INTIM'IDATE, to make fearful.
TIM'ID, fearful.
TIM'OROUS, cowardly.

Ting-o, tinct-um, to dip, to paint, to stain.

ATTAIN'DER,° the act of attainting.
ATTAINT', to corrupt; to find guilty of treason.
TAINT, corruption; blemish.
TINC'TURE, a liquid containing the principal qualities of some substance.
TINGE, to infuse or impregnate slightly
TINT, a dye; a slight coloring.

Titul-us, title, inscription.

[illegible]TI'TLE,° to give a claim.
TI'TLE, an appellation of honor; a claim of right.
TIT'ULAR, relating to a title.
UNTI'TLED, having no title.

Toler-o, tolerat-um, to bear, to suffer.

INTOL'ERABLE, that cannot be borne.
TOLERA'TION, allowance of that which is not approved.

Toll-o, to raise.

EXTOL', to praise ; to exalt.
TOLL', a tax ; a charge for passing.

Torp-eo, to benumb ; to be stiff.

TORPE'DO, an electric fish.
TOR'PID, numbed ; sluggish.
TOR'PITUDE, sluggishness.
TOR'POR, numbness.

Torre-o, to dry, to parch.

TOR'REFY, to dry by fire.
TORREFAC'TION, a drying by fire.
TOR'RENT, a rapid stream.
TOR'RID, parched ; dried.

Tort-um, (a ***torqueo***), to twist ; to writhe.

CONTORT', to writhe.
DISTOR'TION, a twisting out of shape.
EXTOR'TION,° illegal exaction.
RETORT', to throw back a censure or objection.
TOR'MENT, extreme pain.
TOR'TIOUS, wrongful.
TORT'URE, agony.
UNDISTORT'ED, not perverted.

Tot-us, whole, all.

FACTO'TUM, one who can perform all kinds of service.
SURTOUT',° an overcoat.
TO'TAL, the whole.

Trad-o, tradit-um, to deliver, to hand down.

TRADITI'ON, oral account handed down from age to age.
TRAD'ITIVE, transmitted from age to age.

Trah-o, tract-um, to draw.

ABSTRACT',° to draw from.
ABSTRAC'TION, absence of mind.
ATTRACT', to draw to ; to allure.
ATTRACT'IVE, engaging.
BETRAY', to give up treacherously.
CONTRACT', to draw together.
DETRACT', to take from.
DISTRACT',° to draw apart ; to separate ; to perplex.
EXTRACT', to draw out.
POR'TRAIT,° a likeness.
PORTRAY',° to delineate.
PROTRACT',° to prolong.
RETRACT', to draw or take back.
SUBTRACT', to deduct.
TRACT, a region ; a small treatise.
TRAIT, a feature ; a line.
TREAT, to use ; to discuss.

Trem-o, to shake.

TREM'BLE, to shake ; to quiver.
TREMEN'DOUS, terrible ; dreadful.
TRE'MOR, a trembling.
TREM'ULOUS, shaking; quivering

Trepid-us, trembling.

INTREP'ID, fearless ; daring
TREPIDA'TION, fear ; tremor

Tres, tri-a, three.

TRI'AD, the union of three.
TRIAN'GLE, a figure having three angles.
TRI'DENT,°an instrument having three prongs.
TRIEN'NIAL, happening every three years.
TRI'FLE,°a thing of little value.
TRIN'ITY, a union of three in one.
TRI'O, a part in music for three performers.
TRIPH'THONG, a union of three vowels in one sound.
TRIP'LE, threefold.
TRI'REME, a galley with three benches of oars on a side.
TRISECT', divided into three parts.
TRIS'YLLABLE, a word of three syllables.
TRIUNE', three in one.
TRIV'IAL,°trifling; worthless.

Trib-us, a tribe.

TRIBE, a distinct body of people.
TRIBU'NAL, a court of justice.
TRI'BUNE,°a Roman officer.
TRIBUNITI'AL, relating to a tribune.

Tribut-um (*ab* ***Tribuo***), to give.

ATTRIB'UTE, to ascribe.
CONTRIB'UTE, to give in common with others.
DISTRIBU'TION, a giving to several.
RETRIB'UTIVE, repaying.
TRIB'UTE, a tax paid to a conqueror.
TRIB'UTARY, paying tribute.

Trouv-er (Fr.), to find.

CONTRIVE', to plan; to invent.
RETRIEVE', to repair; to regain.
CONTRI'VANCE, a plan; a scheme.

Trud-o, trus-um, to thrust, to push.

ABSTRUSE',°concealed; obscure.
INTRUDE', to thrust one's self in; to encroach.
INTRU'SION, the act of intruding.
OBTRUDE', to thrust in or on.
INTRU'SIVE, entering without invitation.
PROTRUDE', to thrust forward.
PROTRU'SION, a thrusting forward.

Trunc-o, truncat-um, to lop, to cut off.

DETRUN'CATE, to cut off; to lop.
TRUN'CHEON, a short staff; a club.
TRUNC'ATE, maimed; cut off short.
TRUNK, the main body of any thing; a chest.

Tuber, a swelling.

PROTU'BERANCE, a prominence; a swelling.
TU'BER, a knob in roots.
TU'BERCLE, a little tumor.

Tue-or, tuit-us, to keep, to protect, to see.

TUITI'ON, instruction.
INTU'ITIVE, seen instantly by the mind.
TU'TELAGE, guardianship; care.
TU'TOR, a teacher; a guardian.

Tume-o, to swell.

CONTUMA'CEOUS,°stubborn.
CON'TUMELY,° rudeness; insolence.
ENTOMB', to put into a tomb.
TOMB,°a grave; a burial place.
TUM'BLE, to fall; to roll about.
TU'MID, swollen; pompous.
TU'MOR, a swelling.
TU'MULT,°a commotion.
TUMULT'UARY, disorderly.

Tund-o, tus-um, to beat, to bruise, to blunt.

CONTU'SION, a bruise.
OBTUSE', dull; blunted.

Turb-a, a crowd, confusion.

DISTURB', to disquiet.
PERTURBA'TION, disquiet; mental agitation.
TROUB'LE, perplexity.
TUR'BID, muddy; not clear.
TUR'BULENT, tumultuous.

Turg-eo, to swell. TUR'GID, bloated; swollen.

Uber, fertile.

EXU'BERANT, abundant.
U'BERTY, fruitfulness.

Ultim-us, last.

ANTEPENULT', the last syllable but two.
ULTE'RIOR, further.
UL'TIMATE, final; last.
PENULT', the last syllable but one.
ULTIMA'TUM, a final proposition.

Umbr-a, a shadow, or shade.

UM'BRAGE, offence.
UMBRA'GEOUS, shady.
UMBREL'LA, a screen or shade carried in the hand.

Und-o, undat-um, to rise in waves.

ABOUND', to be in great plenty.
ABUND'ANT, plentiful.
INUNDA'TION, a flood.
REDOUND', to conduce; to result.
REDUND'ANCY, superfluity.
SUPERABUND'ANT, very plentiful.
UN'DULATE, to wave; to vibrate.
UN'DULATORY, moving like waves.

Ungu-o, unct-um, to anoint.

UNC'TION, an anointing.
UNC'TUOUS, oily.
UNG'UENT, ointment.
OINT'MENT, a salve.

Un-us, one, alone.

TRIUNE', three in one.
UNAN'IMOUS, of one mind.
U'NICORN, a beast with one horn.
U'NIFORM, even; regular.
U'NION, concord; conjunction.
UNIQUE', sole; peculiar.
U'NISON, agreement; harmony.
U'NIT, a single thing.
UNITE', to concur; to join.
UNIVER'SITY, a universal school in which all branches of learning are taught.
U'NIVERSE, the whole system of things.

Urbs, a city.

SUB'URBS, the outpart of a city.
URBAN'ITY, politeness.

Ust-um, (ab ***uro***), to burn.

COMBUS'TION, a burning.
INCOMBUST'IBLE, not to be burned.

Ut-or, usus, to use.

ABUSE', to make an ill use of.
DISUSE', to cease to use.
INUTIL'ITY, uselessness.
MISU'SAGE, ill use.
PERUSE',° to read.
USE, to employ.
U'SAGE, custom; treatment.
U'SUAL, ordinary.
U'SURY,° illegal interest.
UTEN'SIL, a vessel; an instrument.

Vac-o, vacat-um, to be empty.

EVAC'UATE, to quit; to leave.
VA'CANT, empty.
VACA'TION, recess; leisure.
VAC'UUM, empty space.

Vad-o, vas-um, to go.

EVADE', to avoid; to escape.
INVADE',° to attack; to assail.
INVA'SION, a hostile entrance.
PERVADE', to pass through.

Vag-us, a wandering.

EXTRAV'AGANT,° prodigal; wasteful; excessive.
VAG'ABOND, an idle fellow.
VAGA'RY, a whim; a wild freak
VA'GRANT, an idle wanderer.
VAGUE, uncertain; unsettled.

Val-eo, to be well or strong, to be worth.

AVAIL', to be of use.
CONVALES'CENT, improving in health.
EQUIV'ALENT, equal in value.
IN'VALID, a sick person.
INVAL'IDATE, to weaken.
PREVAIL', to overcome; to be general.
INVAL'UABLE, extremely precious.
PREV'ALENCE, influence; predominance.
VALEDIC'TION, a farewell.
VALID'ITY, strength.
VAL'OR, personal bravery.
VAL'UE, worth; price.

Vall-um, a fence.

IN'TERVAL, space between places.
WALL, a work of stone or brick to enclose or defend a place.

Van-us, vain, empty.

EVANES'CENT, vanishing.
VAIN, empty; worthless.
VAN'ISH, to disappear.
VAN'ITY, idle show.

Vapor, steam; fume. EVAP'ORATE, to disperse in vapors

Vari-us, diverse, changeable.

VA'RY, to change.
VA'RIANCE, dissension.
VA'RIEGATE, to diversify.
VARI'ETY, change; diversity.

Vas, a vessel.

VASE, a vessel.
VAS'CULAR, full of vessels.
VES'SEL, a cask or utensil for holding liquids.

Vast-us, large; desert.

DEV'ASTATE, to ravage.
DEVASTA'TION, a laying waste.
VAST, large; great.
WASTE, a desolate country.

Veh-o, vect-um, to carry.

CONVEY', to carry; to send.
CONVEY'ANCE, that which conveys.
INVEI'GH, to censure.
INVEC'TIVE, angry abuse.
VE'HEMENCE, ardor; violence.
VE'HICLE, a carriage.
VEX, to trouble; to irritate.
VEXA'TIOUS, troublesome.

Vell-o, vuls-um, to pull; to pluck.

CONVULSE', to give violent motion to.
REVUL'SION, a drawing back.

Vel-o, to cover, to conceal.

DEVEL'OPMENT, an unfolding.
ENVEL'OP, to enfold.
REVEAL', to disclose.
REVELA'TION, discovery; disclosure.
VEIL, to hide; to cover.

Velox, veloc-is, swift. VELOCITY, swiftness.

Ven-a, a vein.

VEIN, a tube for the blood.
VENESEC'TION,° blood-letting.

Venen-um, poison.

ENVEN'OM, to poison.
VENEFICI'AL, acting by poison.
VEN'OM, poison.
VEN'OMOUS, poisonous.

Ven-io, vent-um, to come, to go.

AD'VENT, a coming.
ADVENT'URE, an enterprise; a risk.
AV'ENUE, a passage.
CIRCUMVENT',° to deceive; to cheat.
CONVENE', to assemble.
CONVE'NIENT, suitable; fit.
CON'VENT, a nunnery; a monastery.
CONVEN'TION, an assembly.
EVENT'UAL,° ultimate.
EVENT'UATE, to come to an end.
INCONVE'NIENCE, unfitness; disadvantage.
INTERVENE', to come between.
INVENT',° to discover; to feign.
IN'VENTORY, an account of goods.
PREVENT',° to hinder; to obstruct.
REV'ENUE,° income of a state.
SUPERVENE', to come as an addition; to happen to.
VENT, an aperture; a hole.
VEN'TUROUS, daring; bold

Venter, ventr-is, the belly.

VENTRIL'OQUISM,° the art of speaking from the stomach.

Vent-us, the wind. VEN'TILATE, to cause a free circulation of air

Ver, the spring. VER'NAL, belonging to the spring.

Verb-um, a word.

AD'VERB, a part of speech.
PROV'ERB,° a maxim.
VERB'IAGE,° empty discourse.
VERBOSE', full of words.

Verd-is, *for* ***Viridis***, green.

VER'DANT, flourishing; green.
VER'DIGRIS, rust of copper.
VER'DURE, freshness of vegetation; greenness.

Vere-or, to fear, to reverence.

REVERE', to respect highly.
REV'ERENCE, respect mingled with awe.
REV'EREND, worthy of reverence.
REVEREN'TIAL, expressing or feeling reverence.

Verg-o, to tend.

DIVERG'ENT, receding; separating.
CONVERGE', to tend to one point
VERGE, to tend; to incline.

Verm-is, a worm.

VERMICEL'LI, a paste in the form of worms.
VERM'IFORM, in the shape of a worm.
VERMIL'ION, a bright red color; formerly the cochineal.
VERM'IFUGE, a medicine to destroy worms.
VERM'IN, noxious animals, insects, &c.
VERMIP'AROUS, producing worms.

Vert-o, vers-um, to turn.

ADVERT', to turn to.
AD'VERSE, opposite; hostile.
ADVERS'ITY,° misfortune; calamity.
ADVERTISE', to publish a notice.
ANIMADVER'SION, censure.
ANNIVERS'ARY, a stated day coming once in every year.
AVERT', to turn away.
AVER'SION, dislike.
CON'TROVERT,° to dispute.
CONTROVER'SY, disputation.
CONVERSE', to discourse with.
DIVERT', to please; to turn off.
DIVERS'ITY, variety; difference.
DIVERS'IFY, to vary.
INADVERT'ENT, negligent; inattentive.
INVERT', to turn upside down.
INVER'SION, the act of inverting.
PERVERSE',° cross; stubborn.
PERVERT', to distort.
RET'ROVERT, to turn back.
RETROVER'SION, the act of turning back.
REVERT', to turn back.
REVERSE', to repeal; to put in an opposite direction.
REVER'SION, a turning or falling back.
SUBVERT', to overthrow; to ruin.
TRANSVERSE', lying across.
TRA'VERSE, to cross; to pass over.
UNIVERS'ALISM, the doctrine that all men will be saved.
VERS'ATILE, changing; turning with ease from one thing to another.
VERSE, a poetical line; a short division of any composition.
VER'SIFY, to make verse.

VERSIFICA'TION, the art of making verses.
VER'SION, a translation.
VERT'EX, the top; the point overhead.
VERT'ICAL, overhead.
VOR'TEX, a whirlpool.

Ver-us, true.

AVER', to declare positively.
VERAC'ITY, truth.
VER'DICT, the decision of a jury.
VER'IFY, to prove true.
VERISIMIL'ITUDE, resemblance to truth.
VER'ITY, truth.
VER'ILY, certainly; truly.

Vestigi-um, a footstep.

INVEST'IGATE,°to search into.
VES'TIGE, a trace; a mark.

Vest-is, clothing.

DIVEST', to strip; to deprive.
INVEST', to clothe; to confer.
VEST, an outer garment.
VES'TURE, a garment; a robe.

Vet-o, I forbid. VE'TO,° a prohibition.

Vetus, veter-is, old.

INVET'ERATE, old; long established.
VET'ERAN,°an old soldier.

Vi-a, a way.

CON'VOY,°an attendance for defence.
DE'VIATE, to wander; to err.
EN'VOY,°a public messenger.
IMPER'VIOUS, impenetrable.
IN'VOICE, a catalogue of merchandise sent away.
OB'VIATE, to remove; to prevent.
OB'VIOUS, plain; evident.
PRE'VIOUS, antecedent; prior.
VI'ADUCT, a structure supporting a passage way.
WAY, a road; a passage.

Vic-is, a change, in stead.

VIC'AR, a substitute.
VICEGE'RENT, a deputy.
VICE'ROY, a king's deputy governor.
VICIS'SITUDE, change; revolution.
VIS'COUNT,°a degree of nobility next below an earl.

Vid-eo, vis-um, to see.

ADVICE', counsel.
ADVI'SABLE, expedient; fit.
EN'VY,°hatred of another for his success, or excellence.
EV'IDENT, plain; apparent.
IMPRU'DENCE, indiscretion.
INVID'IOUS, exciting envy.
INVIS'IBLE, not to be seen.
PROVIDE', to supply; to prepare.
PROV'ENDER, food for cattle.
PROV'IDENCE, foresight.
PROVIDEN'TIAL, effected by Providence.
PROVISI'ON, victuals; food.
PROVI'SO, a condition.
PRU'DENCE,°practical wisdom.
PURVEY', to provide; to procure.
REVIEW', a critical examination.
REVISE', to re-examine.

REVIS'IT, to visit again.
SUPERVISE', to overlook.
SURVEY', to view; to oversee.
VIEW, prospect.
VIS'AGE, look; countenance.
VIS'IBLE, that may be seen.
VISI'ON, sight.
VIS'IT, to go to see.
VI'SOR, a mask.
VIS'TA, a view; a prospect.

Vidu-o, to deprive of, to part.

AVOID', to shun.
DEVICE', contrivance; design.
DEVOID', empty; free from.
DIVIDE', to separate.
DIV'IDEND, a share.
DIVISI'ON, act of dividing.
INDIVIS'IBLE, that cannot be divided.
INDIVID'UAL, a single person.
SUBDIVIDE', to divide a part into more parts.
SUBDIVISI'ON, the division of a part.
VOID, empty; unoccupied.
WID'OW, a woman whose husband is dead.

Vigil, watchful.

VIG'IL, a watch.
VIG'ILANCE, watchfulness.

Vigor, strength.

INVIG'ORATE, to strengthen.
VIG'OROUS, full of strength.

Vil-is, of small price; base. REVILE', to reproach; to abuse.

Vinc-o, vict-um, to conquer.

CONVINCE',° to satisfy by evidence.
CONVICT', to prove guilty.
EVINCE', to make evident.
INVINC'IBLE, unconquerable.
PROV'INCE,° a subject country; a division of a country.
VAN'QUISH, to conquer.
VIC'TIM, one who is sacrificed; prey.
VIC'TORY, conquest; triumph.

Vindex, vindic-is, an avenger.

AVENGE',° to punish for an injury.
REVENGE', to return an injury.
VINDIC'TIVE, revengeful.
VIN'DICATE, to justify; to support.
VENG'EANCE, recompense of evil.

Vin-um, wine.

VINE, the plant that bears the grape.
VI'NOUS, having the qualities of wine.
VIN'EGAR,° an acid liquor.
VINT'AGE, the time of gathering grapes; the crop of grapes.

Vir, a man.

TRIUM'VIRATE, a coalition of three men.
VIRA'GO,° a turbulent woman.
VI'RILE, manly; bold

Vir-us, poison.

VIR'ULENCE, malignity.
VIR'ULENT, venomous; bitter

Visc-us, viscer-is, an entrail.

EVIS'CERATE, to take out the entrails.
VIS'CERAL, relating to the entrails

Viti-um, vice.

Vici'ous, wicked ; sinful.
Vit'iate, to deprave ; to spoil.

Vit-o, to shun. Inev'itable, that cannot be avoided.

Vitr-um, glass.

Vit'reous, resembling glass.
Vit'rify, to change into glass.
Vit'riol,° copperas.

Viv-o, vict-um, to live.

Conviv'ial, gay ; jovial.
Revive', to live again ; to arouse.
Survive', to outlive.
Vi'and,° an article of food.
Vict'uals,° food ; provisions.
Vi'tal, necessary to life.
Vivac'ity, liveliness.
Viv'id, sprightly ; active.
Viv'ify, to animate.

Voc-o, vocat-um, to call.

Ad'vocate, an intercessor ; a pleader.
Avoca'tion,° the business which calls aside.
Convoca'tion, an assembly.
Convoke', to call together.
Equiv'ocal, ambiguous ; doubtful.
Equiv'ocate, to use doubtful expressions.
Evoke', to call forth.
Invoke', to implore ; to pray to.
Irrev'ocable, not to be recalled.
Invoca'tion, a calling upon solemnly or in prayer.
Provoca'tion, a cause of anger.
Provoke',° to enrage ; to offend.
Revoca'tion, a recalling.
Unequiv'ocal, not equivocal.
Vocab'ulary, a list of words.
Vo'cal, relating to the voice.
Vocif'erate, to make outcries.
Voice, sound from the mouth ; an opinion.
Vow'el, a simple sound.

Vol-o, volat-um, to fly.

Vol'atile,° gay ; lively.
Vol'ley,° a flight of shot.

Vol-o, volit-um, to wish, to will.

Benev'olent, kind ; wishing well.
Invol'untary, not willing.
Malev'olence, ill will.
Voliti'on, the act or power of willing.
Vol'untary, willing ; of choice.
Volunteer', a voluntary soldier.

Volupt-as, pleasure.

Volup'tuary, a man given up to pleasure.
Volup'tuous, indulging to excess in pleasure.

Volv-o, volut-um, to roll.

Circumvolu'tion, a rolling round.
Evolu'tion, act of unfolding ; a displaying.
Involve', to envelop ; to entangle.
Involu'tion, act of infolding.
Revolt',° to throw off subjection ; to shock.
Revolu'tion, rotation ; thorough change.
Revolve', to roll round.
Vol'uble, rolling ; fluent.
Vol'ume,° a book ; a roll.
Volu'minous, consisting of many volumes.

Vor-o, to eat, to devour.

CARNIV'OROUS, eating flesh.
DEVOUR', to eat up greedily.
OMNIV'OROUS, eating all things.
OSSIV'OROUS, devouring bones.
PISCIV'OROUS, eating fish.
VORAC'ITY, greediness.

Vot-um, a vow.

AVOW', to declare openly.
DEVOTE', to dedicate; to set apart.
DEVO'TION,° piety; affection.
DEVOUT',° earnest; sincere.
VO'TARY, one devoted or addicted.
VOTE, suffrage; a ballot.
VO'TIVE, given by vow.
VOW, a solemn promise.

Vulcan-us, the god of fire.

VOLCA'NO, a burning mountain.
VOLCAN'IC, relating to a volcano.

Vulg-us, the common people.

DIVULGE', to make public.
PROMULGA'TION, publication; exhibition
VUL'GAR, unrefined; rude.
VUL'GATE,° an ancient Latin version of the Bible.

PART III.

PREFIXES AND ROOTS FROM THE GREEK.

PREFIXES.

A, An (*a* privative),

Signifies *want of*, *not*, or *without*.

*A*BYSS'—(*byssos*), *without* a bottom.
*A*CEPH'ALOUS—(*cephale*), *without* a head.
An'ARCHY—(*arche*), *want of* government.
*An*OM'ALY—(*omalos*), *not* or *none* like.
*A*P'ATHY—(*pathos*), *want of* feeling.
A'THEIST—(*theos*), one *without* a God.

Amphi, Ambi (ἀμφι and *ambo*, Lat. both),

Signifies *both* or *double*.

*Amphi*B'IOUS—(*bios*), living *both* on land and in water.
*Ambi*DEX'TROUS—(*dexter*), using *both* hands.

Ana (ἀνα),

Signifies *through*, *up*, *back*, or *again*.

*Ana*L'YSIS—(*lysis*), a loosing *back* or *again*.
*Ana*T'OMY—(*tomos*), a cutting *through* or *up*.

Anti, Ant (ἀντι),

Signifies *opposite to*, *against*.

*Ant*ARC'TIC—(*arctos*), *opposite to* the north.
*Anti*AC'ID—(*acidus*), *against* or *opposing* acid.
*Anti*BIL'IOUS—(*bilis*), *against* bile.
*Anti*P'ATHY—(*pathos*), feeling *against*.
*Anti*P'ODES—(*pous*), those who have their feet *opposite to*.

Apo, Aph (ἀπο),

Signifies *from* or *away*.

*Apo*C'RYPHA—(*crypto*), writings concealed *from*.
*Apo*S'TATE—(*sto*), one who stands *from* or *away*.
*Apo*S'TLE—(*stello*), one sent *from*.
*Aph*ELION—the point farthest *from* the sun.

Cata, Cat (κατα),

Signifies *down, from side to side.*

*Cat'a*LOGUE—(*logos*), words or names written *down.*
*Cata*RRH'—(*rheo*), a flowing *down.*
*Cat'*ECHISE—(*echeo*), to make sounds *from side to side.*

Dia, Di (δια),

Signifies *through, asunder.*

*Di*ÆR'ESIS—(*aeresis*), a taking *asunder* or separately.
*Dia*G'ONAL—(*gonia*), *through* the opposite angles.
*Di'a*LOGUE—(*logos*), words *through* or between persons.
*Dia*M'ETER—(*metrum*), the measure *through.*
*Dia*PH'ANOUS—(*phano*), appearing *through.*

En, Em,

Signifies *in* or *on.*

*En*DEM'IC—(*demos*), arising *in* or *among* the people.
*En*THU'SIAST—(*theos*), one who believes that God is *in* him.
*Em*PHASIS—(*phano*), a stress of voice *on* (a word or sentence).

Epi (επι),

Signifies *upon.*

*Epi*DEM'IC—(*demos*), *upon* the people.
*Ep'i*GRAM—(*grapho*), something written *upon.*
*Ep'i*LOGUE—(*logos*), what is spoken *upon* or *after.*
*Epi*GLOT'TIS—(*glossa*), *upon* the tongue.
*Ep'i*TAPH—(*taphos*), *upon* one who is buried.

Hyper (ὑπερ),

Signifies *above, over,* or *beyond.*

*Hyper*BO'REAN—(*boreas*), *beyond* the north.
*Hyper*CRIT'ICAL—*over* critical.

Hypo (ὑπο),

Signifies *under.*

*Hypo*TH'ESIS—(*thesis*), what is placed under.

Meta (μετα),

Signifies *beyond, according to.*

*Met'a*PHOR—(*phero*), a word carried *beyond* its ordinary meaning
*Meta*PHYS'ICS—(*physis*), the science of things *beyond* nature.
*Meth'*OD—(*odos*), *according to* a way or plan.

Para, Par (παρα),

Signifies *beside, like,* or *similar.*

*Par'*ALLEL—(*allelon*), *beside* one another.
*Par'a*PHRASE—(*phrasis*), a phrase *beside* or *like* another.
*Par'*ODY—(*ode*), a song or poem, *like* or in imitation of another.

Peri (περι),
Signifies *round, about.*

*Peri*CRA'NIUM—(*cranium*), *round* the cranium.
*Peri*M'ETER—(*metrum*), the measure *round.*

Syn (συν),
Signifies *together, with.*

*Syn'*OD—(*odos*), a way or coming *together.*
*Syn*ON'YMOUS—(*onoma*), named *together* or like.
*Syn*OP'SIS—(*opto*), a looking *together.*
*Syn'*TAX—(*tactos*), a putting together.

Sy, for **Syn**,
Signifies *together, with.*

*Sy*S'TEM—(*stasis*), a standing *together.*
*Sy*S'TOLE—(*stello*), a sending *together.*

Syl, for **Syn**,
Signifies *together, with.*

*Syl'*LABLE—(*labo*), a taking *together.*

Sym, for **Syn**,
Signifies *together with.*

*Sym'*METRY—(*metrum*), a measuring *together.*
*Sym'*PATHY—(*pathos*), a feeling *with.*

GREEK ALPHABET.

Α α	Alpha	a	Ν ν	Nu	n
Β β ϐ	Beta	b	Ξ ξ	Xi	x
Γ γ	Gamma	g	Ο ο	Omicron	ŏ short
Δ δ	Delta	d	Π π	Pi	p
Ε ε	Epsilon	ĕ short	Ρ ρ	Rho	r
Ζ ζ	Zeta	z	Σ σ, final ς	Sigma	s
Η η	Eta	ē long	Τ τ	Tau	t
Θ ϑ θ	Theta	th	Υ υ	Upsilon	u or y
Ι ι	Iota	i	Φ φ	Phi	ph
Κ κ	Kappa	k* or c	Χ χ	Chi	ch
Λ λ	Lambda	l *	Ψ ψ	Psi	ps
Μ μ	Mu	m	Ω ω	Omega	ō long

* Kappa and Upsilon are much more frequently changed into *c* and *y* in English, than into *k* and *u:* the latter is of very rare occurrence.

GREEK ROOTS.

Academ-ia (ἀκαδημια), a grove near Athens where Plato taught philosophy.

ACAD'EMY, a place of instruction.
ACADEM'IC, relating to an academy.

Acou-o (ἀκουω), to hear. ACOU'STICS, the science of sounds.

Acr-on (ἀκρον), end, summit.

ACROP'OLIS, the citadel.
ACROS'TIC, a kind of poem.

Adelph-os (ἀδελφος), a brother. PHILADEL'PHIA, brotherly love.

Aer (ἀηρ), the air.

A'EROLITE, a stone that falls from the atmosphere.
A'ERONAUT, one who sails in the air.

Aeresis (αἱρεσις), a taking.

DIÆR'ESIS, the mark [··] used to separate syllables.

Agoge-us (ἀγωγεύς), a leader.

DEM'AGOGUE, a leader of the populace.
PED'AGOGUE, a school-master.
SYN'AGOGUE, a Jewish church.

Agon (ἀγων), a combat.

AG'ONY, violent pain.
AG'ONIZE, to afflict with agony.
ANTAG'ONIST, an opponent; an enemy.

Alg-os (ἀλγος), pain.

CEPHALAL'GIA, headache.
ODONTAL'GIA, toothache.

Allel-on (ἀλληλων), one another, each other.

PAR'ALLEL, equidistant at all points.
UNPAR'ALLELED, unequalled; unmatched.

All-os (ἀλλος), another.

AL'LEGORY, a figurative composition.
ALLEGOR'ICAL, not literal.

Alpha (ἀλφα), the first letter in the Greek alphabet.

AL'PHABET, the letters of a language.
ALPHABET'ICAL, belonging to the alphabet.

Anem-os (ἀνεμος), the wind.

ANEMOG'RAPHY, a description of the wind.
ANEMOM'ETER, a wind-gauge

Angel-lo* (ἀγγελλω), to bring tidings.

ANGEL, a celestial spirit.
EVAN'GELIST, a writer or preacher of the gospel.
ARCHAN'GEL, a chief angel.
EVANGEL'ICAL, agreeable to the gospel.

Anth-os (ἀνθος), a flower.

ANTHOL'OGY, a collection of flowers or poems.
POLYAN'THUS, a plant with flowers in clusters.

Anthrop-os (ἀνθρωπος), a man.

ANTHROPOPH'AGI, man-eaters; cannibals.
MIS'ANTHROPE, a hater of mankind.
PHILAN'THROPIST, one who loves mankind.
PHILANTHROP'IC, benevolent.

Arche (ἀρχη), the beginning; government.

AN'ARCH, an author of confusion.
ARCH, chief; principal; shrewd.
ARCHBISH'OP, the chief bishop.
ARCHDEA'CON, a church dignitary, next in rank to a bishop.
ARCHDUKE', a chief prince.
AR'CHITECT, a professor of the art of building; a builder.
AR'CHIVES, ancient or public records.
ARCHITEC'TURE, the art of building.
HEP'TARCHY, a sevenfold government.
HI'ERARCH, the chief of a sacred order.
MON'ARCH, a sovereign; a king.
PA'TRIARCH, a head of a family or church.

Arct-os, (ἀρκτος), a bear, the north.

ARC'TIC, northern; lying under the constellation the Bear.
ANTARC'TIC, relating to the south pole.

Arist-os (ἀριστος), noblest, best.

ARISTOC'RACY, the government of the nobles.
ARIST'OCRAT, one who favors aristocracy.

Arithm-os (ἀριθμος), number.

ARITH'METIC, the science of numbers.
ARITHMETICI'AN, a master of arithmetic.

Aromat-a (ἀρωματα), spices.

AROMAT'ICS, spices; fragrant drugs.
AROMAT'IC, spicy; fragrant.
AR'OMATIZE, to give a spicy taste.

Arteri-a (ἀρτηρια), an artery.

AR'TERY, a blood vessel.
ARTE'RIAL, relating to an artery.

---

* γ or g, before γ g, κ k, χ ch, in Greek, sounds like '*ng*,' and accordingly, in English, it assumes that *form*.

Astr-on (ἀστρον), a star.

As'terisk, a mark [*] in printing.
As'tral, starry.
Astrol'ogy, the science of foretelling by the stars.
Astron'omy, the science of the heavenly bodies.
Disas'ter, misfortune; grief.

Atm-os (ἀτμος), vapor, air.

At'mosphere, the mass of air, &c., surrounding the earth.

Aul-os (ἀυλος), a pipe.

Hydrau'lics,° the science of the force and motion of fluids.

Authent-eo (ἀυθεντεω), to authorize.

Authen'tic, genuine; true.
Authentic'ity, authority; genuineness.

Aut-os (ἀυτος), one's self.

Autobiog'raphy, biography of a person written by himself.
Au'tocrat, a sole ruler.
Au'topsy, ocular demonstration.
Au'tograph, one's own hand writing.
Autom'aton, a self-moving machine.

Balsam-on (βαλσαμον), fragrant ointment.

Balm, a plant.
Bal'sam, a soothing ointment.

Bapt-o (βαπτω), to dip, to wash.

Baptize', to administer baptism.
Bap'tism, a Christian sacrament.

Bas-is (βασις), the base or foundation.

Base, the bottom; mean; vile.
Debase', to degrade; to lower.

Bar-os (βαρος), weight.

Barom'eter, an instrument to measure the weight of the atmosphere.

Beta (β), the second letter in the Greek alphabet. See *Alpha.*

Bibl-os (βιβλος), a book.

Bi'ble, the sacred Scriptures.
Bibliog'rapher, a man skilled in the knowledge of books.
Biblioma'nia, the rage for possessing scarce or curious books.

Bi-os (βιος), life.

Amphib'ious, living in two elements, air and water.
Biog'raphy, an account of one's life.

Blapt-o (βλαπτω), to injure.

Blaspheme',° to speak impiously.
Blas'phemy, impiety of speech.

Bole-o (βαλλω), to throw.

Diabol'ical,° devilish; atrocious.
Em'blem, a picture.
Emblemat'ic, using emblems; allusive.
Hyper'bole,° an exaggeration.
Par'able, a similitude.
Prob'lem,° a question proposed.
Problemat'ical, uncertain.
Sym'bol, a sign; an emblem

Botan-e (βοτανη), an herb, a plant.

BOT'ANY, the science of plants. | BOTAN'ICAL, relating to plants.

Brach-ys (βραχυς), short. BRACHYG'RAPHY, short-hand writing.

Bronch-os (βρουχος), the wind-pipe.

BRON'CHIAL, belonging to the wind-pipe and its branches. | BRONCHOT'OMY, incision of the wind-pipe.

Byss-os (βυσσος), bottom. ABYSS', a depth without bottom.

Calypt-o (καλυπτω), to cover, to veil.

APOC'ALYPSE, revelation; a vision. | APOCALYP'TICAL, concerning revelation.

Canon (κανων), a rule.

CAN'ON, a rule; a law. | CAN'ONIZE, to declare one a saint.

Cardi-a (καρδια), the heart.

CAR'DIAC, relating to the heart.
CARDIAL'GIA, the heart-burn. | PERICAR'DIUM, a membrane enclosing the heart.

Caustic-os (καυστικος), burning.

CAUS'TIC, burning; corroding. | CAU'TERY, an iron for burning.

Cele (κηλη), a swelling. BRON'CHOCELE, a tumor in the throat.

Centr-um* (κεντρον), the centre.

CEN'TRE, the exact middle.
CEN'TRAL, relating to the centre.
ECCENTRIC'ITY, irregularity. | CONCEN'TRIC, having one common centre.
CONCEN'TRATE, to bring together.

Cephal-e (κεφαλη), the head.

BICEPH'ALOUS, having two heads. | CEPHALAL'GIA, headache.

Chaos (χαος), confusion.

CHA'OS, a confused mass. | CHAOT'IC, confused; indigested.

Character (χαρακτηρ), a mark.

CHARACTERIS'TIC, that which gives character. | CHAR'ACTERIZE, to give a character.

Charis, charit-os (χαρις), grace, joy.

CHAR'ITY, goodwill; alms.
CHAR'ITABLE, kind; bountiful. | EU'CHARIST,† the sacrament of the Lord's Supper.

---

* In this case, as in many others, the Latin form of the word is retained, yet it is placed here because of its Greek origin.

† Literally, the act of giving thanks; so called because it is an occasion of special and solemn thanksgiving to God for the gift of his son, Christ Jesus.

Chimera** for **Chimæra (χιμαιρα), a fictitious monster.

CHIM'ERA, a wild fancy.

CHIMER'ICAL, wild; fanciful.

Chir (χειρ), the hand.

CHIROG'RAPHY, hand-writing.

CHIRUR'GEON, a surgeon.

SUR'GERY, the art of curing by manual operation.

Chol-e (χολη), bile.

CHOL'ER, anger; rage.

CHOL'IC, pain in the bowels.

MEL'ANCHOLY,° sadness; dejection.

Chord-a (χορδη), a gut, a string.

CHORD, the string of a musical instrument.

CLAR'ICHORD, a musical instrument.

COR'DAGE, a quantity of cords.

MON'OCHORD, an instrument of one string.

Christ-os (χριστος), the anointed.

CHRIST, the Savior.

CHRIS'TEN, to baptize and name.

CHRIS'TMAS, the festival of Christ's nativity.

Chron-os (χρονος), time.

ANACH'RONISM, an error in dates.

CHRON'IC, of long duration.

CHRON'ICLE, a register; a record.

CHRONOL'OGY, the science of computing time.

CHRONOM'ETER, an exact time-piece.

Chym-os (χυμος), juice.

CHEM'ISTRY, the science of the nature and properties of bodies.

CHEM'ICAL, concerning chemistry.

Cler-os (κληρος), a lot, a portion.

CLER'GY,* the body or order of divines.

CLER'ICAL, relating to the clergy.

CLERK, a secretary or book-keeper.

Com-os (κωμος), a jovial meeting.

COM'EDY,° an amusing dramatic piece.

COM'IC, raising mirth.

ENCO'MIUM, praise; eulogy.

Conch-a (κογχα), a shell. CONCHOL'OGY, the science of shells.

Cone-o (κονεω), to manage. DEA'CON, a church officer.

Con-os (κονος), a cone.

CON'IC, of the form of a cone.

CO'NOID, a figure like a cone.

---

* So styled from the practice of heathen *priests*, who used to draw *lots*, either to ascertain the will of the Deity, or prognosticate future events. Formerly *clerk* was the usual term for a scholar; most situations of talent or trust being filled by the *clergy*.

Cope (κοπη), a cutting.

APOC'OPE, an omission of the last syllable or letter of a word.
SYN'COPE, a contraction of a word.

Cosm-os (χοσμος), order, ornament, the world.

COSMET'IC, beautifying.
COS'MICAL, relating to the world.
COSMOP'OLITE, a citizen of the world.

Crani-um (κρανιον), the skull.

CRANIOL'OGY, the science of skulls.
PERICRA'NIUM, a membrane covering the skull.

Crat-os (κρατος), power, government.

ARISTOC'RACY, the government of the nobles.
ARIST'OCRAT, one who favours aristocracy.
AU'TOCRAT, a sole ruler.
DEMOC'RACY, government by the people.
THEOC'RACY, government directed by God.

Crit-es (κριτης), a judge.

CRI'SIS, the deciding point.
CRITE'RION, a standard of judging.
CRIT'IC, a judge in literature or art.
CRIT'ICISE, to censure; to judge.
HYPOC'RISY, dissimulation.
HYP'OCRITE, a dissembler.

Crystall-us (κρυσταλλος), congealed like ice.

CRYS'TAL, a regular solid body.
CRYS'TALLINE, bright; clear.

Crypt-o (κρυπτω), to hide. APOC'RYPHAL, of doubtful authority.

Cycl-us (κυκλος), a circle.

CY'CLE, a period of time.
CYCLOPE'DIA, a circle of the arts and sciences.
ENCYC'LICAL, sent round.
ENCYCLOPE'DIA, see Cyclopedia.

Cylindr-os (κυλινδρος), a roller.

CYL'INDER, a roller.
CYLIN'DRICAL, like a cylinder.

Cyon, cyn-os (κυων, κυνος), a dog.

CYN'IC, snarling; satirical.
CYN'OSURE,* a constellation.

Dam-ao (δαμαω), to tame.

AD'AMANT, a very hard stone.
ADAMAN'TINE, made of adamant.
DI'AMOND, the most valuable of gems.

---

* *Literally*, the dog's tail. The north star. Figuratively, any thing that attracts general notice or admiration.

Deca, decem (δεκα), ten.

DEAN,* one next to a bishop.
DEC'ADE, the sum of ten.
DEC'AGON, a plane figure having ten angles.
DEC'ALOGUE, the ten commandments.
DECEM'BER,† the twelfth month.
DEC'IMAL, numbered by ten.
DEC'IMATE, to take the tenth.
DECU'RION, a commander over ten.
DUODEC'IMO, having twelve leaves to a sheet.

Dem-os (δημος), the people.

DEM'AGOGUE, a popular leader.
DEM'OCRAT, one advocating government by the people.
ENDEM'IC,° peculiar to a place.
EPIDEM'IC,° a prevailing disease.

Demon (δαιμων), a spirit.

DEMONOL'OGY, a treatise on evil spirits.
DE'MON, a devil.

Deuter-os (δευτερος), second.

DEUTERON'OMY,‡ the fifth book of Moses, or second of the law.

Didasc-o (διδασκω), to teach. DIDAC'TIC, instructive.

Diploma (διπλωμα), a duplicate.

DIPLO'MA,°a paper conferring a literary honor.
DIPLO'MACY, negotiation.
DIPLO'MATIST, one versed in diplomacy.
DIPLOMAT'IC, respecting diplomacy.

Dis, Di (δις), two.

DILEM'MA, difficulty.
DIP'HTHONG, a union of two vowels in one sound.
DISSEV'ER, to part in two.
DIS'SYLLABLE, a word of two syllables.

Dot-os (δοτος), given.

AN'ECDOTE,° a biographical incident.
AN'TIDOTE, a medicine that counteracts poison.

Dox-a (δοξα), an opinion, glory.

DOXOL'OGY, words of glory to God.
HET'ERODOX,°not of sound doctrine.
ORTHODOX'Y, soundness in doctrine.
PAR'ADOX, an opinion apparently absurd.

Drama (δραμα), an action, a play.

DRA'MA, a poem suited for representation on the stage.
DRAMAT'IC, relating to plays.
DRAM'ATIST, a writer of plays.

---

* So called, because he was anciently set over *ten* canons or prebendaries, at least in some cathedral churches.

† Formerly, March was taken as the first month, and consequently September would be the *seventh* month; October, the *eighth*; November, the *ninth* and December the *tenth*.

‡ The *second* book of the law.

Drom-os (δρομος), a running.

DROM'EDARY, a sort of camel.
PAL'INDROME, a word or sentence which is the same read forwards or backwards.

Drus (δρυς), the oak-tree.

DRU'ID, an ancient priest.
DRY'AD, a wood nymph.

Dynasti-a (δυναστεια), power.

DY'NASTY, a race of princes.
DYNAM'ICS, the science of moving powers.

Dys (δυς), weakness.

DYS'ENTERY, disease of the bowels.
DYSPEP'SY, difficulty of digestion.

Ech-eo (ἠχεω), to sound. CAT'ECHISE, to question.

Ec-eo (οἰκεω), to dwell.

DI'OCESE, a bishop's jurisdiction.
DI'OCESAN, pertaining to a diocese.
ECON'OMY, frugality.
ECONOM'ICAL, frugal; thrifty.

Edr-a (ἑδρα), a seat, a side.

CATHE'DRAL, the head church in a diocese.
POLYE'DRON, a figure having many sides.

Egor-a, *for* **Agora** (ἀγορα), a public place.

AL'LEGORY, a figurative discourse.
CAT'EGORY,* an order of ideas.
PANEGYR'IC, a eulogy.

Elegi-a (ἐλεγεια), a mournful poem.

EL'EGY, a dirge.
ELEGI'AC, mournful.

Eme-o (ἐμεω), to vomit. EMET'IC, causing to vomit.

Enter-on (ἐντερον), the bowels.

DYS'ENTERY, a disease of the bowels.
MES'ENTERY, a membrane supporting the intestines.

Entom-on (ἐντομον), an insect.

ENTOMOL'OGY, the science which treats of insects.

Epicur-us ('Επικουρος), a sensual philosopher.

EP'ICURE, one given to luxury.
EP'ICURISM, sensual enjoyment.

---

* *Category* (in Logic), a name for the *predicates* or *attributes* contained under any genus, which, according to the computation of Aristotle, are ten, viz.: *substance, quantity, quality, relation, acting, suffering, time, place, situation,* and *habit.*

Ep-os (ἔπος), a word.

EP'IC, narrative; heroic.

ORTHO'EPY, the art of pronouncing words properly.

Erem-os (ἔρημος), lonely, alone.

ER'EMITE, HER'MIT, one who lives in seclusion.

Erg-on (ἔργον), a work.

LIT'URGY, a formulary of public prayer.

CHIRUR'GEON, a surgeon.

EN'ERGY,° force; vigor.

MET'ALLURGY, the art of working metals.

Eth-os (ἔθος), custom.

ETH'ICS, the doctrine or system of morality.

ETH'ICAL, relating to morals.

Ethn-os (ἔθνος), a people.

ETH'NICAL, relating to the human races.

ETHNOG'RAPHY, a description of nations or races.

Etymon (ἔτυμον), the true meaning of a word.

ETYMOL'OGY, the descent, or derivation of words.

Eu (εὖ), well.

EU'LOGIZE, to commend; to praise.

EULO'GIUM, praise; panegyric.

EU'PHONY, agreeable sound.

Gam-eo (γαμεω), to marry.

AMAL'GAMATE,° to mix or unite metals.

CRYPTOG'AMY, concealed union.

BIG'AMY, the crime of having two wives at once.

POLYG'AMY, plurality of wives.

Gaster, gastr-os (γαστηρ, γαστρος), the belly or stomach.

GAS'TRIC, belonging to the stomach.

GASTRIL'OQUY, a speaking from the stomach.

Ge (γῆ), the earth.

AP'OGEE,° greatest distance from the earth.

GEOCEN'TRIC, having the earth for its centre.

GEOG'RAPHY, a description of the earth's surface.

GEOL'OGY, the science of the structure of the earth.

GEOM'ETRY,° the science of dimensions.

GEOPON'ICS, agriculture.

Genea (γενεα), a generation, a birth.

GENEAL'OGY, an account of the succession of families.

GEN'ESIS, the first book of Scripture.

HETEROGE'NEOUS, dissimilar.

HY'DROGEN,° a gas.

OX'YGEN,° a gas which generates acids.

Gloss-a (γλωσσα), the tongue.

EPIGLOT'TIS, a tongue-shaped cartilage over the opening into the wind-pipe.

GLOS'SARY, a dictionary of difficult words or phrases.

POL'YGLOT, in many languages.

Glyph-o (γλυφω), to carve. HI'EROGLYPH, a symbolical character.

Gnomon (γνωμων), a pointer, a thing that serves to make known.

GNOME, an imaginary being.

GNO'MON, the hand of a dial.

PHYSIOG'NOMY, the art of discovering the character by the features of the face.

PROGNOS'TIC, a sign by which a future event may be known.

Gon-ia (γωνια), an angle.

DIAG'ONAL, a line from angle to angle.

DEC'AGON, a plane figure having ten angles.

PEN'TAGON, a plane figure of five angles.

POL'YGON, a figure of many angles.

TRIGONOM'ETRY, the art of measuring triangles.

Graph-o (γραφω), to write: **Gramma** (γραμμα), a writing.

AN'AGRAM,° the change of one word into another by the transposition of its letters.

AP'OGRAPH, a copy; a transcript.

AU'TOGRAPH, one's own handwriting.

BIOG'RAPHY, an account of lives.

CHIR'OGRAPH,° a deed; a writing.

COSMOG'RAPHY, the science of the general system of the world.

DIA'GRAM, a figure; a drawing.

ENGRAVE', to impress, to imprint; to cut with a graver.

EP'IGRAM,° a short, witty poem.

EPIGRAMMAT'IC, like an epigram.

GEOG'RAPHY, a description of the surface of the earth.

GRAM'MAR,° the science of language.

GRAPH'IC, well delineated.

LEXICOG'RAPHY, the writing of dictionaries.

LITHOG'RAPHY, the art of drawing on and printing from stone.

ORTHOG'RAPHY, correct spelling.

PAR'AGRAPH, a distinct part of a discourse, or writing.

STENOG'RAPHY, the art of writing in short-hand.

TEL'EGRAPH, a machine for conveying intelligence to a distance by signals.

TOPOG'RAPHY, a description of a place.

TYPOG'RAPHY, the art of printing.

Gymn-os (γυμνος), naked.

GYMNA'SIUM, a place for athletic exercises.

GYMNAS'TIC,* pertaining to athletic exercises.

GYMNOS'OPHIST, one of a sect of Indian philosophers who went nearly naked.

Gyn-e (γυνη), a woman. MISOG'YNIST, a woman-hater.

* Among the ancients there were five kinds of gymnastic exercises: 1. running (*cursus*); 2. leaping (*saltus*); 3. boxing (*pugillatus*); 4. wrestling (*lucta*); and throwing the dart or quoit (*disci jactus*); hence called *certamen athleticum* or *gymnicum*, because they contended naked (γυμνοι), with nothing on but trousers or drawers.

Gyr-us (γυρος), a circle.

GY'ROMANCY, divination by walking in a circle.

GYRA'TION, a whirling round

Harmoni-a (ἁρμονια), harmony.

HAR'MONY, musical concord.

HARMON'IC, musical.

HAR'MONIZE, to agree.

HARMO'NIOUS, peaceful, musical.

Heli-os (ἡλιος), the sun.

APHE'LION,° the point most remote from the sun.

HE'LIOTROPE, a plant that turns to the sun.

PARHE'LION, a mock sun.

PERIHE'LION,° the point of a planet's orbit nearest the sun.

Hellen (Ἑλλην), a Greek.

HEL'LENIC, Grecian.

HEL'LENISM, a Greek idiom.

HEL'LENIST,° one skilled in the Greek language.

Hem-a (αἱμα), blood.

HEM'ORRHAGE, a flow of blood.

Hemer-a (ἡμερα), a day.

EPHEM'ERAL, lasting a day.

EPHEM'ERIS,* an almanac.

Hemis-us (ἡμισυς), half.

HEM'ICYCLE, a half circle.

HEM'ISPHERE, half a globe.

Hept-a (ἑπτα), seven.

HEP'TAGON, a plane figure with seven angles.

HEP'TARCHY, a government by seven persons.

Heres-is (αἱρεσις), an opinion.

HER'ESY,° error in religion.

HER'ETIC, one guilty of heresy.

Hero-s (ἡρως), a hero.

HE'RO, a brave man.

HER'OISM, great bravery.

Heter-os (ἑτερος), other, dissimilar.

HET'ERODOXY, unsoundness of doctrine.

HETEROGE'NEOUS, dissimilar.

Hex (ἑξ), six.

HEXAM'ETER, a verse of six feet.

HEX'AGON, a figure of six angles.

HEXAN'GULAR, having six angles

Hier-os (ἱερος), sacred.

HI'ERARCHY, ecclesiastical government.

HIEROGLYPH'IC,† a sacred character or symbol.

---

* *Ephemerides*, (the plural of Ephemeris,) astronomical tables, showing the present state of the heavens for every *day* at noon.

† See the Introduction.

Hipp-os (ἱππος), a horse.

HIPPOCEN'TAUR, a fabulous monster, half man and half horse.

HIPPOPOT'AMUS, the river-horse.

HIP'POGRIFF, a winged horse.

Hol-os (ὁλος), the whole, all.

CATH'OLIC, universal; general.

CATHOL'ICISM, adherence to the Catholic church.

Hom-os (ὁμος), like, equal.

HOMOGE'NEOUS of the same kind.

HOMOL'OGOUS, proportional to each other.

Hor-a (ὡρα), an hour.

HOR'OLOGE, an instrument that marks the hour.

HOR'OSCOPE, aspect of the planets at the hour of birth.

Hor-os (ὁρος), a boundary.

APH'ORISM,° a maxim; a precept.

APH'ORIST, a writer of maxims.

HORI'ZON, the line that bounds the view.

Hydor (ὑδωρ), water.

CLEPSY'DRA, a water-clock.

DROP'SY, a disease.

HYDRAU'LICS, the science of the motion and force of fluids.

HYDROCEPH'ALUS, a dropsy in the head.

HY'DROGEN, a gas. (° p. 160.)

HYDROPHO'BIA, a dread of water; canine madness.

HYDROSTAT'ICS, the science of the weight and equilibrium of fluids.

Idea (ἰδεα), a mental image.

IDE'A, thought; notion.

IDE'ALIZE, to form ideas.

Idi-os (ἰδιος), peculiar, private.

ID'IOCY, want of understanding.

IDIOP'ATHY, a primary disease.

ID'IOM, peculiarity of speech.

IDIOMAT'ICAL, containing an idiom.

IDIOSYN'CRASY, peculiar temperament.

Ironi-a (εἰρωνια), irony.

I'RONY, taunting speech.

IRON'ICAL, containing irony.

Lab-o (λαβω *for* λαμβανω), to take.

AS'TROLABE, an instrument for taking the altitude of stars.

DIS'SYLLABLE, a word of two syllables.

MON'OSYLLABLE, a word of one syllable.

POL'YSYLLABLE, a word of many syllables.

SYL'LABLE, a letter or combination of letters uttered or taken together.

La-os (λαος), the people.

LA'ITY, the people, as distinguished from the clergy.

LAY, not clerical; pertaining to the laity.

Latri-a (λατρεια), worship.

IDOL'ATER, a worshipper of idols; a pagan.

Lepr-a (λεπρα), leprosy, a disease.

LEP'ER, one infected with a leprosy.
LEP'ROSY, a loathsome disease of the skin.

Leps-is (λεψις), a taking or receiving.

DILEM'MA,° a difficult, vexatious alternative.
EP'ILEPSY,° a convulsion.
EPILEP'TIC, convulsed.

Lethe (ληθη), forgetfulness.

LETH'ARGY, morbid sleepiness.
LETHAR'GIC, sleepy by disease.

Lip-o (λειπω), to leave out, to fail.

ECLIPSE',° obscuration.
ELLIP'SIS,° an omission.
ELLIP'TICAL, pertaining to an ellipsis.

Lith-os (λιθος), a stone.

A'EROLITE, a meteoric stone.
LITH'ARGE,° the scum of lead.
LITHOG'RAPHY, drawing on and printing from stone.

Log-os (λογος), reason, a word, a discourse.

ANAL'OGY,° correspondence.
ANTHOL'OGY, a collection of flowers or poems.
APOL'OGY, an excuse.
APOLOGET'IC, given as an excuse.
AP'OLOGUE,° a fable.
ASTROL'OGY,° the practice of foretelling by the stars.
CAT'ALOGUE, a list.
CHRONOL'OGY, the science of dates.
CHRONOLOG'ICAL, relating to chronology.
DEC'ALOGUE, the ten commandments.
DI'ALOGUE,° a conference.
DOXOL'OGY, words of glory to God.
EL'OGY, praise.
EP'ILOGUE, the speech at the end of a play.
ETYMOL'OGY, derivation of words.
EULO'GIUM, praise.
EU'LOGIZE, to commend.
GEOL'OGY, the science of the structure of the earth.
HOMOL'OGOUS, proportionate to each other.
LOG'IC,° the art of reasoning.
MINERAL'OGY, the science of minerals.
MYTHOL'OGY,° a system of fables.
ORNITHOL'OGY, the science of birds.
OSTEOL'OGY, a description of the bones.
PHILOL'OGY, grammatical learning.
PHRASEOL'OGY, style ; diction.
PROL'OGUE,° a preface.
PSYCHOL'OGY, the science which treats of the nature of the soul.
SYL'LOGISM,° a form of reasoning.
TAUTOL'OGY, repetition of the same sense in different words.
THEOL'OGY, the science of God and divine things.
ZOOL'OGY, the science of animals.

Lys-is (λυσις), a loosing.

ANAL'YSIS, the separation of a compound body into its constituent parts.
AN'ALYZE, to make an analysis.
PAL'SY,° a privation of motion.
PARALYT'IC, one struck by palsy.
PAR'ALYZE, to affect as with palsy.

Mach-omai (μαχομαι), to fight.

LOGOM'ACHY, a contention about words.

THEOM'ACHY,° a fight against the gods.

Manci-a *for* **Mantia** (μαντεια), a divining, prediction.

ARITH'MANCY, a foretelling by numbers.

CHIR'OMANCY, the act of foretelling by inspecting the hand.

PYR'OMANCY, divination by fire.

GE'OMANCY, divination by casting figures.

NEC'ROMANCY,° conjuration.

NECROMAN'TIC, relating to necromancy.

Mani-a (μανια), madness.

BIBLIOMA'NIA, a rage for possessing scarce and curious books.

MA'NIAC, mad; raving.

MA'NIA, madness.

Martyr (μαρτυρ), a witness, a martyr.

MAR'TYR, one put to death for adherence to a cause.

MAR'TYRDOM, the death of a martyr.

Mathem-a (μαθημα), learning.

MATHEMAT'ICAL, relating to mathematics.

MATHEMAT'ICS,° the science of quantity.

Mat-os (ματος), a moving. AUTOM'ATON, a self-moving machine.

Mechan-ao (μηχαναω), to contrive, to invent.

MECHAN'ICS,° the science of motion.

MECHANICI'AN, a maker of machines.

Mel, mell-is (μελι), honey.

MELLIF'EROUS, yielding honey.

MELLIF'LUENT, sweetly flowing.

OX'YMEL, a mixture of vinegar and honey.

Melan (μελαν), black, dark. MEL'ANCHOLY, sadness; dejection.

Mel-os (μελος), a song or poem.

MELO'DIOUS, musical.

MEL'ODY, sweetness of sound.

MEL'ODRAME, a drama containing songs.

PHILOME'LA,° the nightingale.

Men (μην), a month. AL'MANAC, an annual calendar.

Mes-os (μεσος), middle. MES'ENTERY,° a membrane in the intestines

Metall-um (μεταλλον), a metal.

MET'AL,° a hard fossil substance.

METALLIF'EROUS, producing metals.

MET'ALLOID, a substance resembling a metal.

MET'ALLURGY, the art of working metals.

Meteor-a (μετεωρα), flying luminous bodies in the air.

ME'TEOR, a shooting star.

METEOROL'OGY, the science of the atmosphere and its phenomena.

Meter, metr-os (μητηρ, μητρος), a mother.

METROP'OLIS, the chief city.

METROPOL'ITAN, belonging to a metropolis.

Metr-um (μετρον), a measure.

BAROM'ETER,° an instrument to measure the weight of the atmosphere.

CHRONOM'ETER, a timepiece.

DIAM'ETER,° the measure through any thing.

DIAMET'RICAL, describing a diameter; direct.

GASOM'ETER, an instrument to measure gas.

ME'TER,° a measurer.

GEOM'ETRY,° the science of dimensions.

GEOMETRICI'AN, one skilled in [geometry.

PERIM'ETER, the bounding line of a figure.

SYM'METRY,° due proportion of parts.

SYMMET'RICAL, having symmetry.

THERMOM'ETER, an instrument to measure heat.

Micr-os (μικρος), little, small.

MICROM'ETER, an instrument to measure small spaces.

MI'CROSCOPE, an instrument for viewing the smallest objects.

Mis-os (μισος), hatred, enmity.

MIS'ANTHROPE, a hater of mankind.

Mne-o, *for* ***Mnao*** (μναω), to remind.

AM'NESTY,° an act of general pardon.

MNEMON'ICS, the art of memory.

Mon-os (μονος), one, alone.

MON'AD, an atom.

MON'ARCH,° a sovereign.

MON'ASTERY, a convent.

MONAS'TIC, pertaining to monks.

MONK, one living in a monastery.

MONOP'OLIZE, to engross.

MON'ODY, a poem sung by one person.

MONOSYL'LABLE, a word of one syllable.

MONOT'ONY, sameness of sound.

MONOT'ONOUS, wanting variety.

Morph-e (μορφη), a form or figure.

AMORPH'OUS, shapeless.

METAMORPH'OSE, to change the form of.

Mus-a (μουσα), a muse, a poem.

AMUSE', to divert.

MUSE, to think.

MU'SIC, harmony; melody.

MUSE'UM,° a repository of curiosities.

MUSIC'IAN, one skilled in music

Myst-es (μυστης), hidden, secret.

MYS'TERY, something secret; an enigma.

MYS'TIC, obscure; secret.

Myth-os (μυθος), a word, a fable.

MYTHOL'OGY, a system of fables. (° p. 214.)

Narc-e (ναρκη), numbness or torpidness.

Narcis'sus, the daffodil.
Narco'sis, stupefaction.
Narcot'ic, soporific; causing sleep.

Naus (ναυς), *Nav-is* (Lat.), a ship.

Nau'sea, loathing; sea-sickness.
Circumnav'igate, to sail round.
Na'vy, a fleet.
Nau'seous, loathsome; sickening.
Nav'igate, to pass by ships.
Renav'igate, to sail again.

Necr-os (νεκρος), a dead body.

Necrol'ogy, a register of deaths.
Nec'romancy, conjuration.

Nectar (νεκταρ), the drink of the gods.

Nec'tar, the feigned drink of the gods.
Nec'tary, the melliferous part of a flower.

Ne-os (νεος), new.

Neol'ogy, a system of new words.
Ne'ophyte,° a new convert; a novice.

Neur-on (νευρον), a nerve, a sinew.

En'ervate,° to weaken.
Nerve, an organ of sensation.
Neural'gia, a diseased state of the nerves.

Nom-os (νομος), a law, a management.

Astron'omy, the science of the heavenly bodies.
Econ'omy,° frugality.
Econ'omize, to employ with economy.

Octo (οκτω), eight.

Oc'tagon, a plane figure of eight angles.
Octang'ular, having eight angles.
Octo'ber, tenth month. (p. 165.)
Octa'vo, a book in which a sheet is folded into eight leaves.

Ode (ῳδη), an ode, a hymn.

Com'edy,° an amusing dramatic piece.
Mel'ody, sweetness of sound.
Ode, a poem; a song.
Pal'inode, a recantation.
Par'ody,° a humorous imitation.
Pros'ody,° the laws of versification.
Rhap'sody,° an irregular composition.
Rhap'sodist, one who writes rhapsodies.
Trag'edy,* a dramatic representation.

Od-os (οδος), a road, a journey.

Ep'isode,° incidental narrative.
Meth'od, a manner; a way.
Pe'riod,° a circuit; an epoch.
Syn'od,° a church assembly.

---

* *Tragedy*, originally, a *song* or *poem* sung in honor of Bacchus, by a chorus of music, with dances and the sacrifice of a *goat*.

Oid-os (εἰδος), a form, a figure.

Co'noid,° a figure like a cone.
O'void, egg-shaped.
Rhom'boid,° a figure like a rhomb.
Spheroid', a body like a sphere.
Va'rioloid, a disease resembling the smallpox.

Olig-os (ὀλιγος), few. Ol'igarchy, the goverment of a few.

Omal-os (ὀμαλος), even, regular.

Anom'aly, irregularity; deviation from rule.
Anom'alous, irregular; out of rule.

Onom-a (ὀνομα), a name.

Anon'ymous, wanting a name.
Patronym'ic, a name derived from a father.
Syn'onyme, a word of the same meaning with another.

Ophthalm-os (ὀφθαλμος), the eye.

Ophthal'mic, relating to the eye.
Oph'thalmia, a disease of the eyes.

Opt-o (ὀπτω), to see.

Au'topsy, ocular demonstration.
Catop'trics, the science of the reflection of light.
Diop'trics, the science of the refraction of light.
Drop'sy, a collection of water in the body.
Op'tics, the science of light and vision.
Optici'an, one skilled in optics.
Synop'sis, a general view.

Oram-a (ὀραμα), the thing seen.

Diora'ma, a transparent painting showing the effect of light.
Panora'ma,° a large circular painting.

Ornis, ornith-os (ὀρνιι, ὀρνιθος), a bird.

Ornithol'ogy, the science of birds.

Orth-os (ὀρθος), erect, straight, right.

Or'thoepy, correct pronunciation.
Or'thodox, sound in opinion.
Orthog'raphy, correct spelling.
Orthograph'ical, relating to spelling.

Oste-on (ὀστεον), a bone. Osteol'ogy, a description of the bones.

Ous, ot-os (οὐς, ὠτος), the ear.

Otacou'stic, an instrument to assist hearing.
Parot'id, relating to glands situated below the ears.

Oxy-s (ὀξυς), sharp, sour.

Ox'ydize, to convert into an oxyde.
Ox'yde,° a substance combined with oxygen.
Ox'ygen, a gas which generates acids.
Par'oxysm, temporary violence of a disease.

Palin (παλιν), back, again.

PAL'INODE, a recantation or withdrawal of a former assertion.

PAL'INDROME,* a word or sentence that is the same when read *backwards* or *forwards*.

Pap-as (παπας), a father.

PA'PACY, the office of the pope.

PA'PAL, popish.

POPE, the bishop of Rome.

POPE'DOM, papal jurisdiction.

Pas, pant-os; Pan (πας), all, whole.

PANACE'A, a universal medicine.

PAN'DECT,† a digest of law.

PANEGYR'IC, a eulogy.

PAN'OPLY, complete armor.

PAN'ORAMA, a large circular painting.

PAN'THEISM, the doctrine that the universe is God.

PANTHE'ON, a temple dedicated to all the gods.

PAN'TOMIME, a play in which only gesture and dumb show are used.

Pat-eo (πατεω), to tread, to walk.

PATROL', a guard.

PERIPATET'IC, a follower of Aristotle.

PERIPATET'ICISM,‡ the Peripatetic doctrine.

Pater (πατηρ), a father.

COMPA'TRIOT, one of the same country.

EXPA'TRIATE, to banish from one's country.

PAR'RICIDE, the murder of a parent.

PATER'NAL, fatherly; kind.

PATRICI'AN,°a nobleman.

PA'TRIARCH, the father and ruler of a family.

PAT'RIMONY, an inherited estate.

PA'TRIOT, a lover of his country.

PA'TRON,°a supporter.

PAT'RONIZE, to protect; to support.

Path-os (παθος), feeling.

ANTIP'ATHY, aversion.

AP'ATHY, want of feeling.

APATHET'IC, without feeling.

PA'THOS, passion; warmth.

PATHOL'OGY, the science of diseases.

SYM'PATHY, fellow feeling.

Pedi-a (παιδεια), learning.

PED'AGOGUE, a schoolmaster.

PED'ANT, a man vain of low knowledge.

PED'ANTRY, vain show of learning.

PEDOBAP'TIST, one that holds to infant baptism.

---

* As, *madam*, or "Roma tibi subito motibus ibit amor."

† *Pandect, all* the words, *all* the sayings. *Pandects*, in the plural, the digest or collection of civil or Roman law, made by order of the Emperor Justinian, and containing 534 decisions or judgments of lawyers, to which the emperor gave the force and authority of law. This compilation consists of fifty books, forming the first parts of the civil law.

‡ Aristotle was the founder of this sect of philosophers. They were called *peripatetics*, because their great teacher delivered his instructions, *walking up and down* the shaded paths of the Lyceum, a public grove at Athens.

Pent-e (πεντε), five.

PEN'TAGON, a plane figure with five angles.

PENTAM'ETER, a verse of five feet.

PEN'TATEUCH, the five books of Moses.

PEN'TECOST,* a Jewish feast.

Pept-os (πεπτος), boiled, digested.

DYSPEP'SY, difficulty of digestion.

EUPEP'TIC, having good digestion.

Petal-on (πεταλον), a flower leaf.

APET'ALOUS, without petals.

PET'AL, a flower-leaf.

MONOPET'ALOUS, having but one petal.

Petr-a (πετρα), a rock, a stone

PE'TER, a man's name.

PETRES'CENT, turning to stone.

PET'RIFY, to harden.

PETRIFAC'TION, the process of turning to stone.

SALTPE'TRE,°a mineral salt.

Phag-o (φαγω), to eat.

ANTHROPOPH'AGI, man-eaters; cannibals.

SARCOPH'AGUS,† a sort of stone coffin.

Phan-o, or *Phen-o* (φαινω), to appear, to show.

BLAS'PHEMY, impious language.

EM'PHASIS, stress laid on a word or sentence.

EMPHAT'IC, forcible.

EPIPH'ANY,‡ the manifestation.

PHAN'TOM, an apparition.

PHAN'TASM, a fancied appearance.

PHENOM'ENON,°an appearance.

PROPH'ECY, a foretelling.

PROPH'ET, a foreteller.

SYC'OPHANT,°a low flatterer.

Pharmac-on (φαρμακον), a medicine or drug.

PHARMACEU'TIC, relating to pharmacy.

PHAR'MACY, the art of preparing medicines.

Pher-o (φερω), to carry, to bring.

MET'APHOR,°a short similitude.

METAPHOR'ICAL, figurative.

PERIPH'ERY,°circumference.

PHOS'PHORUS, a luminous substance.

PHOSPHORES'CENT, shining.

---

* *Pentecost*—so called because it was celebrated on the *fiftieth* day after the sixteenth of the month Nisan, which was the second day of the passover.

† This word is derived from the name of a calcareous stone (λιθος σαρκοφαγος), anciently used by the Greeks, which decomposed the bodies deposited in it in a very short time.

‡ *Epiphany*, a Christian festival celebrated on 6th January, the 12th day after Christmas, in commemoration of the *appearance* of our Savior to the wise men or philosophers of the east who came to adore him with presents; or of the *manifestation* of Christ to the Gentiles.

Phil-os (φιλος), a lover.

PHILADEL'PHIA, brotherly love.
PHILAN'THROPIST, one who loves mankind.
PHILOME'LA, the nightingale.
PHILOL'OGY,° the knowledge and study of language.
PHILOS'OPHY,° knowledge; the study of general laws.

Phleps, phleb-os (φλεψ, φλεβος), a vein.

PHLEBOT'OMY, the art of blood-letting.

Phob-os (φοβος), fear, dread.

HYDROPHO'BIA, dread of water; canine madness.

Phon-e (φωνη), a sound, a voice.

EU'PHONY, agreeable sound.
SYM'PHONY, harmony of sounds.

Phras-is (φρασις), a saying, a speech.

PAR'APHRASE, an explanation in other words.
PER'IPHRASE, circumlocution.
PHRASE, an expression; a short sentence.
PHRASEOL'OGY, style; diction.

Phren (φρην), the mind.

PHRENOL'OGY, the science of the mind as connected with the brain.

Phtheg-ma (φθεγμα), a saying.

AP'OPHTHEGM, a remarkable saying.
DIPH'THONG, a union of two vowels in one sound.

Phys-is (φυσις), a bringing forth, nature.

EPIPH'YSIS,° a growing upon.
METAPHYS'ICS,° the science of mind.
PHYSICI'AN, a professor of medicine.
PHYS'ICS, natural philosophy.
PHYS'ICAL, natural; not moral.
PHYSIOG'NOMY, the art of discovering the temper by the face.
PHYSIOL'OGY, the science of animals and plants.
SYM'PHYSIS,° a growing together.

Phyt-on (φυτον), a plant.

ZO'OPHYTE, a body partaking of the nature of both animal and vegetable.

Plan-e (πλανη), a wandering about.

PLAN'ET,° a wandering celestial body.
PLAN'ETARY, pertaining to the planets.

Plass-o (πλασσω), to smear, to form in clay.

CAT'APLASM, a poultice.
PLAS'TER, lime to cover walls.

Plect-os (πληκτος), struck, seized.

AP'OPLEXY, a sudden loss of sense and the power of motion.
APOPLEC'TIC, relating to apoplexy.

Poie-o (ποιεω), to make, to compose.

PO'EM, a metrical composition.

PO'ET, a writer of poems.

Pol-eo (πωλεω), to sell.

MONOP'OLY, exclusive sale.

MONOP'OLIZE, to engross.

Pol-is (πολις), a city, a town.

CONSTAN'TINOPLE, the city of Constantine.

IMPOL'ICY, imprudence.

IMPOLITE', rude; uncivil.

POLICE', the government of a city.

POL'ISH, to smooth; to brighten.

POLITE', refined; genteel.

POLIT'ICAL, relating to politics.

POL'ITICS, the science of government.

POL'ITY, form of government.

Poly (πολυ), many.

POL'YGLOT, having many languages.

POL'YGON, a figure having many angles.

POLYNE'SIA, a division of the earth consisting of many isles.

POLYG'AMY, a plurality of wives.

POL'YPUS, a sea animal with many feet.

POL'YTHEISM, the doctrine of a plurality of gods.

Por-os (πορος), a passage or way.

EMPO'RIUM,°a place of commerce.

PORE, a small passage in the skin.

PO'ROUS, having pores.

POROS'ITY, the quality of having pores.

Pous, pod-os (πους, ποδος), the foot, a foot.

ANTIP'ODES, those on the opposite side of the globe, whose feet are opposite to ours.

POL'YPUS, a sea animal with many feet.

TRI'POD,°a seat with three feet.

Pract-os (πρακτος), done: **Pragma** (πραγμα), a deed.

IMPRAC'TICABLE, that cannot be done.

PRAC'TICE,°habit; use.

PRACTITI'ONER, he who is engaged in any art.

PRAGMAT'IC, impertinent; meddling.

Presbyter-os (πρεσβυτερος), older, a priest.

PRESBYTE'RIAN, one who holds to church government by presbyters.

Prot-os (πρωτος), first.

PROTHON'OTARY, the head registrar.

PRO'TOTYPE, an exemplar; a model.

Psalm-a (ψαλμα), a sacred song.

PSAL'MIST, a writer of psalms.

PSAL'MODY, a singing of psalms.

Psych-e (ψυχη), the breath, the soul.

METEMPSYCHO'SIS,* transmigration of souls.

PSYCHOL'OGY, the science which treats of the nature of the soul.

* Pythagoras, and his followers, held that after death, the *souls* of men pass

Ptom-a (πτωμα), a fall.

MONOP'TOTE,* a noun used only in one oblique case.

SYM'PTOM,° a token; an indication.

Pty-o (πτυω), to spit. HEMOP'TYSIS, the spitting of blood.

Pyr, pyros (πυρ, πυρος), fire.

EMPYRE'AN, the highest heaven.

PYR'AMID,° a solid figure, ending in a point.

PYRE, a funeral pile.

PYROM'ETER, an instrument to measure heat.

PYR'OMANCY, divination by fire.

PYROTECH'NICS, the art of making fireworks.

Rhe-o (ῥεω), to flow, to speak.

CATARR'H,° influenza.

DIARRHE'A, a flux; a purging.

HEM'ORRHAGE, a flux of blood.

RHEUM, a thin watery humor.

Rhomb-os (ῥομβος), a rhomb.

RHOMB,° a quadrangular figure.

Rhythm-os (ῥυθμος), measured movement.

RHYME, to agree in sound.

RHYTHM,° meter; verse.

Sarx, sarc-os (σαρξ, σαρκος), flesh.

SAR'CASM,° a keen reproach.

SARCAS'TIC, keen; severe.

Scariph-os (σκαριφος), a pointed instrument.

SCAR'IFY, to let blood by cutting the skin.

SCARIFICA'TOR, an instrument for scarifying.

Scen-a (σκηνη), the stage, a representation.

SCENE, an appearance.

SCE'NERY, a collection of scenes.

Scept-omai (σκεπτομαι), to look about, to doubt.

SCEP'TIC, a doubter; an infidel.

SCEP'TICISM, doubt; infidelity.

Schism-a (σχισμα), division in the church.

SCHISM, a division in a church or society.

SCHISMAT'IC, one guilty of schism.

Schol-a (σχολη), a school.

SCHOL'AR, a man of letters.

SCHOOL, a place of education.

---

into other bodies; and this doctrine still prevails in some parts of Asia, particularly in India, and China.

* Nouns, in the Latin Language, have six cases: the Nominative, Genitive, Dative, Accusative, Vocative, and Ablative. The first was called *Casus rectus*, the straight case, and the others *Casus obliqui*, the oblique cases, because they seem to *fall* or *lean* from the Nominative.

Scop-eo (σκοπεω), to look, to observe narrowly.

ARCHBISH'OP, the principal of the bishops.
BISH'OPRIC, the diocese of a bishop.
TEL'ESCOPE, a glass used for distant views.
EPISCOPACY, a government by bishops.
SCOPE, aim ; intention.

Selen-e (σεληνη), the moon. PARASELENE', a mock moon.

Sep-o (σηπω), to make putrid.

ANTISEP'TIC, counteracting putrefaction.

Sit-os (σιτος), bread. PAR'ASITE,° a low, mercenary flatterer.

Soph-ia (σοφια), wisdom.

GYMNOS'OPHIST*, an Indian philosopher.
PHILOS'OPHY, knowledge ; the study of first principles.
SOPH'ISM, a fallacious argument.
SOPH'ISTRY, fallacious reasoning.
UNSOPHIST'ICATED, not acquainted with evil ; pure.

Spasm-a (σπασμα), a convulsion.

SPASM, a violent contraction.
SPASMOD'IC, convulsive.

Sperm-a (σπερμα), seed.

GYMNOSPERM'OUS, having naked seeds.
MONOSPERM'OUS, having one seed.

Spher-a, *for* **Sphæra** (σφαιρα), a sphere or globe.

AT'MOSPHERE, the air around the earth.
HEM'ISPHERE, a half globe.
SPHE'ROID,° a body like a sphere
SPHER'ULE, a little globe.

Stas-is (στασις), a standing, a weighing.

APOS'TASY, departure from one's profession.
APOS'TATIZE, to forsake one's faith or religion.
EC'STASY,° rapture; enthusiasm.
ECSTAT'IC, rapturous.
HYDROSTAT'ICS, the science of the weight, motion, and equilibrium of fluids.
SYS'TEM,° regular method.
UNSYSTEMAT'IC, without system.

Stegan-os (στεγανος), concealed.

STEGANOG'RAPHY, the art of writing in secret characters.

Stell-o (στελλω), to send.

APOS'TLE,° a messenger.
DIAS'TOLE,° the dilation of the heart.
EPIS'TLE, a letter sent.
SYS'TOLE,° the contraction of the heart.

---

* The *Gymnosophists*—so called from their going with bare feet, or with little clothing—lived on wild productions of the earth. They never drank wine, nor married. Some of them travelled about, and practised physic. They believed the immortality and transmigration of the soul, and placed the chief happiness of man in a contempt of the goods of fortune, and of the pleasures of sense.

Sten-os (στενος), short.

STENOG'RAPHY, the art of writing in short-hand.

Stere-os (στερεος), solid. STER'EOTYPE,° solid type.

Stich-os (στιχος), a row, a line.

ACROS'TIC,° a kind of poem.

DIS'TICH, a couplet.

Stigma, stigmat-os (στιγμα), a mark of infamy.

STIG'MA, a blot; a reproach.

STIG'MATIZE, to disgrace, to censure.

Strat-os (στρατος), an army. STRAT'AGEM, a military artifice.

Strophe (στροφη), a turning round.

APOS'TROPHE,° a figure of speech; an address.

CATAS'TROPHE,° an unfortunate accident; a final event.

Syc-os (σοκος), a fig. SYC'OPHANT,° a mean flatterer.

Tact-os (τακτος), put in order.

SYN'TAX, the construction of sentences.

TAC'TICS,° the art of directing movements in war.

Taph-os (ταφος), a tomb.

CEN'OTAPH, a monument for one buried elsewhere.

EP'ITAPH, an inscription upon a tomb.

Taut-os (ταυτος), the same.

TAUTOL'OGY, repetition of the same words, or the same sense in different words.

TAUTOLOG'ICAL, containing tautology.

Techn-e (τεχνη), an art or science.

POLYTECH'NIC, embracing many arts.

PYR'OTECHNY, the art of making fireworks.

TECH'NICAL, belonging to art.

TECHNOL'OGY, a discourse upon the arts.

Tect-on (τεκτων), an artist, a fabricator.

ARCHITEC'TURE, the science of building.

AR'CHITECT, a builder; a former

Tel-os (τελος), the end, distance.

TEL'EGRAPH, a machine for conveying intelligence to a distance by signals.

TEL'ESCOPE, an instrument for viewing distant objects.

Teuch-os (τευχος), a vessel; a book.

PEN'TATEUCH, the five books of Moses.

Theatr-um (θεατρον), a theatre.

AMPHITHE'ATRE,° a theatre of circular form.

THE'ATRE, a place of action or exhibition.

Thec-e (θηκη), a place of deposit.

APOTH'ECARY, one who sells drugs.

BIBLIOTH'ECAL, pertaining to a library.

Theor-os (θεωρος), a beholder, a speculator.

THE'OREM,° a proposition to be demonstrated.

THE'ORY, speculation.

THEORET'IC, speculative; not practical.

THE'ORIZE, to form theories.

The-os (θεος), a god.

A'THEIST, one who denies the existence of a God.

ENTHU'SIASM,° violence of passion.

THEOC'RACY, government directed by God.

THEOL'OGY, the science of God and divine things.

Therm-os (θερμος), warm. THERMOM'ETER, a measurer of heat.

Thesis (θεσις), a placing or putting.

ANATH'EMA,°ecclesiastical curse.

ANTITH'ESIS,°opposition of words or sentiments.

EP'ITHET, a descriptive word.

PAREN'THESIS, a sentence or clause within another.

HYPOTH'ESIS, a supposition.

SYN'THESIS,°a putting together; combination.

SYNTHET'ICAL, relating to synthesis.

THEME,°a subject.

THE'SIS,° a position; a proposition advanced.

Tom-os (τομος), a cutting.

ANAT'OMY, the art of dissecting.

ENTOMOL'OGY, a treatise upon insects.

AT'OM, an indivisible particle.

EPIT'OME, an abridgment; a compendium.

Ton-os (τονος), a stretching, a sound.

ASTON'ISH, to surprise; to amaze.

ASTOUND', to strike dumb.

ATTUNE', to put in tune.

INTONA'TION, manner of sounding.

TONE, tension; vigor; sound.

MONOT'ONY, uniformity of tone or sound.

TON'IC, increasing tension or vigor; imparting tone.

TUNE, sound; note; harmony.

Top-os (τοπος), a place.

TOPOG'RAPHY, a description of a place.

TOP'IC, a subject of discourse.

Trop-os (τροπος), a turning.

HE'LIOTROPE, a plant that turns to the sun.

TROPE,°a figure of speech which changes a word from its ordinary meaning.

TROP'IC,°the point at which the sun appears to turn again towards the north or from it.

TRO'PHY, a monument of victory.

Typ-us (τυπος), a type, a mark.

AN'TITYPE, the model of a type.
STER'EOTYPE, solid type.
TYP'ICAL, symbolical.
TYPE, an emblem; a printing letter.
TYPOG'RAPHY, the art of printing.

_Zo-on_ (ζωον), an animal.

ZO'DIAC,° a broad circle in the heavens.
ZOOL'OGY, the science of animals.
ZO'OPHYTE, a body which partakes of the nature of both vegetables and animals.

DERIVATION FROM THE LATIN THROUGH THE FRENCH.

As most of the English words of Latin origin are derived through the French, it is both interesting and important to trace the changes which the Latin words underwent in their transition to French. Without some attention to this subject, it will be difficult to appreciate the connection between many English words and the Latin roots to which they are referred.

Almost all Latin words, in passing into the French, were modified by *apocope*, or the loss of their final syllable; many by *syncope*, or the loss of their middle syllable; and the *commutation*, *addition*, and *transposition* of letters, occasioned various other differences in the derivative words.

I.

In the following list, the consonants, *c*, *g*, *d*, or *t*, when preceded and followed by a vowel, are dropped; and, as usual, the final syllable is rejected.

Latin.		French.	English.
Publi*c*are,	(publiare,)	publier,	to publish.
Pre*c*ari,	(preari,)	prier,	to pray.
Dupli*c*are,	(dupliare,)	doubler	to double.
Dene*g*are,	(deneare,)	denier,	to deny.
Alli*g*are,	(alliare,)	allier,	to ally.
Pli*c*are,	(pliare,)	plier,	to ply.
Fri*g*ere,	(friere,)	frire,	to fry.
Desi*d*erare,	(desierare,)	desirer,	to desire.
Invi*d*ere,	(inviere,)	envier,	to envy.
Do*t*are,	(doare,)	douer,	to endow.
Mari*t*are,	(mariare,)	marier,	to marry.
Peri*c*ulum,	(periulum,)	peril,	peril.
Foeni*c*ulum,	(foeniulum,)	fenouil	fennel.
Cuni*c*ulum,	(cuniulum,)	connil,	a cony.
O*c*ulus,	(oulus,)	œil,	an eye.
Se*c*urus,	(seurus,)	sur,	sure.
Te*g*ula,	(teula,)	tuile,	a tile.
Re*g*ula,	(reula,)	——	a rule.
Re*g*ina,	(reina,)	reine,	——
Sa*g*ena,	(saena,)	seine,	a seine.
Fra*g*ilis,	(frailis,)	frêle,	frail.
Inte*g*er,	(inteer,)	entière,	entire.
Cru*d*elis,	(cruelis,)	cruel,	cruel.
Vo*c*alis,	(voalis,)	voyelle,	a vowel

Latin.		French.	English.
Le*g*alis,	(lealis,)	loyal,	loyal.
Re*g*alis,	(realis,)	royal,	royal.
Ro*t*ula,	(roula,)	rouelle,	rowel, roll.
Ro*t*undus,	(roundus,)	rond,	round.
Arma*t*ura,	(armaura,)	armure,	armor.
Ra*d*ius,	(raius,)	rayon,	a ray.
Me*d*ius,	(meius,)	moyen,	a mean.

*** This *syncope* is observable, also, in the modern proper names of towns, rivers, places, and persons; as in TRENT, from *Tridentum*, by apocope of *um*, (*Trident*) and syncope of *d* (*Trient*); YORK, from *Eboracum*, (E-*b*-orac, *Eorac*;) RHONE from *Rhodanus*, (Rho-*d*-an, *Rhoan*;) the LOIRE, from (Li-*g*-er) *Ligeris*; the MARRO, from *Me-t-aurus*; AUSTIN, from (A-*g*-ustin) *Augustinus*; BENNET, from (Bene-*d*-it, Bene-*d*-ict) *Benedictinus*, &c.

II.

CHANGE OF VOWELS AND DIPHTHONGS.

A is changed into E and A I.*

Latin.	French.	English.
Arm*a*re,	arm*e*r,	to arm.
Ador*a*re,	ador*e*r,	to adore.
Cit*a*re,	cit*e*r,	to cite.
Err*a*re,	err*e*r,	to err.
Sign*a*re,	sign*e*r,	to sign.
S*a*l,	s*e*l,	salt.
N*a*sus,	n*e*z,	the nose.
Gr*a*num,	gr*ai*n,	grain.
Rom*a*nus,	Rom*ai*n,	Roman.
Hum*a*nus,	hum*ai*n,	human.

E is changed into A, I, and OI.

*E*mendare,	*a*mender,	to amend.
Retinēre,	reten*i*r,	to retain.
Pallēre,	pal*i*r,	to be pale.
Prevalēre,	preval*oi*r,	to prevail.
Condolēre,	condoul*oi*r,	to condole.
M*e*,	m*oi*,	me.
T*e*,	t*oi*,	thee.

I is changed into E, AI, and EI.

*I*ntrare.	*e*ntrer,	to enter.
*I*nvidēre,	*e*nvier,	to envy.
N*i*ger,	n*e*gre,	negro.
Car*i*na, *s.*	car*e*ner, *v.*	to careen.

*The interchange of vowels is so frequent, and so obvious, that it is almost unnecessary to adduce examples. Thus, in our own language, we have B*a*nd, B*i*nd, B*o*nd, B*u*ndle, B*ou*nd; S*i*ng, S*a*ng, S*u*ng, S*o*ng; L*o*ng, L*e*ngth; Br*oa*d, Br*ea*dth, &c.

Latin.	French.	English.
D*i*gnari,	d*a*igner,	to deign.
*I*ns*i*gne,	*enseigne*,	an ensign
Cons*i*lium,	cons*e*il,	counsel.
Dom*i*nium,	dom*a*in,	domain.

O changed into OU, EU, and OI.

Latin.	French.	English.
Pr*o*bare,	pr*ou*ver,	to prove.
Dem*o*rari,	dem*eu*rer,	to demur.
Amor,	am*ou*r,	amor.
H*o*ra,	h*eu*re,	an hour.
S*o*lus,	s*eu*l,	sole.
F*o*lium,	f*oi*l,	foil (leaf.)

U changed into O, OI, and OU.

Latin.	French.	English.
Ann*u*nciare,	ann*o*ncer,	to announce
Ab*u*ndare,	ab*o*nder,	to abound.
F*u*ndare,	f*o*nder,	to found.
*U*ngere,	*oi*ndre,*	to anoint.
*U*ncia,	*o*nce,	an ounce.
M*u*sca,	m*ou*sse,	moss.
Cr*u*x,	cr*oi*x,	cross.

COMMUTATION OF CONSONANTS.

Interchange of B, P, F, and V.

Latin.	French.	English.
Deli*b*erare,	deli*v*rer,	to deliver.
Gu*b*ernare,	gou*v*erner,	to govern.
Pro*b*are,	prou*v*er,	to prove.
Du*p*licare,	dou*b*ler,	to double.
Se*p*arare,	se*v*rer,	to sever.
Recu*p*erare,	recou*v*rer,	to recover.
Reci*p*ere,	rece*v*oir,	to receive.
Coö*p*erire,	cou*v*rir,	to COVER.
Canna*b*is,	cane*v*as,	canvass.
Fe*b*ris,	fiè*v*re,	fever.
Li*b*ra,	li*v*re,	livre.
Ver*b*ena,	ver*v*eine,	vervain.
Dia*b*olus,	dia*b*le,	de*v*il.
*F*i*b*er,	*b*ie*v*re,	a beaver.
Ne*p*os,	ne*v*eu,	a nephew.
A*p*rilis,	A*v*ril,	April.
Sa*p*or,	sa*v*eur,	savour.
Pau*p*ertas,	pau*v*reté,	poverty.
Pau*p*er,	pau*v*re,	poor.
*V*ara,	*b*arre,	a bar.
Vannus,	*v*an,	*f*an.
Bre*v*is,	bre*f*,	brief.

* *Oindre.* See below, for the change of *g* into *d*.

Interchange of B, V, and G *soft*.

Latin.	French.	English.
Ra*b*ies,	ra*g*e,	rage.
Ti*b*ia,	ti*g*e,	——
Lum*b*us,	lon*g*e,	the loin.
Ru*b*eus,	rou*g*e,	rouge.
Abbre*v*iare,	abre*g*er,	to ABRIDGE.*
Suble*v*are,	soula*g*er,	——
Dilu*v*ium,	delu*g*e,	deluge.
Ca*v*ea,	ca*g*e,	a cage.
Reple*g*ium,	reple*v*in,	replevin.
Ser*v*iente,†	ser*g*ent,	a sergeant.
Ni*v*e,	nie*g*e,	——
Sal*v*ia,	sau*g*e,	sage.
*V*espa, (*guespe*,)	*g*uêpe,	a wasp.
*V*astare, (*gaster*,)	*g*âter,	to waste
In *g*yro,	en*v*iron,	environs.

Interchange of C *hard*, G *hard*, Q and K.

Lo*c*are,	lo*g*er,	to LODGE.
A*c*er,	ai*g*re,	eager.
Ala*c*er,	alle*g*ro,	allegro.
Ma*c*er,	mai*g*re,	meagre.
*C*rassus,	*g*ros,	gross.
*C*rypta.	*g*rotte,	a grot.
Fi*c*us,	fi*g*ue,	a fig.
Su*g*ere,	su*c*er,	to suck.
*Q*uadrare,	*c*adrer,	to square.
A*q*uila,	ai*g*le,	an eagle.

C changed into CH,‡

Cantare,	*ch*anter,	to chant.
Carmen,	*ch*arme,	a charm.
Castus,	*ch*aste,	chaste,
Camera,	*ch*ambre,	chamber.
Carrus,	*ch*ar,	car, chariot

Interchange of C *soft*, S, and T.

Pla*c*ens,	plai*s*ant,	pleasing.
Ra*c*emus,	rai*s*in,	a raisin.
Ra*t*ione,	rai*s*on,	reason.
Po*t*ione,	poi*s*on,	poison.

---

* *Abridge*. In this, and in several other words borrowed from the French, *d* has been inserted before *g* to strengthen the sound; as in to *lodge*, from *loger; judge*, from *juger; budge*, from *bouger; budget*, from *bougette;* and *pledge*, from *pleige*. Hence the disposition to pronounce, and sometimes to write, the words *allege* and *oblige*, alle*d*ge, obli*d*ge.

† *Serviente*, ablative of serviens. (See Observation III.)

‡ Hence we derive CHEST from *cista;* CHEESE from *caseus:* and from our own word *care*, CHARY and CHARILY, i. e., *careful* and *carefully*.

Latin.	French.	English.
Fac*t*ione,	fa*ç*on,	fashion.
Lec*t*ione,	le*ç*on,	lesson.
Gra*t*ia,	gra*c*e,	grace.
Distan*t*ia,	distan*c*e,	distance.
	Interchange of D and G.	
Jun*g*ere,	join*d*re,	to join.
Tin*g*ere,	tein*d*re,	to tinge.
Pin*g*ere,	pein*d*re,	to paint.
Man*d*ere,	man*g*er,	to munch.
Ro*d*ere,	ron*g*er,	——
Se*d*e,	sie*g*e,	siege.
Ju*d*ice,	ju*g*e,	judge.
Diurnalis,*	journal,	a journal
Sta*d*ium, (*estage*,)	etage,	a stage.
	Interchange of L, M, N, R.	
Chartu*l*a,	chart*r*e,	a chapter.
Capitu*l*um,	chapit*r*e,	a chapter.
Titu*l*us,	tit*r*e,	a title.
U*l*mus,	o*r*me,	the elm.
Tempo*r*a,	tempes,	the temp*l*es.
Turtu*r*,	tourt*r*e,	turt*l*e.
G*r*anum, *s*.	g*l*aner,	to GLEAN.
F*r*agrare,	f*l*airer,	——
Pe*r*egrinus,	pé*l*erin,	pilgrim.
*M*atta,	*n*atte,	a mat.
*M*appa,	*n*appe,	napkin.
Pu*m*ice,	po*n*ce,	pumice-stone.
Pampi*n*us,	pamp*r*e,	pamper ?
Diaco*n*us,	diac*r*e,	a deacon.
Tympa*n*um,	timb*r*e,	timbre*l*.
Cophi*n*us,	coff*r*e,	a coffer and coffin.

The frequent substitution of the vowel U for the consonant L deserves particular notice.

So*l*idare,	so*u*der,	to SODER or solder.
Sa*l*vare,	sa*u*ver,	to save.
Abso*l*vere,	absoudre,	to absolve.
Ba*l*samum,	ba*û*me,	balm.
A*l*tare,	a*u*tel,	an altar.
Falsus,	fa*u*x,†	false.

* *Diurnalis*, L., giornàll, It., *j*ournal, F.

† Hence the formation of the plural number of French nouns ending in *al* or *ail*; which, with a few exceptions, pass into *aux*. Hence, also, such changes as Nouve*ll*e, Nouve*au*, Be*l*, Be*au*, &c.; and, in our language, Em*bell*ish and *Beau*tify. In several English words, as in *Walk*, *Talk*, *Chalk*, *Balk*, this letter, though it is still retained, is pronounced exactly like *u*. See he word PIANO, in which *i* has taken the place of *l*.

Latin.	French.	English.
A*l*tus,	ha*u*t,	high.
U*l*tra,	outre,	OUT.
Penici*ll*us,	pincea*u*,	a pencil.
A*l*ter,	a*u*tre,	OTHER.
	T changed into D.	
Arcua*t*um,	arca*d*e,	arcade.
Para*t*um,	para*d*e,	parade.
Grana*t*um,	grena*d*e,	grenade.
Ca*t*ena,	ca*d*enas,	——
Renegatus,	renéga*t*,	renega*d*e.
Charta,	car*t*e,	car*d*.
Sali*t*um,	sala*d*e,	sala*d*e.
Arma*t*a,	arma*d*a,*	armada.
	Interchange of X, S, Z.	
No*x*a,	noi*s*e,	noise.
Co*x*a,	cui*ss*e,	cuisse.
A*x*is,	e*ssi*eu,	axis.
E*x*ire,	issue,	to issue.
Te*x*tus,	ti*ss*u,	tissue.
Nasus,	nez,	the nose.
Oryza,	ri*s*,	ri*c*e.

EXAMPLES OF LETTERS INSERTED.

	B inserted.	
Numerare,	nom*b*rer,	to number.
Cumulare,	com*b*ler,	to accumulate.
Simulare,	sem*b*ler,	to seem.
Tremulare,	trem*b*ler,	to tremble.
Camera,	*ch*ambre,	a chamber.
Humilis,	hum*b*le,	humble.
	D inserted.	
Cinere,†	cen*d*re,	a cinder.
Sicera,	ci*d*re,	cider.
Genere (*gendre*),	genre,	gen*d*er.
Pulvere,	pou*d*re,	pow*d*er.
	G inserted.	
Hispania,	Espa*g*ne,	Spain.
Britannia,	Breta*g*ne,	Britain.

* *Armada.* It is almost unnecessary to remark that this word is properly Spanish, in which language the change of *d* into *t* is very frequent; as in Pe*d*ro, from *Petro;* Pa*d*re, from *Patre;* Trini*d*a*d*a, from *Trinitate.*—But we need not go farther than our own language for examples of the change of *d* into *t;* as bereave*d*, bereav'd, *bereft:* weave*d*, weav'd, *weft;* cleave*d*, cleav'd, *cleft;* gived, giv'd, *gift*, &c. The change of *v* into its kindred letter *f* is also exemplified by these words.

† The ablative case.

Latin.	French.	English.
Campaneus,	campagne,	campaign.
Montanus,	montagne,	mountain.
Linea,	lignea,	a line.
Vinea,	vigne,	a vine.
Linum,	ligne,	linen.
Simia,	singe,	——
Granum,	grange,	GRANGE.
Somnium,	songe,	——
Damnum,	danger,	DANGER.
Vindemia,	vendange,	vintage.

EXAMPLES OF LETTERS PREFIXED.

E prefixed.

This letter was very frequently prefixed to French-Latin words commencing with *s*.

Latin.	French.	English.
Sperare,	esperer,	——
Spicare (*espier*),	épier,*	to spire
Specere,	épier,	to SPY.
Status,	état,	estate.
Species,	espèce,	species.
Spiritus,	esprit,	sprite.
Scriptorium,	écritoire,	scrutoire
Schola,	école,	school.
Studium,	étude,	study.
Stola,	étole,	a stole.
Stomachus,	éstomac,	stomach.

H prefixed.

Latin.	French.	English.
U*l*ulare,	*h*u*r*ler,	to howl.
Audire,	ouir,	to *h*ear.
Oleum,	*h*uile,	oil.
Octo,	*h*uit,	eight.
Ostrea (*huistre*),	huitre,	an oyster.
Ostiarius,	huissier,	an usher.
Ascia,	*h*ache (hachette),	a hatchet.
Aula,	*h*alle,	a hall.

III.

It is necessary to observe, that it is from the *ablative* case that French-Latin nouns are generally formed.

EXAMPLES.

Latin.	French.	English.
Bos, *bove*,	bœu*f*,†	beef.
Calix, *calice*,	calice,	a chalice.

* *Epier.* In this, and in most of the French words which follow, the *s* has been dropped. For the elision of the middle consonant, see Observation I.

† For the commutation of *b*, *f*, and *v*, see above.

Latin.	French.	English.
Ars, *arte,*	art,	art.
Ebur, *ebore,*	*i*v*oire,*	ivory.
Ratio, *ratione,*	raison,	reason.

IV.

Latin verbs became French generally by *apocope*, or the omission of the final letter.

EXAMPLES.

Latin.	French.	English.
Armar*e*,*	armer,	to arm.
Errar*e*,	errer,	to err.
Damnar*e*,	damner,	to damn.
Taxar*e*,	taxer,	to tax.
Admirar*i*,	admirer,	to admire.
Assignar*e*,	assigner,	to assign.
Prohibēr*e*,	prohiber,	to prohibit.
Abhorrēr*e*,	abhorrer,	to abhor.
Absorbēr*e*,	absorber,	to absorb.
Accedĕr*e*,	acceder,	to accede.
Assistĕr*e*,	assister,	to assist.
Arguĕr*e*,	arguer,	to argue.
Finir*e*,	finir,	to finish.
Punir*e*,	punir,	to punish.
Consentir*e*,	consentir,	to consent.

Many French-Latin verbs are formed differently; but their irregularities may, in general, be explained by the preceding principles. Thus, from DEBERE, by dropping the final letter, and changing *b* into *v*, we have *dever*, which becomes dev*oi*r by the same analogy as *moi* from *me*, *toi* from *te*, &c. Thus, also, VALERE (valer), *valoir*. HABERE (ha*b*er, ha*v*er, aver), *avoir*, to HAVE, the asperate being restored. ASSIDERE (assi*d*er, assier), *asseoir*. VIDERE (vi*d*er, vier), *voir*. SAPERE (sa*p*er, sa*v*er), *savoir*. DECĬDERE (de*c*ider, decier, de*ch*ier), *déchoir*. SOLVERE (so*l*ver, sou*v*er), *soudre*. AUDIRE (au*d*ir, auir), *ouir*, to HEAR, the asperate being prefixed.

---

* In Latin verbs of the first conjugation, the *a* before *re* was changed into *e*. See above.

THE KEY.

ABB

Abbreviate. *Ab; brevis*
Abdicate. *Ab; dica*
Aberration. *Ab; erro.*
Abhor. *Ab; horreo.*
Ability *Habeo.*
Abject, *Ab; jacio.*
Abjure. *Ab; juro.*
Able. *Habeo.*
Ablution. *Ab; luo.*
Abolish, abolition. *Ab; oleo.*
Abominable, abominate. *Ab; omen.*
Abortion. *Ab; orior.*
Abound. *Ab; undo.*
Abrade. *Ab; rado.*
Abridge. *Ab; brevis.*
Abrogate, abrogable. *Ab; rogo.*
Abrupt. *Ab; ruptum.*
Abscond. *Abs; con; do.*
Absence, absent. *Abs; ens.*
Absolute, absolution, absolve. *Ab; solvo.*
Absorb, absorption. *Ab; sorbeo.*
Abstain, abstemious. *Abs; teneo.*
Abstinent. *Abs; teneo.*
Abstract, abstraction. *Abs; traho.*
Abstruse. *Abs; trudo.*
Abundant. *Ab; undo.*
Abuse. *Ab; utor.*
Accede. *Ac; cedo.*
Accelerate. *Ac; celer.*
Accent, accentuate. *Ac; cano.*
Accept, acceptable. *Ac; capio.*
Access. *Ac; cedo.*
Accident. *Ac; cado.*
Acclaim, acclamation. *Ac; clamo.*
Acclivity. *Ac; clivus.*
Accommodate. *Ac; com; modus.*
Accompany. *Ac; com; pannus.*
Accomplice. *Ac; com; plico.*
Accomplish. *Ac; com; pleo.*
Accord. *Ac; cor.*
Accrue. *Ac; cresco.*
Accumulate. *Ac; cumulo.*
Accuracy, accurate. *Ac; cura.*
Accuse. *Ac; causa.*
Accustom. *Ac; coutume.*
Acerbity. *Acerbus.*
Acescent, acetous. *Aceo.*
Acidity, acidulate. *Acidus.*
Acquiesce. *Ac; quies.*
Acquire, acquisition. *Ac; quæro.*
Acrid, acrimony. *Acris.*
Acrostic. *Acron; stichos.*
Act, active, actor, actuate. *Ago.*
Acumen, acute. *Acuo.*
Adamant, adamantine. *A; damao.*
Adapt. *Ad; aptus.*
Add. *Ad; do.*
Addict. *Ad; dico.*
Addition. *Ad; do.*
Adduce. *Ad; duco.*
Adequate. *Ad; equus.*

ALP

Adhere. *Ad; hæreo.*
Adjective. *Ad; jacio.*
Adjoin. *Ad; jungo.*
Adjourn. *Ad; jour.*
Adjudge, adjudicate. *Ad; judico.*
Adjunct. *Ad; jungo.*
Adjust. *Ad; justus.*
Adjutant. *Ad; juvo.*
Administer, administration. *Ad; minister*
Admiration, admire. *Ad; mirus.*
Admission, admit, admittance. *Ad; mitto*
Admixture. *Ad; misceo.*
Admonish, admonition. *Ad; moneo.*
Adopt. *Ad; opto.*
Adore. *Ad; oro.*
Adorn. *Ad; orno.*
Adulation. *Adulatum.*
Adult. *Ad; oleo.*
Advance, advantage. *Avant.*
Advent, adventure. *Ad; venio.*
Adverb. *Ad; verbum.*
Adverse, adversity, advert, advertize. *Ad, verto.*
Advice, advisable. *Ad; video.*
Advocate. *Ad; voco.*
Aerolite. *Aer; lithos.*
Affable. *Af; fari.*
Affect, affection. *Af; facio.*
Affiance. *Af; fides.*
Affinity. *Af; finis.*
Affirm. *Af; firmus.*
Affix. *Af; fixus.*
Afflict. *Af; fligo.*
Affluence, afflux. *Af; fluo.*
Affront. *Af; frons.*
Agent. *Ago.*
Agglutinate. *Ag; gluten.*
Aggrandize. *Ag; grandis.*
Aggravate. *Ag; gravis.*
Aggregate. *Ag; grex.*
Aggression. *Ag; gradior.*
Aggrieve. *Ag; gravis.*
Agile, agility. *Agilis.*
Agitate, agitation. *Agito.*
Agrarian. *Ager.*
Agree. *A; gratia.*
Agriculture. *Ager; colo.*
Alien. *Alius.*
Aliment, alimony. *Alo.*
Aliquot. *Alius; quot.*
Allege, allegiance. *Al; lego*
Allegory. *Allos; egora.*
Alleviate. *Al; levo.*
Allow. *Al; laus.*
Allude. *Al; ludo;*
Allure. *Al; lure.*
Allusion. *Al; ludo.*
Alluvial. *Al; luo.*
Almanac. *Al; men.*
Almoner, alms. *Alo*
Alpine. *Alpes.*

Alter. *Alter.*
Alternate, alternative. *Alternus.*
Altiloquence. *Altus; loquor.*
Altisonant. *Altus; sonus.*
Altitude. *Altus.*
Amalgamate. (*Hama*, together); *gameo.*
Amanuensis. *A; manus.*
Amateur, amatory. *Amo.*
Ambition. *Am; eo.*
Amble. *Ambulo.*
Ameliorate. *A; melior.*
Amend. *A; menda.*
Amiable. *Amo.*
Ammunition. *Am; munio.*
Amnesty. *A; mneo.*
Amorous. *Amo.*
Amorphous. *A; morphe.*
Amour. *Amo.*
Amphitheatre. *Amphi; theatrum.*
Ample. *Amplus.*
Amplification. *Amplus; facio.*
Amplify. *Amplus.*
Amuse. *A; musa.*
Anagram. *Ana; grapho.*
Analogy. *Ana; logos.*
Analysis, analytical, analyze. *Ana; lysis.*
Anathema. *Ana; thesis.*
Anatomy. *Ana; tomas.*
Ancestor, ancestral, ancestry. *Ante; cedo.*
Ancient. *Antiquus.*
Anecdote. *An; ec; dotos.*
Anemoscope. *Anemos; scopeo.*
Anger. *Ango.*
Angle. *Angulus.*
Anguish. *Ango.*
Angular. *Angulus.*
Animadversion, animadvert. *Animus; verto.*
Animal, animalcule, animate. *Anima.*
Animosity. *Animus.*
Annalist, annals. *Annus.*
Annex. *An; necto.*
Annihilate. *An; nihil.*
Anniversary. *Annus; verto.*
Announce. *An; nuncio.*
Annual, annuitant, annuity. *Annus.*
Annul. *An; nullus.*
Annular. *Annulus.*
Annunciation. *An; nuncio.*
Anomalous, anomaly. *An; omalos.*
Anonymous. *A; onoma.*
Antecedent. *Ante; cedo.*
Antediluvian. *Ante; diluvium.*
Antemeridian. *Ante; meridies.*
Antemundane. *Ante; mundus.*
Antepenult. *Ante; pene; ultimus.*
Anthology. *Anthos; logos.*
Anthropophagi. *Anthropos; phago.*
Antibilious. *Anti; bilis.*
Antic. *Antiquus.*
Anticipate. *Anti; capio.*
Antidote. *Anti; dotos.*
Antiparalytic. *Anti; para; lysis.*
Antipathy. *Anti; pathos.*
Antipodes. *Anti; pous.*
Antiquary antiquate, antique, antiquity. *Antiquus.*
Antithesis. *Anti; thesis.*
Antitype. *Anti; typus.*
Anxiety, anxious. *Ango.*
Apart. *A; pars.*
Apathetic, apathy. *A; pathos.*
Aperient, aperture. *Aperio.*
Apetalous. *A; petalon.*
Aphelion. *Apo; helios.*
Aphorism, aphoristical. *Apo; horos.*
Apiary. *Apis.*
Apocope. *Apo; cope.*
Apogee. *Apo; ge.*
Apograph. *Apo; grapho.*
Apologetic, apology, apologue. *Apo; logos*
Apoplectic, apoplexy. *Apo; plectos.*
Apostasy, apostatize. *Apo; stasis.*
Apostle. *Apo; stello.*
Apostrophe. *Apo; strophe.*
Apophthegm, apothecary. *Apo; phthegma.*
Apparatus, apparel. *Ap; paro.*
Apparent, apparition, apparition. *Ap; pareo.*
Appeal. *Ap; pello.*
Appear. *Ap; pareo.*
Appease. *Ap; pax.*
Append, appendix. *Ap; pendeo.*
Appertain. *Ap; per; tenio.*
Appetite. *Ap; peto.*
Applaud, applause. *Ap; plaudo.*
Applicable, applicant, application, apply. *Ap; plico.*
Apportion. *Ap; pars.*
Appraise. *Ap; precium.*
Apprehend, apprehension, apprentice. ap-prize. *Ap; prehendo.*
Approach. *Ap; prope.*
Approbation. *Ap; probo*
Appropriate. *Ap; proprius.*
Approve. *Ap; probo.*
Approximate. *Ap; prope.*
Apt, aptitude. *Aptus.*
Aquatic. *Aqua.*
Aqueduct. *Aqua; duco.*
Aqueous. *Aqua.*
Aquiline. *Aquila.*
Arable. *Aro.*
Arbiter, arbitrament, arbitrary, arbitrate. *Arbiter.*
Arbor, arborary, arborist. *Arbor.*
Arch. *Arche.*
Arch. *Arcus.*
Archbishop. *Arche; epi; scopeo.*
Archer. *Arcus.*
Architect, architecture. *Arche; tecton.*
Ardency, ardent, ardor. *Ardeo.*
Arefaction. *Areo; facio.*
Arefy. *Areo.*
Arenaceous, arenose. *Arena.*
Argue, argument. *Arguo.*
Arid. *Aridus.*
Aristocracy, aristocrat. *Aristos; cratos.*
Arithmancy. *Arithmos; mancia.*
Arm, armada, armament. *Arma.*
Armistice. *Arma; sto.*
Armor, arms, army. *Arma.*
Arrange. *Ar; rang.*
Arrant. *Erro.*
Arrest. *Ar; re; sto.*
Arrive. *Ar; rivus.*
Arrogant. *Ar; rogo.*
Arson. *Ardeo.*
Art. *Ars.*
Article, articulate. *Articulus.*
Artifice. *Ars; facio.*
Artisan, artist. *Ars.*
Ascend, ascension, ascent. *A; scando*
Ascertain. *As; certus.*
Ascribe, ascription. *A; scribo.*
Asinine. *Asinus.*
Aspect. *A; specto.*
Asperity. *Asper.*
Asperse. *A; spargo.*
Aspirate, aspire. *A; spiro.*
Ass. *Asinus.*
Assail, assault. *As; salio.*
Assent. *As; sentio.*
Assert. *As; sertum.*
Assess. *As; sedeo.*

Assiduous. *As; sedeo.*
Assign, assignment. *As; signum.*
Assimilate. *As; similis.*
Assist. *As; sisto.*
Associate. *As; socio.*
Assort. *As; sors.*
Assuage, assuasive. *As; suadeo.*
Astonish, astound. *As; tonos.*
Astringent. *A; stringo.*
Astrolabe. *Astron; labo.*
Astrology. *Astron; logos.*
Astronomy. *Astron; nomos.*
Atheist. *A; theos.*
Atmosphere. *Atmos; sphæra.*
Atom. *A; tomos.*
Atrobilarian. *Atra; bilis.*
Atrocious, atrocity. *Atrox.*
Attain. *At; tango.*
Attainder, attaint. *At; tingo.*
Attempt. *At; tento.*
Attend, attention. *At; tendo.*
Attenuate. *At; tenuis.*
Attest. *At; testis.*
Attract, attractive. *At; traho.*
Attribute. *At; tributum.*
Attune. *At; tonos.*
Auction. *Augeo.*
Audacious, audacity. *Audax.*
Audible, audience, auditory. *Audio.*
Augment. *Augeo.*
Augur, augury. *Augur.*
Auricle, auricular. *Auris.*
Auspicious. *Avis; specio.*
Austere, austerity. *Austerus.*
Author, authoritative, authorize. *Augeo.*
Autocrat. *Autos; cratos.*
Autograph. *Autos; grapho.*
Automaton. *Autos; matos.*
Autopsy. *Autos; opto.*
Auxiliar, auxiliary. *Auxilium.*
Avantguard. *Avant; guarder.*
Avenge. *A; vindex.*
Avenue. *A; venio.*
Aver. *A; verus.*
Aversion, avert. *A; verto.*
Aviary. *Avis.*
Avidity. *Avidus.*
Avocation. *A; voco.*
Avoid. *A; viduo.*
Avouch. *A; voco.*

B.

Babel, Babylon. *Babel.*
Bacchanalian. *Bacchus.*
Bankrupt. (*Abacus*, a bench); *ruptum.*
Bar. *Barre.*
Barber. *Barba.*
Barbaric, barbarity, barbarous. *Barbarus.*
Barometer, barometrical. *Baros; metrum.*
Barricade, barrier. *Barre.*
Beatific. *Beatus; facio.*
Beatify, beatitude. *Beatus.*
Beau, beauty, belle. *Beau.*
Belligerent. *Bellum; gero.*
Bellipotent. *Bellum; posse; ens.*
Benediction. *Bene; dico.*
Benefaction, benefice, benefit. *Bene; facio.*
Benevolence, benevolent. *Bene; volo.*
Benign, benignity. *Benignus.*
Besiege. *Be; sedeo.*
Betray. *Be; traho.*
Bibber. *Bibo.*
Bibliomania. *Biblos; mania.*
Bilious. *Bilis.*
Biennial. *Bini; annus.*
Bifid. *Bini; findo.*
Bigamist, bigamy. *Bini; gameo*
Binary. *Bini.*
Binocular. *Bini; oculus.*
Biography. *Bios; grapho.*
Biped. *Bini; pes.*
Biscuit. *Bini; coquo.*
Bisect. *Bini; seco.*
Bishopric. *Epi; scopeo.*
Bland, blandish. *Blandus.*
Blasphemy. *Blapto; phano.*
Boil. *Bulla.*
Bounty, bounteous. *Bonus.*
Brachial. *Brachium.*
Breviary, brevity, brief. *Brevis.*
Brilliancy, brilliant. *Briller.*
Brutal, brutish. *Brutus.*
Bubble. *Bulla.*

C.

Cachexy. *Cacos; exis.*
Cadence. *Cado.*
Calamitous, calamity. *Calamitas.*
Calculate. *Calculus.*
Caldron. *Caleo.*
Calefaction. *Caleo; facio.*
Caloric. *Caleo.*
Calorific. *Caleo; facio.*
Calumniate, calumnious, calumny. *Calumnia.*
Camp, campaign. *Campus.*
Candid, candidate, candle, candor. *Candeo*
Cant, canticle, canto. *Cano.*
Cap. *Caput.*
Capable, capacious, capacitate, capacity *Capio.*
Capillary. *Capillus.*
Capital, capitation, capitulate. *Caput*
Captain. *Caput.*
Captivate, captive, captor, capture. *Capio*
Carbonic. *Carbo.*
Carbuncle. *Carbo.*
Cardinal. *Cardo.*
Care. *Cura.*
Career. *Curro.*
Caress. *Carus.*
Carnage, carnal. *Caro.*
Carnivorous. *Caro; voro.*
Carry. *Curro.*
Cascade, case. *Cado.*
Castigate. *Castigo.*
Casual. *Cado.*
Catalogue. *Cata; logos.*
Cataplasm. *Cata; plasso.*
Catarrh. *Cata; rheo.*
Catastrophe. *Cata; strophe.*
Catechise. *Cata; echeo.*
Category. *Cata; egora.*
Catenarian. *Catena.*
Cathedral. *Cata; edra.*
Catholic. *Cata; holos.*
Cause. *Causa.*
Caution. *Cautio.*
Cavalcade, cavalier, cavalry. *Cavallo.*
Cavern. *Cavus.*
Cavity. *Cavus.*
Cease, cede. *Cedo.*
Celebrate, celebrity. *Celebris.*
Celerity. *Celer.*
Cell, cellar, cellular. *Cella.*
Cenotaph. (*Cenos*, empty); *taphos.*
Censorious, censure, census. *Censeo*
Cent. *Centum.*
Centennial. *Centum; annus.*
Centipede. *Centum; pes.*
Centurion, century. *Centum.*

Cerate, cere. *Cera.*
Certain. *Certus.*
Certificate. *Certus; facio.*
Certify. *Certus.*
Cerulean. *Ceruleus.*
Cession. *Cedo.*
Cetaceous. *Cetus.*
Chandelier. *Candeo.*
Chant. *Cano.*
Chapter. *Caput.*
Charnel. *Caro.*
Chaste. *Castus.*
Chasten, chastise. *Castigo.*
Chemical, chemist. *Chymos.*
Cherish. *Carus.*
Chevalier. *Cheval.*
Chirograph. *Chir; grapho.*
Chiromancy. *Chir; mancia.*
Chirurgeon, chirurgical. *Chir; ergon.*
Chivalry. *Cheval.*
Choir, choral, chorister, chorus. *Chorus.*
Chronological, chronology. *Chronos; logos.*
Chronometer. *Chronos; metrum.*
Cincture. *Cingo.*
Circle. *Circulus.*
Circuit. *Circum; eo.*
Circular, circulate. *Circulus.*
Circumference. *Circum; fero.*
Circumflex. *Circum; flecto.*
Circumlocution. *Circum; loquor.*
Circumnavigate. *Circum; navis; ago.*
Circumpolar. *Circum; polus.*
Circumscribe. *Circum; scribo.*
Circumspect. *Circum; specio.*
Circumstance, circumstantial. *Circum; sto.*
Circumvent. *Circum; venio.*
Circumvolution. *Circum; volvo.*
Cisalpine. *Cis; Alpes.*
Cite. *Cito.*
Citizen, city, civic, civil. *Civis.*
Claim, clamor. *Clamo.*
Clarification. *Clarus; facio.*
Clarify, clarion. *Clarus.*
Class, classic. *Classis.*
Classification. *Classis; facio.*
Classify. *Classis.*
Clause. *Claudo.*
Clear. *Clarus.*
Clemency. *Clemens.*
Clepsydra. (*Clepto*, to steal); *hydor.*
Clergy, clerical, clerk. *Cleros.*
Cliff. *Clivus.*
Close, closet. *Claudo.*
Coact. *Co; ago.*
Coadjutor. *Co; ad; juvo.*
Coalition. *Co; alo.*
Coequal. *Co; equus.*
Coerce, coercive. *Co; erceo.*
Coeternal. *Co; eternus.*
Coeval. *Co; evum.*
Cogent. *Co; ago.*
Cogitate. *Co; agito.*
Cohesive. *Co; hæreo.*
Coincide. *Co; in; cado.*
Collapse. *Col; labor.*
Collateral. *Col; latus.*
Colleague. *Col; lego.*
Collect. *Col; lego.*
College. *Col; lego.*
Collision. *Col; lido.*
Colloquial, colloquy. *Col; loquor.*
Collusion. *Col; ludo*
Colony. *Colo.*
Color. *Color.*
Combine. *Com; bini.*
Combustion. *Com; ustum.*
Comedy. *Comos; ode.*
Comfort. *Com; fortis.*
Comic. *Comos.*
Command. *Com; mando.*
Commemorable, commemorate. *Com; memor.*
Commend, commendation. *Com; mando.*
Commensurate. *Com; mensura.*
Comment, commentary, commentator. *Com, mens.*
Commerce, commercial. *Com; mercor.*
Commiserate. *Com; miser.*
Commissary, commission, committee, commitment. *Com; mitto.*
Commix. *Com; misceo.*
Commodious, commodity. *Com; modus.*
Common, commonalty. *Com; munus.*
Commotion. *Com; moveo.*
Commune, communication, communion, community. *Com; munus.*
Commute. *Com; muto.*
Companion, company. *Com; pannus.*
Comparative, compare. *Com; par.*
Compass. *Com; passus.*
Compatible. *Com; peto.*
Compatriot. *Com; pater.*
Compeer. *Com; par.*
Compel. *Com; pello.*
Compendium, compensate. *Com; pendo.*
Compete, competence, competitor. *Com; peto.*
Compile. *Com; pilo.*
Complacency. *Com; placeo.*
Complain, complaint. *Com; plango.*
Complaisant. *Com; placeo.*
Complement, complete. *Com; pleo.*
Complex, compliance, complicate, complexion, comply. *Com; plico.*
Compliment. *Com; pleo.*
Comport. *Com; porto.*
Compose, compositor, compost, composure. *Com; pono.*
Comprehend, comprehension. *Com; prehendo.*
Compress. *Com; premo.*
Comprise. *Com; prehendo.*
Compromise. *Com; pro; mitto.*
Compulsory. *Com; pello.*
Concatenate. *Con; catena.*
Concave. *Con; cavus.*
Conceal. *Con; celo.*
Concede. *Con; cedo.*
Conceit, conceive, conception. *Con; capio.*
Concern. *Con; cerno.*
Concession. *Con; cedo.*
Conch. *Concha.*
Conchology. *Concha; logos.*
Conciliate. *Concilio.*
Concise. *Con; cædo.*
Conclude, conclusion. *Con; claudo.*
Concoct. *Con; coquo.*
Concomitant. *Con; comes.*
Concord. *Con; cor.*
Concourse. *Con; curro.*
Concrete. *Con; cresco.*
Concur. *Con; curro.*
Concussion. *Con; cutio.*
Condemn. *Con; damnum.*
Condense. *Con; densus.* [*do*
Condescend, condescension. *Con; de; scan-*
Condign. *Con; dignus.*
Condition. *Con; do.*
Condole. *Con; doleo.*
Conduce, conduct, conduit. *Con; duco.*
Confection. *Con; facio.*
Confederacy, confederate. *Con; fedus.*
Confer. *Con; fero.*

Confess. *Con; fessum.*
Confide. *Con; fides.*
Confine. *Con; finis.*
Confirm. *Con; firmus.*
Confiscate. *Con; fiscus.*
Conflagration. *Con; flagro*
Conflict. *Con; fligo.*
Confluence. *Con; fluo.*
Conform. *Con; forma.*
Confound. *Con; fundo.*
Confraternity. *Con; frater.*
Confront. *Con; frons.*
Confuse. *Con; fundo.*
Congenial. *Con; genus.*
Congestion. *Con; gero.*
Congratulate. *Con; gratia.*
Congregate, congregation. *Con; grex.*
Congress. *Con; gradior.*
Congruity. *Con; grus.*
Conic. *Conos.*
Conjecture. *Con; jacio.*
Conjoin. *Con; jungo.*
Conjugal, conjugate. *Con; jugum.*
Conjūre. *Con; juro.*
Connect, connection. *Con; necto.*
Connubial. *Con; nubo.*
Conoid. *Conos; oidos.*
Conquer, conquest. *Con; quæro.*
Consanguinity. *Con; sanguis.*
Conscience, conscientious, conscious. *Con; scio.*
Conscript. *Con; scribo.*
Consecrate. *Con; sacer.*
Consecutive. *Con; sequor.*
Consent. *Con; sentio.*
Consequent, consequential. *Con; sequor.*
Consider. *Con; sedeo,* or *sidus.*
Consignment. *Con; signum.*
Consist. *Con; sisto.*
Console. *Con; solor.*
Consonance. *Con; sonus.*
Consort. *Con; sors.*
Conspicuous. *Con; specio.*
Conspiracy, conspirator, conspire. *Con spiro.*
Constable, constant. *Con; sto.*
Constantinople. (*Constantine*); *polis.*
Constellation. *Con; stella.*
Consternation. *Con; sterno.*
Constitute, constitution. *Con; sto.*
Constrain, constriction. *Con, stringo.*
Construct, construe. *Con; struo.*
Consul, consulate, consult. *Con; salio.*
Consume. *Con; sumo.*
Consummate. *Con; summa.*
Consumption. *Con; sumo.*
Contact, contagion. *Con; tango.*
Contain. *Con; teneo.*
Contemn. *Con; temno.*
Contemporaneous, contemporary. *Con; tempus.*
Contempt. *Con; temno.*
Contend. *Con; tendo.*
Contention. *Con; tendo.*
Contest. *Con; testis.*
Context. *Con; textus.*
Contiguity. *Con; tango.*
Contingent. *Con; tango.*
Continual, continue. *Con; teneo.*
Contort. *Con; tortum.*
Contract. *Con; traho.*
Contradict. *Contra; dico.*
Contrary. *Contra.*
Contrast. *Contra; sto.*
Contribute. *Con, tributum.*
Contrite. *Con; tero.*
Contrivance, contrive. *Con; trouver.*
Controverse, controvert. *Contra; verto.*
Contumacious, contumely. *Con; tumeo.*
Contund, contusion. *Con; tundo.*
Convalescent. *Con; valeo.*
Convene, convenient, convent, convention. *Con; venio.*
Converge. *Con; vergo.*
Converse. *Con; verto.*
Convey, conveyance. *Con; veho.*
Convict, convince. *Con; vinco.*
Convivial. *Con; vivo.*
Convocation, convoke. *Con; voco.*
Convoy. *Con; via.*
Convulse. *Con; vello.*
Cook. *Coquo.*
Co-operate. *Co; opera.*
Co-ordinate. *Co; ordo.*
Co-partner. *Co; pars.*
Copious. *Copia.*
Copula, copulate. *Copula.*
Cordial, core. *Cor.*
Coriaceous. *Corium.*
Cornea, cornet. *Cornu.*
Cornigerous. *Cornu; gero.*
Cornu-copiæ. *Cornu; copia.*
Coronet. *Corona.*
Corporal, corporeal. *Corpus.*
Corps, corpulence. *Corpus.*
Correct. *Cor; rego.*
Corroborate. *Cor; robur.*
Corrode, corrosion. *Cor; rodo.*
Corrupt, corruption. *Cor; ruptum.*
Cosmetic, cosmical. *Cosmos.*
Cosmography. *Cosmos; grapho.*
Cosmopolite. *Cosmos; polis.*
Counsel. *Con; salio.*
Count. *Con; puto.*
Count. *Comes.*
Countenance. *Con; teneo.*
Counter. *Contra.*
Counteract. *Counter; ago*
Counterfeit. *Counter; facio.*
Countermand. *Counter; mando.*
Couple. *Copula.*
Courage. *Cor.*
Courier, course. *Curro.*
Covet. *Cupio.*
Craniology. *Cranium; logos.*
Create, creature. *Creo.*
Credence, credible, credit, credulity, credulous, creed. *Credo.*
Crescent. *Cresco.*
Crevice. *Crepo.*
Crime, criminal. *Crimen.*
Crisis, criterion, critic, criticise. *Crites.*
Crosier, cross. *Crux.*
Crown. *Corona.*
Crucible. *Crux.*
Crucifix. *Crux; fixus.*
Crucify. *Crux.*
Crust. *Crusta.*
Cryptogamy. *Crypto; gameo.*
Crystal, crystallize. *Crystallus.*
Cub. *Cubo.*
Culinary. *Culina.*
Culpable. *Culpa.*
Cultivate, culture. *Colo.*
Cumulative. *Cumulo.*
Cuneal. *Cuneus.*
Cuneiform. *Cuneus; forma.*
Cupidity. *Cupio.*
Curacy, curate, cure, curious. *Cura*
Current. *Curro.*
Currier. *Corium*
Cursory. *Curro.*
Curvature, curve. *Curvus.*
Curvilinear. *Curvus; linea.*

Custom. *Coutume.*
Cutaneous, cuticle. *Cutis.*
Cycle. *Cyclus.*
Cyclopedia. *Cyclus; pedia.*
Cylinder, cylindrical. *Cylindros.*
Cynic. *Cyon.*
Cynosure. *Cyon;* (*oura*, the tail).

D.

Damn. *Damnum.*
Date. *Do.*
Deacon. *Dia; coneo.*
Dean. *Deca.*
Debauch, debauchee. *De; Bacchus.*
Debilitate, debility. *Debilis.*
Debt, debtor. *Debitus.*
Decade. *Deca.*
Decagon. *Deca; gonia.*
Decalogue. *Deca; logos.*
Decamp. *De; campus.*
Decant. *De; cano.*
Decapitate. *De; caput.*
Decay. *De; cado.*
Decease. *De; cedo.*
Deceit, deceive. *De; capio.*
December. *Deca.*
Decent. *Decens.*
Deception. *De; capio.*
Decide, deciduous. *De; cædo.*
Decimal, decimate. *Deca.*
Decision, decisive. *De; cædo.*
Declaim. *De; clamo.*
Declare. *De; clarus.*
Declension, decline. *De; clino.*
Declivity. *De; clivus.*
Decoction. *De; coquo.*
Decompose. *De; com; pono.*
Decoration. *Decor.*
Decorum. *Decor.*
Decrease. *De; cresco.*
Decree. *De; cerno.*
Decrepit. *De; crepo*
Decretal. *De; cerno.*
Decurion. *Deca.*
Dedicate. *De; dico.*
Deduce, deduction. *De; duco.*
Deface. *De; facio.*
Defalcation. *De; falcatus.*
Defame. *De; fama.*
Defeat. *De; facio.*
Defect. *De; facio.*
Defend, defense. *De; fendo.*
Defer, deference. *De; fero.*
Deficient, deficit. *De; facio.*
Define, definite. *De; finis.*
Deform. *De; forma.*
Defraud. *De; fraus.*
Defunct. *De; functus.*
Defy. *De; fides.*
Degeneracy, degenerate. *De; genus.*
Deglutition. *De; glutio.*
Degradation, degrade, degree. *De; gradior.*
Deity. *Deus.*
Deign. *Dignus.*
Deist. *Deus.*
Dejection. *De; jacio*
Delegate. *De; lego.*
Deleterious. *De; leo.*
Delicacy, delicate, delicious. *Deliciæ.*
Delineate. *De; linea.*
Delinquent. *De; linquo.*
Deliver. *De; livrer.*
Delude. *De; ludo.*
Deluge. *Diluvium.*
Delusive. *De; ludo.*
Demagogue. *Demos; agogeus.*
Demand. *De; mando.*
Demerit. *De; meritum.*
Demise. *De; mitto.*
Democracy, democrat. *Demos; cratos.*
Demolish, demolition. *De; molior.*
Demon. *Demon.*
Demonology. *Demon; logos.*
Demonstrate. *De; monstro.*
Demoralize. *De; mos.*
Denomination. *De; nomen.*
Denote. *De; nota.*
Denounce. *De; nuncio.*
Dense. *Densus.*
Dental, denticulated. *Dens.*
Dentifrice. *Dens; frico.*
Denude. *De; nudus.*
Denunciation. *De; nuncio.*
Deny. *De; nego.*
Depart, departure. *De; pars.*
Depend, dependence. *De; pendeo.*
Depict. *De; pingo.*
Deplorable, deplore. *De; ploro.*
Deponent. *De; pono.*
Depopulate. *De; populus.*
Deportment. *De; porto.*
Depose, deposit, depot. *De; pono.*
Deprave, depravity. *De; pravus*
Deprecate. *De; precor.*
Depression. *De; premo.*
Deprive. *De; privus.*
Derange. *De; rang.*
Dereliction. *De; re; linquo.*
Deride, derision. *De; rideo.*
Derive. *De; rivus.*
Derogate. *De; rogo.*
Descant. *De; cano.*
Descend, descent. *De; scando.*
Describe. *De; scribo.*
Desecration. *De; sacer.*
Desert. *De; sertum.*
Deserve *De; servio.*
Desideratum. *De; sidus.*
Design, designate. *De; signum.*
Desire. *De; sidus.*
Desist. *De; sisto.*
Desolate. *De; solus.*
Despair, desperado, desperate. *De; spero*
Despicable, despise, despite. *De; specio.*
Despoil. *De; spolium.*
Despond, despondent. *De; spondeo.*
Despot, despotism. *Despotes.*
Destination, destine. *De; stino.*
Destitution. *De; sto.*
Destroy, destruction. *De; struo.*
Desultory. *De; salio.*
Detail. *De; tailler.*
Detain. *De; teneo.*
Detention. *De; teneo.*
Deter. *De; terreo*
Deterioration, deteriorate. *Deterior.*
Determine. *De; terminus.*
Detestation. *De; testis.*
Dethrone. *De; thronus.*
Detract. *De; traho.*
Detriment, detritus. *De; tero.*
Deuteronomy. *Deuteros; nomos.*
Devastate, devastation. *De; vastus.*
Development. *De; velo.*
Deviate. *De; via.*
Device. *De; viduo.*
Devoid. *De; viduo.*
Devote, devotion. *De; votum.*
Devour. *De; voro.*
Dexterity. *Dexter.*
Diaconal. *Dia; coneo.*
Diagonal. *Dia; gonia.*

Diagram. *Dia ; grapho.*
Dialect. *Dia ; lego.*
Dialogue. *Dia ; logos.*
Diameter, diametrical. *Dia ; metrum.*
Diamond. *A ; damao.*
Diarrhea. *Dia ; rheo.*
Diary. *Dies.*
Diastole. *Dia ; stello.*
Dictate, diction, dictionary. *Dico.*
Didactic. *Didasco.*
Differ. *Dif ; fero.*
Difficult. *Dif ; facilis.*
Diffident. *Dif ; fides.*
Diffuse. *Dif ; fundo.*
Digest. *Di ; gero.*
Dignify, dignity. *Dignus.*
Digress. *Di ; gradior.*
Dilapidation. *Di ; lapis.*
Dilate, dilatation. *Di ; latus.*
Dilatory. *Di ; latum.*
Dilemma. *Dis ; lepsis.*
Diligent. *Di ; lego.*
Diluent, dilute. *Di ; luo.*
Dimension. *Di ; mensura.*
Diocese, diocesan. *Dia ; eceo.*
Dioptrics. *Dia ; opto.*
Diorama. *Dia ; orama.*
Diphtnong. *Dis ; phthegma.*
Diploma, diplomacy, diplomatic. *Diploma.*
Dire. *Deus ; ira.*
Direct *Di ; rego.*
Disable. *Dis ; habeo.*
Disadvantage. *Dis ; ad ; avant.*
Disaffection. *Dis ; af ; facio.*
Disagreeable. *Dis ; a ; gratia.*
Disappearance. *Dis ; ap ; pareo.*
Disapprove. *Dis ; ap ; probo.*
Disarm. *Dis ; arma.*
Discern. *Dis ; cerno.*
Disciple, discipline. *Discipulus.*
Disclaim. *Dis ; clamo.*
Disclose. *Dis ; claudo.*
Discolor. *Dis ; color.*
Discommode. *Dis ; commodus.*
Discompose. *Dis ; com ; pono.*
Disconsolate. *Dis ; con ; solor.*
Discontented, discontinuance. *Dis ; con ; [teneo.*
Discord. *Dis ; cor.*
Discourage. *Dis ; cor.*
Discourse. *Dis ; curro.*
Discredit. *Dis ; credo.*
Discrepancy. *Dis ; crepo.*
Discretion, discriminate. *Dis ; cerno.*
Discuss. *Dis ; cutio.*
Disdain. *Dis ; dignus.*
Disease. *Dis ; otium.*
Disfigure. *Dis ; figura.*
Disgrace. *Dis ; gratia.*
Dishonest, dishonor. *Dis ; honor.*
Disinter. *Dis ; in ; terra.*
Disinterested. *Dis ; inter ; ens.*
Disjoin. *Dis ; jungo.*
Dislocation. *Dis ; locus.*
Disloyalty. *Dis ; loy.*
Dismal. *Dies ; male.*
Dismission. *Dis ; mitto.*
Dismount. *Dis ; mons.*
Disobey. *Dis ; ob ; audio.*
Disoblige. *Dis ; ob ; ligo.*
Disorder. *Dis ; ordo.*
Disparage, disparity. *Dis ; par.*
Dispel. *Dis ; pello.*
Dispensary, dispensation, dispense. *Dis ; [pendo.*
Disperse. *Di ; spargo.*
Dispirit. *Di ; spiro.*
Displant. *Dis ; planta.*
Display. *Dis ; plico.*
Displease. *Dis ; placeo.*
Disposal, disposition. *Dis ; pono.*
Dispossess. *Dis ; posse.*
Disprove. *Dis ; probo.*
Disqualification. *Dis ; qualis ; facio.*
Disqualify. *Dis ; qualis.*
Disquiet. *Dis ; quies.*
Disrespect. *Dis ; re ; specio.*
Dissect, dissection. *Dis ; seco.*
Dissemble. *Dis ; similis.*
Dissemination. *Dis ; semen.*
Dissension, dissent. *Dis ; sentio.*
Dissertation. *Dis ; sertum.*
Dissever. *Dis ; se ; paro.*
Dissimilar, dissimulation. *Dis ; similis*
Dissolute, dissolve. *Dis ; solvo.*
Dissonant. *Dis ; sonus.*
Dissuade, dissuasion. *Dis ; suadeo*
Dissyllable. *Dis ; syl ; labo.*
Distant. *Di ; sto.*
Distemper. *Dis ; tempero.*
Distend. *Dis ; tendo.*
Distich. *Dis ; stichos.*
Distil, distillery. *Di ; stilla.*
Distinct, distinguish. *Di ; stinguo.*
Distortion. *Dis ; tortum.*
Distract. *Dis ; traho.*
Distribution. *Dis ; tributum.*
Disturb. *Dis ; turba.*
Disuse. *Dis ; utor.*
Diurnal. *Dies.*
Divergent. *Di ; vergo.*
Diversify, diversity, divert. *Di ; verto*
Divest. *Di ; vestis.*
Divide, dividend. *Di ; viduo.*
Divine, divinity. *Divus.*
Division. *Di ; viduo.*
Divulge. *Di ; vulgus.*
Docile, docility. *Doceo.*
Doctor, doctrine, document. *Doceo.*
Dogma, dogmatist. *Dogma.*
Doleful. *Doleo.*
Dolor. *Doleo ; facio.*
Domain. *Dominus.*
Domestic, domicile. *Domus.*
Domineer, dominion, don. *Dominus.*
Donation, donative, donee, donor. *Do*
Dormant, dormitory. *Dormio.*
Dorsal. *Dorsum.*
Dotal. *Dos.*
Double. *Duo ; plico.*
Doubt. *Dubius.*
Doxology. *Doxa ; logos.*
Drama, dramatics, dramatist. *Drama*
Dromedary. *Dromos.*
Dropsy. *Hydor ; opto.*
Druid, dryad. *Drus.*
Dubious. *Dubius.*
Ducal, ducat, duct, ductile. *Duco.*
Duel, duet. *Duo.*
Duke. *Duco.*
Dulcet. *Dulcis.*
Dulcify. *Dulcis.*
Duodecimo. *Duo ; deca.*
Duplicate, duplicity. *Duo ; plico.*
Durable, duration. *Durus.*
Dynamics, dynasty. *Dynastia.*
Dysentery. *Dys ; enteron.*
Dyspepsy. *Dys ; peptos.*

E.

Ease. *Otium.*
Eclipse. *Ec ; lipo.*
Economical, economy. *Eceo ; nomos.*

Ecstasy, ecstatic. *Ec; sto.*
Edible. *Edo.*
Edifice. *Edes; facio.*
Edify. *Edes.*
Edit. *E; do.*
Educate, educe. *E; duco*
Efface. *Ef; facies.*
Effect. *Ef; facio.*
Efflux. *Ef; fluo.*
Effort. *Ef; fortis.*
Effrontery. *Ef; frons.*
Effusion. *Ef; fundo.*
Egotist. *Ego.*
Egregious. *E; grex.*
Egress. *E; gradior.*
Ejaculate, eject. *E; jacio.*
Elaborate. *E; labor.*
Elapse. *E; labor.*
Elated. *E; latum.*
Election, electorate. *E; lego.*
Electric, electricity. *Electrum.*
Electrify. *Electrum.*
Elegance. *Elegans.*
Elegiac. *Elegia.*
Elegy. *Elegia.*
Elevate. *E; levo.*
Elicit. *E; licio.*
Eligible. *E; lego.*
Eliminate. *E; limen.*
Elision. *E; lido.*
Ellipsis, elliptical. *El; lipo.*
Elocution. *E; loquor.*
Eloge. *E; logos.*
Elongation. *E; longus.*
Eloquent. *E; loquor.*
Elucidate. *E; luceo.*
Elude. *E; ludo.*
Elysium. *Elysium.*
Emaciate. *E; maceo.*
Emaculate. *E; macula.*
Emancipate. *E; manus; capio.*
Embarrass. *Em; barre.*
Embellish. *Em; beau.*
Emerge, emergency. *E; mergo.*
Emetic. *Emeo.*
Emigrate, emigrant. *E; migro.*
Eminent. *E; mineo.*
Emissary, emission, emit. *E; mitto.*
Emollient. *E; mollis.*
Emotion. *E; moveo.*
Emperor. *Em; paro:* or *Impero.*
Emphasis, emphatic. *Em; phano.*
Empire. *Em; paro:* or *Impero.*
Empiric, empiricism. *Em; pirates.*
Emporium. *Em; poros.*
Empyrean. *Em; pyr.*
Emulate, emulous. *Emulus.*
Enable. *En; habeo.*
Enact. *En; ago.*
Enamor. *En; amo.*
Encamp. *En; campus.*
Enchant. *En; cano.*
Encircle. *En; circulus.*
Enclose. *En; claudo.*
Encomium. *En; comos.*
Encompass. *En; com; passus.*
Encourage. *En; cor.*
Encumber. *En; cubo.*
Encyclical. *En; cyclus.*
Encyclopedia. *En; cyclus; pedia.*
Endemic. *En; demos.*
Endite. *En; dico.*
Endorse. *En; dorsum.*
Endow. *En; dos.*
Endure. *En; durus.*
Energy. *En; ergon.*
Enervate. *E; neuron*
Enforce. *En; fortis.*
Enfranchise. *En; franc.*
Engender. *En; genus.*
Engrave. *En; grapho.*
Enigma, enigmatic. *Enigma.*
Enjoin. *En; jungo.*
Enlarge. *En; largus.*
Enmity. *In; amicus.*
Enormous. *E; norma.*
Enrapture, enravish. *En; rapio.*
Ensiform. *Ensis; forma.*
Ensue. *En; sequor.*
Entail. *En; tailler.*
Enterprise. *Inter; prehendo.*
Entertain. *Inter; teneo.*
Enthrone. *En; thronus.*
Enthusiasm. *En; theos.*
Entire. *In; tango.*
Entitle. *In; titulus.*
Entomb. *En; tumeo.*
Entomology. *Entomon; logos.*
Enumerate. *E; numerus.*
Enunciate. *E; nuncio.*
Envelope. *En; velo.*
Envenom. *En; venenum.*
Envoy. *En; via.*
Envy. *In; video.*
Ephemeral, ephemeris. *Epi; hemera.*
Epic. *Epos.*
Epicure, epicurism. *Epicurus.*
Epidemic. *Epi; demos.*
Epiglottis. *Epi; glossa.*
Epigram, epigrammatic. *Epi; grapho.*
Epilepsy, epileptic. *Epi; lepsis.*
Epilogue. *Epi; logos.*
Epiphysis. *Epi; physis.*
Episcopacy. *Epi; scopeo.*
Episode. *Epi; odos.*
Epistle. *Epi; stello.*
Epitaph. *Epi; taphos.*
Epithet. *Epi; thesis.*
Epitome. *Epi; tomos.*
Epoch. *Epi; exis.*
Equable, equal, equalize. *Equus.*
Equanimity. *Equus; animus.*
Equator. *Equus.*
Equery, equestrian. *Eques.*
Equidistant. *Equus; di; sto.*
Equilateral. *Equus; latus.*
Equilibrate, equilibrium. *Equus; libra.*
Equinox. *Equus; nox.*
Equip. *Eques.*
Equity. *Equus.*
Equivalent. *Equus; valeo.*
Equivocal, equivocate. *Equus; vox.*
Eradiate. *E; radius.*
Eradicate. *E; radix.*
Erase. *E; rado.*
Erect. *E; rego.*
Eremite. *Eremos.*
Err, erroneous, error. *Error.*
Erudition. *E; rudis.*
Eruptive. *E; ruptum.*
Escalade. *E; scala.*
Especial. *Specio.*
Espouse. *E; spondeo.*
Essence. *Ens.*
Establish. *E; sto.*
Eternize. *Eternus.*
Ether, ethereal. *Ether.*
Ethical, ethics, ethnical. *Ethnos.*
Ethnography. *Ethnos; grapho.*
Etymology. *Etymon; logos.*
Eulogium, eulogize. *Eu; logos.*
Eupeptic. *Eu; peptos.*
Euphony. *Eu; phone.*
Evacuate. *E; vaco.*

Evade. *E; vado.*
Evanescent. *E; vanus.*
Evaporate. *E; vapor.*
Eventual, eventuate. *E; venio.*
Evident. *E; video.*
Evince. *E; vinco.*
Eviscerate. *E; viscus.*
Evoke. *E; voco.*
Evolution. *E; volvo.*
Exacerbate. *Ex; acerbus.*
Exact. *Ex; ago.*
Exaggerate. *Ex; agger.*
Exalt *Ex; altus.*
Example. *Exemplum.*
Exanimate. *Ex; anima.*
Exasperate. *Ex; asper.*
Excandescence. *Ex; candeo.*
Excavate. *Ex; cavus.*
Exceed. *Ex; cedo.*
Excel, excellence. *Ex; celsus.*
Except. *Ex; capio.*
Excess. *Ex; cedo.*
Excise. *Ex; cædo.*
Excite. *Ex; cito.*
Exclaim, exclamation. *Ex; clamo.*
Exclude, exclusion. *Ex; claudo.*
Excommunicate. *Ex; com; munus.*
Excrescence. *Ex; cresco.*
Excruciate. *Ex; crux.*
Exculpate. *Ex; culpa.*
Excursion. *Ex; curro.*
Excuse. *Ex; causa.*
Execrable, execrate. *Ex; sacer.*
Execute. *Ex; sequor.*
Exemplar. *Exemplum.*
Exemplify. *Exemplum.*
Exempt. *Ex; emo.*
Exhale, exhalation. *Ex; halo.*
Exhibit. *Ex; habeo.*
Exhilarate. *Ex; hilaris.*
Exhort. *Ex; hortor.*
Exist. *Ex; sisto.*
Exonerate. *Ex; onus.*
Exorbitant. *Ex; orbis.*
Expand, expansion. *Ex; pando.*
Expatiate. *Ex; spatium.*
Expatriate. *Ex; pater.*
Expect. *Ex; specio.*
Expectorate. *Ex; pectus.*
Expedient, expedite, expeditious. *Ex; pes.*
Expel. *Ex; pello.*
Expend, expenditure, expense. *Ex; pendo.*
Experience,experiment,expert. *Ex; perior.*
Expiate, expiatory. *Ex; pio.*
Expire. *Ex; spiro.*
Explain, explanation. *Ex; planus.*
Expletive. *Ex; pleo.*
Explicit. *Ex; plico.*
Explode. *Ex; plaudo.*
Explore. *Ex; ploro.*
Explosion. *Ex; plaudo.*
Export. *Ex; porto.*
Expose, expositor. *Ex; pono.*
Exposure, expound. *Ex; pono.*
Express, expressive. *Ex; premo.*
Expulsion. *Ex; pello.*
Exquisite. *Ex; quæro.*
Extant. *Ex; sto.*
Extempore. *Ex; tempus.*
Extend, extensive, extent. *Ex; tendo.*
Exterior. *Exterus.*
Exterminate. *Ex; terminus.*
External. *Exterus.*
Extinct, extinguish. *Ex; stinguo.*
Extirpate, extirpation. *Ex; stirps.*
Extol. *Ex; tollo.*
Extortion. *Ex; tortum.*
Extraneous. *Exterus.*
Extraordinary. *Extra; ordo.*
Extravagant. *Extra; vagus.*
Extreme. *Exterus.*
Extrinsic. *Exterus.*
Exuberant. *Ex; uber.*
Exude. *Ex; udo*
Exult. *Ex; salio.*

F.

Fable. *Fabula.*
Fabric, fabricate. *Fabrico.*
Fabulous. *Fabula.*
Face. *Facies.*
Facilitate, facility. *Facilis.*
Fact, faction, factory. *Facio.*
Fair. *Forum.*
Falchion, falcon. *Falcatus.*
Fallacy, fallible, false. *Fallo*
Falsify, falsity. *Fallo.*
Fame, famous. *Fama.*
Familiar, family. *Familia.*
Famine, famish. *Fames.*
Fanatic. *Fanum.*
Fancy. *Fantasia.*
Fane. *Fanum.*
Fantastic. *Fantasia.*
Fashion. *Facies.*
Fatigue. *Fatigo.*
Feat. *Facio.*
Feature. *Facies.*
Federal. *Fedus.*
Feign. *Fingo.*
Felicitate, felicity. *Felix.*
Feminine. *Femina.*
Fencing, fender. *Fendo.*
Ferocity. *Fera.*
Ferry, fertile. *Fero.*
Fervent, fervid, fervor. *Ferveo.*
Festal, festivity. *Festum.*
Fibrile, fibrous. *Fibra.*
Fiction, fictitious. *Fingo.*
Fidelity. *Fides.*
Fierce. *Fera.*
Figure. *Figura.*
Filament. *Filum.*
Filial. *Filius.*
Filter. *Filum.*
Final. *Finis.*
Finance, financial. *Finance.*
Finish. *Finis.*
Firmament. *Firmus.*
Fiscal. *Fiscus.*
Fixture. *Fixus.*
Flagrant. *Flagro.*
Flambeau, *Flamma; beau.*
Flatulent. *Flatus.*
Flexure, flexible. *Flecto.*
Flora, floral, florid. *Flos.*
Floriferous. *Flos; fero.*
Florist, flower. *Flos.*
Fluctuate, fluctuation. *Fluctuo.*
Fluency, fluid, fluor, fluviatic, flux, fluxil. ty. *Fluo.*
Focal, focus. *Focus*
Foil, foliaceous, foliage, folio. *Folium.*
Font. *Fons.*
Forage. *Foris.*
Force. *Fortis.*
Foreign. *Foris.*
Forensic. *Forum.*
Forfeit. *Foris; facio.*
Form. *Forma.*
Fort. *Fortis.*

Fortify, fortress. *Fortis.*
Fortune. *Fors.*
Found, foundation, foundery, foundling. *Fundus.*
Fountain. *Fons.*
Fraction, fracture, fragile. *Frango*
Frail, frailty. *Frango.*
Franchise. *Franc.*
Frank. *Franc.*
Franklin. *Franc.*
Fraternal. *Frater.*
Fratricide. *Frater; cædo.*
Fraud, fraudulence. *Fraus.*
Frequent. *Frequens.*
Friction. *Frico.*
Frigid. *Frigus.*
Frivolity, frivolous. *Frivolus.*
Front, frontal. *Frons.*
Frugal. *Fruges.*
Frugiferous. *Fruges; fero.*
Frumentaceous. *Frumentum.*
Fructify, fruit, fruition. *Fructus.*
Frustrate. *Frustra.*
Fugitive. *Fugio.*
Fume. *Fumus.*
Funambulist. *Funis; ambulo.*
Fundamental. *Fundus.*
Funeral, funereal. *Funus.*
Funicular. *Funis.*
Furious. *Furia.*
Furtive. *Fur.*
Fury. *Furia.*
Futile, futility. *Futilis.*

G.

Gala. *Gala.*
Gallant. *Gala.*
Gallic, gallicism. *Gallica.*
Garrulity, garrulous. *Garrio.*
Gasometer. (*Gas*); *metrum.*
Gastric. *Gaster.*
Gastriloquy. *Gaster; loquor.*
Gelatine, gelid. *Gelu.*
Gender. *Genus.*
Genealogy. *Genea; logos.*
General, generate, generosity, generous. *Genus.*
Genesis. *Genea.*
Genial. *Genus.*
Genius, genteel, gentile, gentility, gentry. *Genus.*
Genuine. *Genus.*
Geocentric. *Ge; centrum.*
Geography. *Ge; grapho.*
Geology. *Ge; logos.*
Geomancy. *Ge; mancia.*
Geometrician, geometry. *Ge; metrum.*
Geoponics. *Ge; ponos.*
Gesticulate, gesture. *Gero.*
Giant. *Gigas.*
Gigantic. *Gigas.*
Glacial, glaciers. *Glacies.*
Gladiator, gladiatorial. *Gladius.*
Gland. *Glans.*
Glandiferous. *Glans; forma.*
Glandule. *Glans.*
Globe, globule. *Globus.*
Glorify, glory. *Gloria.*
Glossary. *Glossa.*
Glossy. *Glossa.*
Glue. *Gluten.*
Glutinous. *Gluten.*
Gnome. *Gnomon.*
Gnomon. *Gnomon.*
Gracious. *Gratia.*
Govern. *Guberno.*
Grace. *Gratia.* [dior.
Gradation, grade, gradual, graduate. *Gra-*
Grain. *Granum.*
Graminivorous. *Gramen; voro.*
Grammar. *Grapho.*
Granary. *Granum.*
Grand, grandeur. *Grandis.*
Granite. *Granum.*
Granulate, granule. *Granum.*
Graphic. *Grapho.*
Grateful. *Gratia.*
Gratification. *Gratia; facio.*
Gratify, gratis, gratitude, gratuitous, gratuity. *Gratia.*
Grave, gravity. *Grapho.*
Gregarious. *Grex.*
Grenadier. *Granum.*
Grief, grievance. *Gravis.*
Guarantee. *Guarantir.*
Guard, guardian. *Guarder.*
Gubernatorial. *Guberno.*
Gusto. *Gustus.*
Guttural. *Guttur.*
Gymnastic, gymnasium. *Gymnos.*
Gymnosophist. *Gymnos; sophia.*
Gymnospermous. *Gymnos; sperma.*
Gyration, gyre. *Gyrus.*
Gyromancy. *Gyrus; mancia.*

H.

Habit, habitation, habituate. *Habeo*
Harmony, harmonic. *Harmonia.*
Heir. *Hæres.*
Heliotrope. *Helios; tropos.*
Hellenic, hellenism, hellenist. *Hellen.*
Hemicycle. *Hemisus; cyclus.*
Hemisphere. *Hemisus; sphæra.*
Hemoptysis. *Hema; ptyo.*
Hemorrhage. *Hema; rheo.*
Heptagon. *Hepta; gonia.*
Heptarchy. *Hepta; arche.*
Herbage. *Herba.*
Hereditary. *Hæres.*
Heresy, heretic. *Heresis.*
Heritable, heritage. *Hæres.*
Hero. *Heros.*
Heroicomic. *Heros; comos.*
Heroism. *Heros.*
Hesitancy, hesitate. *Hæreo.*
Heterodox, heterodoxy. *Heteros; doxa.*
Heterogenous. *Heteros; genea.*
Hexagon. *Hex; gonia.*
Hexameter. *Hex; metrum.*
Hexangular. *Hex; angulus.*
Hierarchy. *Hieros; arche.*
Hieroglyph, hieroglyphic. *Hieros; glypho*
Hilarity. *Hilaris.*
Hippocentaur. *Hippos*; (*centeo*, to spur;) *taurus.*
Hippodrome. *Hippos; dromos.* [bird.)
Hippogriff. *Hippos*; (*gryps*, a fabulous
Hippopotamus. *Hippos; potamos.*
Historian, historic. *Historia.*
History. *Historia.*
Homicidal, homicide. *Homo; cædo.*
Homogeneous. *Homos; genea.*
Homologous. *Homos; logos.*
Honesty, honorary. *Honor.*
Horizon. *Horos.*
Horologe. *Hora; logos.*
Horoscope. *Hora; scopeo.*
Horrible, horrid. *Horreo.*

Horrific. *Horreo; facio.*
Horror. *Horreo.*
Horticulture. *Hortus; cultus.*
Hospitable, hospital, host. *Hospes.*
Host. *Hostis.*
Hostility. *Hostis.*
Hotel. *Hospes.*
Human, humanize. *Homo.*
Humble. *Humus.*
Humid. *Humeo.*
Humiliate, humility. *Humus.*
Humor. *Humeo.*
Hydraulics. *Hydor; aulos.*
Hydrocele. *Hydor; cele.*
Hydrocephalus. *Hydor; cephale.*
Hydrogen. *Hydor; genea.*
Hydrophobia. *Hydor; phobos.*
Hydrostatics. *Hydor; stasis.*
Hypocrisy, hypocrite. *Hypo; crites.*

I.

Idea, idealize. *Idea.*
Identical. *Idem.*
Identify, identity. *Idem.*
Idiocy, idiom, idiomatical. *Idios.*
Idiopathy. *Idios; pathos.*
Idiosyncrasy. *Idios; syn;* (*crasis*, temperament.
Idol. *Idolum.*
Idolater, idolatry. *Idolum; latria.*
Igneus. *Ignis.*
Ignite. *Ignis.*
Ignoble. *Ig; nosco.*
Ignominy. *Ig; nomen.*
Illegal. *Il; lex.*
Illegitimate. *Il; lex.*
Illicit. *Il; liceo.*
Illimitable. *Il; limes.*
Illiterate. *Il; litera.*
Illogical. *Il; logos.*
Illumination. *Il; lumen.*
Illusion. *Il; ludo.*
Illustrate, illustrious. *Il; lustrum.*
Image, imagine. *Imago.*
Imbecile, imbecility. *Imbecillis.*
Imitate. *Imitor.*
Immaculate. *Im; macula.*
Immaterial. *Im; materia.*
Immature. *Im; maturus.*
Immediate. *Im; medius.*
Immemorial. *Im; memor.*
Immense, immensity. *Im; mensura.*
Immerse. *Im; mergo.*
Immigration, immigrant. *Im; migro.*
Imminent. *Im; mineo.*
Immoderate, immodest. *Im; modus.*
Immoral. *Im; mos.*
Immortal, immortalize. *Im; mors.*
Immovable. *Im; moveo.*
Immunity. *Im; munus.*
Immure. *Im; murus.*
Immutable. *Im; muto.*
Impannel. *Im; pannus.*
Impart, impartial. *Im; pars.*
Impassioned, impatient. *Im; patior.*
Impede, impediment. *Im; pes.*
Impel. *Im; pello.*
Impend. *Im; pendeo.*
Impenitent. *Im; peniteo*
Imperative. *Impero*: or *Im*; *paro.*
Imperceptible. *Im; per; capio.*
Imperfect. *Im; per; facio.*
Imperial, imperious. *Impero*: or *Im*; *paro.*
Imperishable. *Im; per; eo.*
Impersonal. *Im; persona.*
Impertinence. *Im; per; teneo.*
Impervious. *Im; per; via.*
Impetus, impetuous. *Im; peto.*
Impiety. *Im; pius.*
Impious. *Im; pius.*
Implacable. *Im; placo.*
Implant. *Im; planta.*
Implement. *Im; pleo.*
Implicit. *Im; plico.*
Implore. *Im; ploro.*
Imply. *Im; plico.*
Impolicy, impolite. *Im; polis.*
Imponderable. *Im; pondus.*
Importer, important, importune. *Im; porto*
Impose, imposition. *Im; pono.*
Impossible. *Im; posse.*
Impost, impostor. *Im; pono.*
Impotence. *Im; posse.*
Impoverish. *Im; pauper.*
Impracticable. *Im; practos.*
Imprecate. *Im; precor.*
Impress, impression. *Im; premo.*
Imprint. *Im; premo.*
Imprison. *Im; prehendo.*
Improper. *Im; proprius.*
Impropriety. *Im; proprius.*
Improve, improvement. *Im; probo.*
Imprudence. *Im; pro; video.*
Impulse, impulsive. *Im; pello.*
Inaccessible. *In; ac; cedo.*
Inaccurate. *In; ac; cura.*
Inaction. *In; ago.*
Inadequacy. *In; ad; equus.*
Inadmissible. *In; ad; mitto.*
Inadvertent. *In; ad; verto.*
Inalienable. *In; alius.*
Inanimate. *In; anima.*
Inapplicable. *In; ap; plico.*
Inaptitude. *In; aptus.*
Inarable. *In; aro.*
Inarticulate. *In; articulus.*
Inartificial. *In; ars; facio.*
Inaudible. *In; audio.*
Inaugurate. *In; augur.*
Incalculable. *In; calculus.*
Incalescence. *In; caleo.*
Incantation. *In; cano.*
Incapable, incapacity. *In; capio.*
Incarcerate. *In; carcer.*
Incarnate. *In; caro.*
Incautious. *In; cautio.*
Incendiary, incense, incentive. *In; candeo.*
Incessant. *In; cedo.*
Incident. *In; cado.*
Incised, incision. *In; cædo.*
Incite. *In; cito.*
Inclement. *In; clemens.*
Incline. *In; clino.*
Inclosure, include. *In; claudo.*
Incogitative. *In; co; agito.*
Incoherent. *In; co; hæreo.*
Incombustible. *In; com; ustum.*
Incompetent. *In; com; peto.*
Incomplete. *In; com; pleo.*
Incomprehensible. *In; com; prehendo.*
Inconcealable. *In; con; celo.*
Inconclusive. *In; con; claudo*
Incongelable. *In; con; gelu.*
Incongruous. *In; con; grus.*
Inconsistent. *In; con; sisto.*
Inconsolable. *In; con; solor.*
Incontestable. *In; con; testis.*
Incorporate. *In; corpus.*
Incorrect, incorrigible. *In; cor; rego*
Incorruptible. *In; cor; ruptum.*
Increase. *In; cresco.*

Incredible. ***In ; credo.***
Incrust. *In ; crusta.*
Inculcate. *In ; culco.*
Incumbent. *In ; cubo.*
Incur. *In ; curro.*
Indebt. *In ; debitus.*
Indecency. *In ; decens.*
Indefatigable. *In ; de ; fatigo.*
Indefinite. *In ; de ; finis.*
Indelible. *In ; de ; leo.*
Indelicate. *In ; deliciæ.*
Indemnify, indemnity. *In ; damnum.*
Indent, indenture. *In ; dens.*
Independent. *In ; de ; pendeo.*
Index. *In ; dico.*
Indicate. *In ; dico.*
Indict. *In ; dico.*
Indifference. *In ; dif ; fero.*
Indigent, indigence. *In ; egeo.*
Indigestible. *In ; di ; gero.*
Indignant. *In ; dignus.*
Indirect. *In ; di ; rego.*
Indiscernible. *In ; dis ; cerno.*
Indiscreet. *In ; dis ; cerno.*
Indiscriminate. *In ; dis ; cerno.*
Indispensable. *In ; dis ; pendo.*
Indisposed. *In ; dis ; pono.*
Indissoluble. *In ; dis ; solvo.*
Indistinct. *In ; di ; stinguo.*
Individual, indivisible. *In ; di ; viduo.*
Indoctrinate. *In ; doceo.*
Indolence. *In ; doleo.*
Indomitable. *In ; domo.*
Induce, induct. *In ; duco.*
Inebriate. *In ; ebrius.*
Ineffable. *In ; ef ; fari.*
Inefficiency. *In ; ef ; facio.*
Inelegant. *In ; elegans.*
Inert. *In ; ars.*
Inestimable. *In ; estimo.*
Inevitable. *In ; e ; vito.*
Inexcusable. *In ; ex ; causa.*
Inexhaustible. *In ; ex ; haustum.*
Inexorable. *In ; ex ; oro.*
Inexplicable. *In ; ex ; plico.*
Inextinct, inextinguishable. *In; ex; stinguo.*
Infamy. *In ; fama.*
Infant, infancy. *In ; fari.*
Infanticide. *In ; fari ; cædo.*
Infect infectious. *In ; facio.*
Infer, inference. *In ; fero.*
Inferior, infernal. *Inferus.*
Infidel. *In ; fides.*
Infinite. *In ; finis.*
Infirm, infirmary. *In ; firmus.*
Inflame, inflammation. *In ; flamma.*
Inflate. *In ; flatus.*
Inflict. *In ; fligo.*
Inform. *In ; forma.*
Infraction. *In ; frango.*
Infrequency. *In ; frequens.*
Infringe. *In ; frango.*
Infuriate. *In ; furia.*
Infuse. *In ; fundo.*
Ingenerate, ingenious, ingenuity, ingenuous. *In ; genus.*
Inglorious. *In ; gloria.*
Ingrate, ingratiate. *In ; gratia.*
Ingredient, ingress. *In ; gradior.*
Inhabit. *In ; habeo.*
Inhale. *In ; halo.*
Inherent. *In ; hæreo.*
Inhospitable, inhospitality. *In ; hospes.*
Inhumanity. *In ; homo.*
Inhume. *In ; humus.*
Inimical. *In ; amicus.*
Inimitable. *In ; imitor.*
Iniquity. *In ; equus.*
Injudicious. *In ; judico.*
Injunction. *In ; jungo.*
Injure, injurious. *In ; jus.*
Injustice. *In ; justus*
Innate. *In ; nascor.*
Innocence. *In ; noceo.*
Innovate. *In ; novus.*
Innumerable. *In ; numerus.*
Inoculate. *In ; oculus.*
Inodorous. *In ; odor.*
Inoffensive *In ; of ; fendo.*
Inofficious. *In ; of ; facio.*
Inordinate. *In ; ordo.*
Inorganic. *In ; organum.*
Inquest. *In ; quæro.*
Inquire, inquisition, inquisitive. ***In ; quæro.***
Insane. *In ; sanus.*
Insatiable, insaturable. *In ; satis.*
Inscribe, inscription. *In ; scribo*
Insect. *In ; seco.*
Insecure. *In ; se ; cura.*
Inseparable. *In ; se ; paro.*
Insert. *In ; sertum.*
Insidious. *In ; sedeo.*
Insignia. *In ; signum.*
Insignificance, insignificant. *In ; signum ; facio.*
Insincere. *In ; sine ; cera.*
Insinuate. *In ; sinus.*
Insipid. *In ; sapio*
Insist. *In ; sisto.*
Insolent, insolence. *In ; soleo.*
Insolvent. *In ; solvo.*
Inspect. *In ; specto.*
Instance, instant, instantaneous. ***In ; sto.***
Instigate, instigator. *In ; stigo.*
Instill. *In ; stilla.*
Instinctive. *In ; stinguo.*
Institute. *In ; sto.*
Instruct, instrument. *In ; struo.*
Insubordinacy. *In ; sub ; ordo.*
Insufferable. *In ; suf ; fero.*
Insufficient. *In ; suf ; facio.*
Insular, insulate. *Insula.*
Insult. *In ; salio.*
Insuperable. *In ; super.*
Insurgent, insurrection. *In ; surgo.*
Integer, integral, integrity. *Integer.*
Integument. *In ; tego.*
Intellect, intelligence, intelligible. *Inter ; lego.*
Intend, intense, intent. *In ; tendo.*
Inter. *In ; terra.*
Intercede. *Inter ; cedo.*
Intercept. *Inter ; capio.*
Intercession. *Inter ; cedo.*
Intercourse. *Inter ; curro.*
Interdict. *Inter ; dico.*
Interest. *Inter ; ens.*
Interfere. *Inter ; ferio.*
Interior. *Intus.*
Interjacent. *Inter ; jaceo.*
Interjection. *Inter ; jacio.*
Interline. *Inter ; linea.*
Intermediate. *Inter ; medius.*
Interminable. *In ; terminus.*
Intermission, intermittent. *Inter ; mitto.*
Intermix. *Inter ; misceo.*
Internal. *Intus.*
Interpose. *Inter ; pono.*
Interrogate, interrogative. *Inter ; rogo.*
Interrupt. *Inter ; ruptum.*
Intersect. *Inter ; seco.*
Intersperse. *Inter ; spargo.*
Interstice. *Inter ; sto.*
Interval. *Inter ; vallum.*

J.

K.

L.

M.

Magi, magic, magician. *Magus.*
Magistracy, magistrate. *Magister.*
Magnanimity, magnanimous. *Magnus; animus.*
Magnet, magnetical, magnetism. *Magnes.*
Magnific, magnificent. *Magnus; facio.*
Magnify. *Magnus.*
Magnitude. *Magnus.*
Maintain, maintenance. *Manus; teneo.*
Majestic, majesty, major, majority. *Magnus.*
Malediction. *Male; dico.*
Malefaction, malefactor. *Male; facio.*
Malevolence. *Male; volo.*
Malice, malicious. *Malitia.*
Malignancy, malignant. *Malignus.*
Malleable, mallet. *Malleus.*
Manacle, manage. *Manus.*
Mandate. *Mando.*
Mania, maniac. *Mania.*
Manifest, manifesto. *Manifestus.*
Manipulation. *Manus; plico.*
Manœuvre. *Manus; opera.*
Mansion. *Maneo.*
Manual. *Manus.*
Manufacture. *Manus; facio.*
Manumission, manumit. *Manus; mitto.*
Manure. *Manus; opera.*
Manuscript. *Manus; scribo.*
Margin, marginal. *Margo.*
Marine, mariner. *Mare.*
Maritime. *Mare*
Market. *Mercor.*
Martial. *Mars.*
Martyr, martyrdom. *Martyr.*
Masculine. *Masculus.*
Master. *Magister.*
Maternal. *Mater.*
Mathematical, mathematician, mathematics. *Mathema.*
Matricide. *Mater; cædo.*
Matrimony, matron. *Mater.*
Maturity. *Maturus.*
Measure. *Mensura.*
Meander. *Meo.*
Mechanics, mechanician, mechanism. *Mechanao.*
Mediation, mediator. *Medius.*
Medical. *Medeor.*
Mediocrity. *Medius.*
Meditation. *Meditor.*
Mediterranean. *Medius; terra.*
Medium. *Medius.*
Melioration. *Melior.*
Mellifluent. *Mel; fluo.*
Melliferous. *Mel.*
Melodrame. *Melos; drama.*
Melody. *Melos; ode.*
Memento, memoir, memorandum, memorial, memory. *Memor.*
Menace. *Minæ.*
Menagery. *Menage.*
Mend. *Menda.*
Mendicant. *Mendicus.*
Menial. *Menage.*
Mensuration. *Mensura.*
Mental. *Mens.*
Mention. *Memor.*
Mercantile, mercenary, mercer, merchandize, merchant. *Mercor.*
Mercury. *Mercor.*
Merge. *Mergo.*
Meridian. *Meridies.*
Merit, meritorious. *Meritum.*
Mesentery. *Mesos; enteron.*
Metal. *Metallum.*
Metalliferous. *Metallum; fero*
Metalloid. *Metallum; oidos.*
Metallurgy. *Metallum; ergon.*
Metamorphose. *Meta; morphe.*
Metaphor, metaphorical. *Meta; phero.*
Metaphysics. *Meta; physis.*
Mete, meter. *Mensura.*
Meteor. *Meteora.*
Meteorology. *Meteora; logos.*
Method. *Meta; odos.*
Metonymical, metonymy. *Meta; onoma*
Metropolis, metropolitan. *Meter; polis.*
Microcosm. *Micros; cosmos.*
Micrometer. *Micros; metrum.*
Microscope. *Micros; scopeo.*
Migrate. *Migro.*
Military, militate, militia, militant. *Miles.*
Millennium. *Mille; annus.*
Milleped. *Mille; pes.*
Mimic. *Mimus.*
Mineralogy. *Mineral; logos.*
Mingle. *Misceo.*
Miniature, minimum. *Minuo*
Minister, ministration, ministry. *Minister*
Minor, minuend, minus, minute. *Minuo.*
Miracle, miraculous, mirror. *Mirus.*
Misanthrope. *Misos; anthropos.*
Misapply. *Mis; ap; plico.*
Miscellany. *Misceo.*
Misconception. *Mis; con; capio.*
Misconduct. *Mis; con; duco.*
Misconstrue. *Mis; con; struo.*
Miscreated. *Mis; creo.*
Miser, miserable, misery. *Miser.*
Misfortune. *Mis; fors.*
Misgovernment. *Mis; guberno.*
Misinfer. *Mis; in; fero.*
Misjoin. *Mis; jungo.*
Misjudge. *Mis; judico.*
Mismanage. *Mis; manus.*
Misogynist. *Misos; gyne.*
Mispronounce. *Mis; pro; nuncio.*
Misproportion. *Mis; pro; pars.*
Misrelate. *Mis; re; latum.*
Misrepresent. *Mis; re; pre; ens.*
Missile, mission, missionary, missive. *Mitto.*
Misusage. *Mis; utor.*
Mix, mixture. *Misceo.*
Mnemonics. *Mneo.*
Mob, mobility. *Moveo.*
Mode, model, moderate, modern, modesty, modify. *Modus.*
Modification. *Modus; facio.*
Modulate. *Modus.*
Mollify. *Mollis.*
Moment, momentary, momentum. *Momentum.*
Monad. *Monos; adelphos.*
Monarch. *Monos; arche.*
Monastic, monastery. *Monos.*
Monitor. *Moneo.*
Monk. *Monos*
Monody. *Monos; ode.*
Monopetalous. *Monos; petalon.*
Monopolize, monopoly. *Monos; polis.*
Monospermous. *Monos; sperma.*
Monosyllable. *Monos; syl; labo.*
Monotony, monotonous. *Monos; tonos*
Monster, monstrous. *Monstro.*
Monument. *Moneo.*
Moon. *Men.*
Morality. *Mos.*
Morbid. *Morbus.*
Morsel, morsure. *Mordeo.*
Mortality, mortify. *Mors.*
Motion, motive. *Moveo*

Mound, mountain. *Mons.*
Mountebank. *Mons; (abacus,* a bench).
Move. *Moveo.*
Multangular. *Multus; angulus.*
Multifarious. *Multus; fari.*
Multiple, multiplex, multiplicand, multiplication, multiplicity, multiply. *Multus; plico.*
Mundane. *Mundus.*
Munificent. *Munus; facio.*
Murder. *Mors.*
Muse, museum, music, musician. *Musa.*
Mutation. *Muto.*
Mutinous, mutineer, mutiny. *Muto.*
Mystery, mystic. *Mystes.*
Mythology. *Mythos; logos.*

N.

Name. *Nomen.*
Narcissus, narcosis, narcotic. *Narce.*
Nasal. *Nasus.*
Natal, nation, native, nativity, natural, nature. *Nascor.*
Nausea, nauseous. *Nausea.*
Nautical, nautilus. *Nauta.*
Navigable, navigate. *Navis; ago.*
Navy. *Navis.*
Necessary, necessitate, necessity. *Necesse.*
Necrology. *Necros; logos.*
Necromancy,necromantic. *Necros; mancia.*
Nectar, nectary. *Nectar.*
Nefarious. *Ne; fari.*
Negation, negative. *Nego.*
Neglect, negligent. *Neg; lego.*
Negotiate, negotiation. *Neg; otium.*
Neology. *Neos; logos.*
Neophyte. *Neos; physis.*
Nerve. *Neuron.*
Neuralgia. *Neuron; logos.*
Neuter, neutrality, neutralize. *Neuter.*
Night. *Nox.*
Nobility. *Nosco.*
Nocturnal. *Nox.*
Nomenclature. *Nomen; (calo,* to call).
Nominal, nominate. *Nomen.*
Nonage. *Non; (age).*
Nondescript. *Non; de; scribo.*
Nonplus. *Non; plus.*
Nonsense. *Non; sentio.*
Normal. *Norma.*
Note, notary. *Nota.*
Notice. *Nosco.*
Notification. *Nosco; facio.*
Notify, notion, notoriety, notorious. *Nosco.*
Nourish. *Nutrio.*
Novel, novelty. *Novus.*
Novice, novitiate. *Novus.*
Noxious. *Noceo.*
Nudity. *Nudus.*
Nuisance. *Noceo.*
Null. *Nullus; ibi.*
Nullity. *Nullus; fides.*
Nullify. *Nullus.*
Number, numeral, numeration, numerical, numerous. *Numerus.*
Nuptial. *Nubo.*
Nurse. *Nutrio.*
Nutriment, nutrition. *Nutrio.*

O.

Obdurate. *Ob; durus.*
Obedience. *Ob; audio.*
Obey. *Ob; audio.*
Obituary. *Ob; eo.*
Objective. *Ob; jacio.*
Oblate. *Ob; latum.*
Oblation. *Ob; latum.*
Obligate, obligatory, oblige. *Ob; ligo.*
Obliterate. *Ob; litera.*
Oblong. *Ob; longus.*
Obloquy. *Ob; loquor.*
Obnoxious. *Ob; noceo.*
Obsequious. *Ob; sequor.*
Obsolete. *Ob; oleo.*
Obstacle. *Ob; sto.*
Obstruct. *Ob; struo.*
Obtain. *Ob; teneo.*
Obtrude. *Ob; trudo.*
Obtuse. *Ob; tundo.*
Obviate, obvious. *Ob; via.*
Occasion, occident. *Oc; cado.*
Occult. *Occultus.*
Occupancy, occupy. *Oc; capio.*
Occur, occurrence. *Oc; curro.*
Octagon. *Octo; gonia.*
Octangular. *Octo; angulus.*
Octavo. *Octo.*
Octennial. *Octo; annus.*
October. *Octo.*
Oculist. *Oculus.*
Ode. *Ode.*
Odious, odium. *Odi.*
Odor. *Odor.*
Offend, offence. *Of; fendo.*
Offer. *Of; fero.*
Office, official, officious. *Of; facio.*
Ointment. *Unguo.*
Olfactory. *Oleo; facio.*
Oligarchy. *Oligos; arche.*
Omen, ominous. *Omen.*
Omission, omit. *Ob; mitto.*
Omnific. *Omnis; facio.*
Omnipotence, omnipotent. *Omnis; posse; ens.*
Omnipresence, omnipresent. *Omnis; pre; ens.*
Omniscience. *Omnis; scio.*
Omnivorous. *Omnis; voro.*
Onerous. *Onus.*
Opera. *Opera.*
Operation. *Opera.*
Ophthalmic. *Ophthalmos.*
Ophthalmy. *Ophthalmos.*
Opine, opinion. *Opinor.*
Opponent. *Op; pono.*
Opportunity. *Op; porto.*
Opposite. *Op; pono.*
Oppress. *Op; premo.*
Optics, optician. *Opto.*
Option. *Opto.*
Opulence. *Opulentus.*
Oracle, oracular, oral, orator, orison, orifice. *Oro.*
Orb, orbit. *Orbis.*
Ordain, ordinal, ordinance, ordinary. *Ordo.*
Organ, organical, organism, organize. *Organum.*
Orient. *Orior.*
Orifice. *Oro; facio.*
Origin, originality, originate. *Orior*
Ornament. *Orno.*
Ornithology. *Ornis; logos.*
Orthodox, orthodoxy. *Orthos; doxa.*
Orthoepy, orthoepist. *Orthos; epos.*
Orthography, orthographical. *Orthos; grapho.*
Osseous. *Os.*
Ossification. *Os; facio.*
Ossify. *Os.*
Ossivorous. *Os; voro.*

Ostensible, ostentation. *Ob; tendo.*
Osteology. *Osteon; logos.*
Ostler. *Hospes.*
Otacoustic. *Ous; acouo.*
Oval, ovary, ovoid. *Ovum.*
Overt, overture. *Ob; pario.*
Oviparous. *Ovum; pario.*
Ovoid. *Ovum; oidos.*
Oxyde, oxygen, oxydize. *Oxys.*
Oxymel. *Oxys; mel.*

P.

Pace. *Passus.*
Pacification. *Pax; facio.*
Pacify. *Pax.*
Pain. *Peniteo.*
Paint. *Pingo.*
Pair. *Par.*
Palindrome. *Palin; dromos.*
Palinode. *Palin; ode.*
Pall. *Pallium.*
Palliate. *Pallium.*
Pallid, pallor. *Palleo.*
Palm, palmetto. *Palma.*
Palmiferous. *Palma; fero.*
Palmistry. *Palma.*
Palpable, palpitate. *Palpo.*
Panacea. *Pas;* (*acesis*, a cure).
Panada. *Panis.*
Pandect. *Pas; dechomai.*
Panegyric. *Pas; egora.*
Panoply. *Pas; oplon.*
Panorama. *Pas; orama.*
Pantheism, pantheon. *Pas; theos.*
Pantomime. *Pas; mimus.*
Pantry. *Panis.*
Papacy, papal. *Papas.*
Parade. *Paro.*
Paradox. *Para; doxa.*
Paragraph. *Para; grapho.*
Paralyze. *Para; lysis.*
Paraphrase. *Para; phrasis.*
Parcel. *Pars.*
Parent. *Pario.*
Parhelion. *Para; helios.*
Parley, parliament, parlor. *Parler.*
Parody. *Para; ode.*
Parole. *Parler.*
Parotid. *Para; ous.*
Paroxysm. *Para; oxys.*
Parricide. *Pater; cædo.*
Parse. *Pars.*
Parsimonious, parsimony. *Parsimonia.*
Part. *Pars.*
Partial. *Pars.*
Participate, participle. *Pars; capio.*
Particle, particular, partisan, partition, partner. *Pars.*
Party. *Pars.*
Paschal. *Pascha.*
Passage, passenger, passible. *Passus.*
Passion, passive. *Patior.*
Passport. *Passus; porto.*
Pastime. *Passus; tempus.*
Pastor, pasture. *Pasco.*
Paternal. *Pater.*
Pathology. *Pathos; logos.*
Pathos. *Pathos.*
Patience. *Patior.*
Patriarch. *Pater; arche*
Patrician, patrimony, patriot. *Pater.*
Patrol. *Pateo.*
Patron, patronize. *Pater.*
Patronymic. *Pater; onoma.*
Pauper. *Pauper.*
Peace. *Pax.*
Peccadillo, peccant. *Pecco.*
Pectoral. *Pectus.*
Pecuniary. *Pecunia.*
Pedant, pedantry. *Pedia.*
Pedestal, pedestrian, pedicellate. *Pes*
Pedigree. *Pes; gradior.*
Pedobaptist. *Pes; bapto.*
Peerage, peerless. *Par.*
Pellucid. *Per; luceo.*
Pen. *Penna.*
Penal, penalty, penance. *Peniteo.*
Pendulum. *Pendeo.*
Peninsula. *Pene; insula.*
Penitent, penitentiary. *Peniteo.*
Pennate. *Penna.*
Pennsylvania. *Penn; sylva.*
Pension, pensive, pensionary. *Pendo.*
Pentagon. *Pente; gonia.*
Pentameter. *Pente; metrum.*
Pentangular. *Pente; angulus.*
Pentateuch. *Pente; teuchos.*
Pentecost. *Pente.*
Penult. *Pene; ultimus.*
People. *Populus.*
Perambulate. *Per; ambulo.*
Perceive. *Per; capio.*
Perdition. *Per; do.*
Peregrinate. *Per; ager.*
Peremptory. *Per; emo.*
Perennial. *Per; annus.*
Perfect. *Per; facio.*
Perfidy. *Per; fides.*
Perforate. *Per; foro.*
Perform. *Per; forma.*
Perfume. *Per; fumus.*
Pericranium. *Peri; cranium.*
Perihelion. *Peri; helios.*
Perimeter. *Peri; metrum.*
Period. *Peri; odos.*
Peripatetic, peripateticism. *Peri; pateo.*
Periphery. *Peri; phero.*
Periphrase. *Peri; phrasis.*
Perish. *Per; eo.*
Perjury. *Per; juro.*
Permanence. *Per; maneo.*
Permeate. *Per; meo.*
Permit, permission. *Per; mitto.*
Permutation. *Per; muto.*
Perpendicular. *Per; pendeo.*
Perpetual, perpetuate, perpetuity. *Perpes*
Perplex, perplexity. *Per; plico.*
Perquisite. *Per; quæro.*
Persecute. *Per; sequor.*
Persist. *Per; sisto.*
Person, personify, personate. *Persona.*
Perspective, perspicuity. *Per; specio.*
Perspire. *Per; spiro.*
Persuade, persuasive. *Per; suadeo.*
Pertain. *Per; teneo.*
Pertinacy, pertinent. *Per; teneo.*
Perturbation. *Per; turba.*
Peruse. *Per; utor.*
Pervade. *Per; vado.*
Perverse, pervert. *Per; verto.*
Pest. *Pestis.*
Pestilence. *Pestis.*
Petal. *Petalon.*
Petition. *Peto.*
Peter, petrescent. *Petra.*
Petrifaction. *Petra; facio.*
Petrify. *Petra.*
Pettifogger. *Petit;* (*voguer*, to row).
Petty. *Petit.*
Phantasm, phantom. *Phano.*
Pharmaceutic. *Pharmacon*

Pharmacy. *Pharmacon.*
Phenomenon. *Phano.*
Philadelphian. *Philos; adelphos.*
Philanthropist. *Philos; anthropos.*
Philology. *Philos; logos.*
Philomela. *Philos; melos.*
Philosophy. *Philos; sophia.*
Phlebotomy. *Phleps; tomos.*
Phosphate. *Phos.*
Phosphorescence, phosphorescent, phosphorous. *Phos; phero.*
Phrase. *Phrasis.*
Phraseology. *Phrasis; logos.*
Phrenology. *Phren; logos.*
Physic, physical, physician. *Physis.*
Physiognomy. *Physis; gnomon.*
Physiology. *Physis; logos.*
Pictorial, picture, picturesque. *Pingo.*
Pigment. *Pingo.*
Pilfer. *Pilo.*
Pillage. *Pilo.*
Piracy, pirate. *Pirates.*
Piscatory. *Piscis*
Piscivorous. *Piscis; voro.*
Placid. *Placeo.*
Plague, plaintive, plaintiff. *Plango.*
Planet, planetary. *Plane.*
Plantation. *Planta.*
Plaster. *Plasso.*
Plaudit, plausible. *Plaudo.*
Pleasant, pleasantry, please, pleasure. *Placeo.*
Plebeian. *Plebs.*
Plenary. *Plenus.*
Plenitude, plenty. *Plenus.*
Pliable, pliant, pliers, ply. *Plico.*
Plumb, plumbago. *Plumbum.*
Plume, plumage. *Pluma.*
Plummet. *Plumbum.*
Plural, plus. *Plus.*
Pneumatics. *Pneuma.*
Pneumatology. *Pneuma; logos.*
Poem, poet. *Poieo*
Poise. *Pondus.*
Polarity, pole. *Polus.*
Police, polish, polite, political. *Polis.*
Pollute. *Per; luo.*
Polygamy. *Poly; gameo.*
Polyglot. *Poly; glossa.*
Polygon. *Poly; gonia.*
Polyedron. *Poly; edra.*
Polynesia. *Poly; nesos.*
Polypous. *Poly; pous.*
Polysyllable. *Poly; syl; labo.*
Polytechnic. *Poly; techne.*
Polytheism. *Poly; theos.*
Pomace. *Pomum.*
Pomegranate. *Pomum; granum.*
Pomeroy. *Pomum; roy.*
Pommel. *Pomum.*
Ponder, ponderous. *Pondus.*
Pontiff. *Pons; facio.*
Pontoon. *Pons.*
Poor. *Pauper.*
Pope, popedom. *Papas.*
Populace, popular, population. *Populus.*
Pore, porosity, porous. *Poros.*
Porphyra. *Porphyra.*
Port, portable, portal, portly. *Porto.*
Portend, portent. *Porro; tendo.*
Portfolio. *Porto; folium.*
Portico. *Porto.*
Portion. *Pars.*
Portmanteau. *Porto; manus.*
Portrait, portray. *Pro; traho.*
Position, positive. *Pono.*
Posse, possession. *Posse.*
Post. *Pono.*
Postdiluvian. *Post; diluvium.*
Posterior, postern, posterity. *Posterus.*
Postfix. *Post; fixus.*
Posthumous. *Post; humus.*
Postmeridian. *Post; meridies.*
Postpone. *Post; pono.*
Posture. *Pono.*
Potent, potentate. *Posse; ens.*
Poverty. *Pauper.*
Practice, practitioner. *Practos.*
Pragmatic. *Practos.*
Preach. *Precor.*
Precarious. *Precor.*
Precaution. *Pre; cautio.*
Precede. *Pre; cedo.*
Precept. *Pre; capio.*
Precinct. *Pre; cingo.*
Precious. *Precium.*
Precipice, precipitance. *Pre; capio.*
Precise, precision. *Pre; cædo.*
Preclude. *Pre; claudo.*
Preconceive. *Pre; con; capio.*
Preconcerted. *Pre; con; certo.*
Precursor. *Pre; curro.*
Predatory. *Preda.*
Predecessor. *Pre; de; cedo.*
Predestination, predestine *Pre; de; stino*
Predicament, predicate, predict. *Pre; dico*
Predilection. *Pre; di; lego.*
Predominance, predominate. *Pre; dominus.*
Pre-eminence. *Pre; e; mineo.*
Pre-emption. *Pre; emo.*
Preface. *Pre; fari.*
Prefer. *Pre; fero.*
Prefix. *Pre; fixus.*
Prejudice. *Pre; judico.*
Prelacy, prelate. *Pre; latum.*
Preliminary. *Pre; limen.*
Prelude. *Pre; ludo.*
Premature. *Pre; maturus.*
Premeditate. *Pre; meditor.*
Premise. *Pre; mitto.*
Premonitory. *Pre; moneo.*
Preoccupy. *Pre; oc; capio.*
Preparatory. *Pre; paro.*
Preponderate. *Pre; pondus.*
Preposition. *Pre; pono.*
Prepossessed, prepossession. *Pre; posse*
Preposterous. *Pre; posterus.*
Prerogative. *Pre; rogo.*
Presage. *Pre; sagax.*
Presbyterian. *Presbyteros.*
Prescribe, prescription. *Pre; scribo.*
Present. *Pre; ens.*
Presentiment. *Pre; sentio.*
Preside, presidency. *Pre; sedeo.*
Press. *Premo.*
Presume, presumptuous. *Pre; sumo.*
Pretend, pretense. *Pre; tendo.*
Pretext. *Pre; textus.*
Prevail, prevalent. *Pre; valeo.*
Previous. *Pre; via.*
Price. *Precium.*
Prim, primacy, primary, primate, prime. primer. *Primus.*
Primeval. *Primus; evum.*
Primitive. *Primus.*
Primogeniture. *Primus; genus.*
Prince, principal, principle. *Primus; capio.*
Print. *Premo.*
Prior, priory. *Primus.*
Prison. *Prehendo.*
Pristine. *Primus.*
Privacy, private privateer, privation *Privus.*

Privilege. *Privus; lex.*
Privy. *Privus.*
Prize. *Prehendo.*
Prize. *Precium.*
Probable, probationer. *Probo.*
Probe, probity. *Probo.*
Proceed, process. *Pro; cedo.*
Proclaim, proclamation. *Pro; clamo.*
Procrastinate. *Pro; cras.*
Procumbent. *Pro; cubo.*
Procure. *Pro; cura.*
Produce, product, productive. *Pro; duco.*
Profane. *Pro; fanum.*
Profess. *Pro; fessum.*
Proffer. *Pro; fero.*
Proficient, profit. *Pro; facio.*
Profound, profundity. *Pro; fundus.*
Profuse. *Pro; fundo.*
Progenitor, progeny. *Pro; genus*
Prognostic. *Pro; gnomon.*
Progress. *Pro; gradior.*
Prohibit. *Pro; habeo.*
Project. *Pro; jacio.*
Prolific. *Proles; facio.*
Prolixity. *Pro; laxus.*
Prologue. *Pro; logos.*
Prolong, prolongation. *Pro; longus.*
Prominent. *Pro; mineo.*
Promiscuous. *Pro; misceo.*
Promise, promissory. *Pro; mitto.*
Promontory. *Pro; mons.*
Promote. *Pro; moveo.*
Prompt. *Pro; emo.*
Promulgation. *Pro; vulgus.*
Pronoun. *Pro; nomen.*
Pronounce, pronunciation. *Pro; nuncio.*
Proof. *Probo.*
Propel. *Pro; pello.*
Propensity. *Pro; pendeo.*
Proper, property. *Proprius.*
Prophecy, prophet. *Pro; phano.*
Propitiate, propitious. *Prope.*
Proportion. *Pro; pars.*
Proposal, proposition. *Pro; pono.*
Propriety. *Proprius.*
Prorogue. *Pro; rogo.*
Prosaic. *Prosa.*
Proscribe, proscription, proscriptive. *Pro; scribo.*
Prosecute. *Pro; sequor.*
Proselyte, proselytism. *Proselytos.*
Prosody. (*Pros*, to); *ode.*
Prospect. *Pro; specio.*
Prosper, prosperity. *Prosper.*
Prostitute. *Pro; sto.*
Prostrate. *Pro; sterno.*
Protect, protectorate. *Pro; tego.*
Protest, protestant. *Pro; testis.*
Prothonotary. *Protos; nosco.*
Prototype. *Protos; typus.*
Protract. *Pro; traho.*
Protrude, protrusion. *Pro; trudo.*
Protuberance. *Pro; tuber.*
Prove. *Probo.*
Provender. *Pro; video.*
Proverb. *Pro; verbum.*
Provide, providence, providential. *Pro; video.*
Province. *Pro; vinco.*
Provision, proviso. *Pro; video.*
Provocation, provoke. *Pro; voco.*
Provost. *Pro; pono.*
Proximity. *Prope.*
Proxy. *Pro; cura.*
Prudence. *Pro; video.*
Psalmist. *Psalma.*
Psalmody. *Psalma; ode.*
Psalmography. *Psalma; grapho.*
Psychology. *Psyche; logos.*
Public, publish. *Populus.*
Pulsation, pulse. *Pello.*
Purify, puritan, purity. *Purus.*
Purpose. *Pro; pono.*
Pursue, pursuit. *Per; sequor.*
Purvey. *Pro; video.*
Pusillanimity. *Pusillus; animus.*
Putrefy, putrescent, putridity, putrefactive. *Putris.*
Pyramid, pyre. *Pyr.*
Pyromancy. *Pyr; mancia.*
Pyrometer. *Pyr; metrum.*
Pyrotechnics. *Pyr; techne.*

Q.

Quadrangular. *Quadra; angulus.*
Quadruped. *Quadra; pes.*
Qualification. *Qualis; facio.*
Qualify, quality. *Qualis.*
Quarrel. *Queror.*
Querimonious. *Queror.*
Quietude. *Quies.*
Quintessence. *Quinque; ens.*
Quintuple. *Quinque; plico.*
Quorum, quota. *Quot.*
Quotidian. *Quot; dies.*
Quotient. *Quot.*

R.

Radiance. *Radius.*
Radical. *Radix.*
Radius. *Radius.*
Ramification. *Ramus; facio.*
Ramify. *Ramus.*
Rancid, rancor, rank, rankle. *Ranceo.*
Rank, range. *Rang.*
Rap, rapacious, rapid, rapier, rapture *Rapio.*
Rarefy, rarity. *Rarus.*
Ratify, ratio, ration, rationality. *Ratus.*
Ravage, ravish. *Rapio.*
Raze, razor. *Rado.*
React. *Re; ago.*
Readmit. *Re; ad; mitto.*
Real, reality, realize. *Res.*
Reanimate. *Re; anima.*
Reason. *Ratus.*
Rebel. *Re; bellum.*
Recant. *Re; cano.*
Recapitulate. *Re; caput*
Recede. *Re; cedo.*
Receipt, receive. *Re; capio.*
Receptacle, reception. *Re; capio.*
Recess. *Re; cedo.*
Recite, recipient. *Re; capio.*
Recite. *Re; cito.*
Reclaim. *Re; clamo.*
Recline. *Re; clino.*
Recluse. *Re; claudo.*
Recognition, recognize. *Re; cog; nosco.*
Recollect. *Re; col; lego.*
Recommend. *Re; com; mando.*
Recommit. *Re; com; mitto.*
Recompense. *Re; com; pendo.*
Recompose. *Re; com; pono.*
Reconcile. *Re; concilio.*
Reconnoitre. *Re; con; nosco.*
Record. *Re; cor.*
Recourse. *Re; curro.*
Recreant, recreation. *Re; creo.*
Recruit. *Re; cresco.*
Rectangle. *Rego; angulus.*

Rectify. *Rego.*
Rectilinear. *Rego; linea.*
Rectitude, rector. *Rego.*
Recumbence. *Re; cubo.*
Recur. *Re; curro.*
Redeem. *Re; emo.*
Redolent. *Re; olio.*
Redound. *Re; undo.*
Reduce, reduction. *Re; duco.*
Redundancy. *Re; undo.*
Re-election. *Re; e; lego.*
Refectory. *Re; facio.*
Refer, reference. *Re; fero.*
Refine. *Re; finis.*
Refit. *Re; facio.*
Reflect. *Re; flecto.*
Reform, reformation. *Re; forma.*
Refract. *Re; frango.*
Refrain. *Re; frenum.*
Refrigerate. *Re; frigus.*
Refuge. *Re; fugio.*
Refulgence, refulgent. *Re; fulgeo.*
Refund, refusal. *Re; fundo.*
Refute. *Re; futo.*
Regal, regalia. *Rego.*
Regenerated. *Re; genus.*
Regent. *Rego.*
Regicide. *Rego; cædo.*
Regimen, regiment, region. *Rego.*
Regularity, regulation, reign. *Rego.*
Reinsert. *Re; in; sertum.*
Reinstate. *Re; in; sto.*
Reiterate. *Re; iter.*
Reject. *Re; jacio.*
Relapse. *Re; labor.*
Relate, relative. *Re; latum.*
Relax, relaxation. *Re; laxus.*
Relevant. *Re; levo.*
Relict, relic. *Re; linquo.*
Relief, relieve. *Re; levo.*
Religion. *Re; ligo.*
Relinquish. *Re; linquo.*
Remain. *Re; maneo.*
Remand. *Re; mando.*
Remedial, remedy. *Re; medeor.*
Remember. *Re; memor.*
Reminiscence. *Re; memor.*
Remiss, remission, remittance. *Re; mitto.*
Remnant. *Re; maneo.*
Remodel. *Re; modus.*
Remonstrance, remonstrate. *Re; monstro.*
Remorse. *Re; mordeo.*
Remote. *Re; moveo.*
Remount. *Re; mons.*
Remove. *Re; moveo.*
Remunerate. *Re; munus.*
Renavigate. *Re; navis; ago.*
Render. *Re; do.*
Renegade. *Re; nego.*
Renew. *Re; novus.*
Renounce. *Re; nuncio.*
Renovation. *Re; novus.*
Renunciation. *Re; nuncio.*
Repair, reparation. *Re; paro.*
Repartee. *Re; pars.*
Repast. *Re; pasco*
Repeal. *Re; pello.*
Repeat. *Re; peto.*
Repel. *Re; pello.*
Repent. *Re; peniteo.*
Repeople. *Re; populus.*
Replenish. *Re; plenus.*
Replete *Re; pleo.*
Reply. *Re; plico.*
Report. *Re; porto.*
Repose, repository. *Re; pono.*
Reprehend. *Re; prehendo.*
Represent. *Re; pre; ens.*
Repress. *Re; premo.*
Reprieve. *Re; prehendo.*
Reprisal. *Re; prehendo.*
Reproach. *Re; prope.*
Reprobate. *Re; probo.*
Reproof, reprove. *Re; probo.*
Reptile. *Reptum.*
Republic. *Re; populus.*
Repulse, repulsive. *Re; pello.*
Request. *Re; quæro.*
Requiem. *Re; quies.*
Require, requisite. *Re; quæro.*
Rescind. *Re; scindo.*
Resent. *Re; sentio.*
Reside, resident, residue. *Re; sedeo.*
Resign. *Re; signum.*
Resist. *Re; sisto.*
Resolution, resolve. *Re; solvo.*
Resort. *Re; sors.*
Resound. *Re; sonus.*
Respect. *Re; specio.*
Respire. *Re; spiro.*
Resplendent. *Re; splendeo.*
Respond, response, responsible. *Re; spondeo.*
Rest. *Re; sto.*
Restitution. *Re; sto.*
Restraint, restrict. *Re; stringo.*
Result. *Re; salio.*
Resume, resumption. *Re; sumo.*
Resuscitate. *Re; sus; cito.*
Retail. *Re; tailler.*
Retain. *Re; teneo.*
Retaliate. *Re; talis.*
Retard. *Re; tardus.*
Retentive. *Re; teneo.*
Reticule. *Rete.*
Retiform. *Rete; forma.*
Retina. *Rete.*
Retinue. *Re; teneo.*
Retort. *Re; tortum.*
Retract. *Re; traho.*
Retributive. *Re; tribuo.*
Retrieve. *Re; trouver.*
Retrograde, retrogression. *Retro; gradior.*
Retrospective. *Retro; specio.*
Retroversion, retrovert. *Retro; verto.*
Reveal. *Re; velo.*
Revelation. *Re; velo.*
Revenge. *Re; vindex.*
Revenue. *Re; venio.*
Reverence, revere, reverend, reverential. *Re; vereor.*
Reverse, reversion, revert. *Re; verto.*
Review. *Re; video.*
Revile. *Re; vilis.*
Revise, revisit. *Re; video.*
Revive. *Re; vivo.*
Revocation. *Re; voco.*
Revolt, revolution, revolve. *Re; volvo*
Revulsion. *Re; vello.*
Rhapsody, rhapsodist. *Rhapto; ode.*
Rheum. *Rheo.*
Rhomb. *Rhombos.*
Rhomboid. *Rhombos; oidos.*
Rhyme, rhythm. *Rhythmos.*
Ridicule. *Rideo.*
Right. *Rego.*
Rigid, rigor. *Rigeo.*
Risible. *Rideo.*
Rivalry, rivulet. *Rivus.*
Robust. *Robur.*
Roseate. *Rosa.*
Rosy. *Rosa.*
Rotation, rote, rotund. *Roto*
Routine. *Rota.*

Royal. *Roy.*
Rubicund, ruby. *Ruber.*
Rudiment. *Rudis.*
Rule. *Rego.*
Rupture. *Ruptum.*
Rural, rustic. *Rus.*

S.

Sacerdotal. *Sacer; dos.*
Sacrament, sacred. *Sacer.*
Sacrifice. *Sacer; facio.*
Sacrilege. *Sacer; lex.*
Sacristy. *Sacer.*
Safe. *Salus.*
Sagacious, sagacity, sage. *Sagax.*
Saint. *Sanctus.*
Salad, salary. *Sal.*
Saline. *Sal.*
Salivary. *Saliva.*
Sally. *Salio.*
Saltpetre. *Sal; petra.*
Salubrity, salutary, salutation, salute. *Salus.*
Salvage, salvation, salve, salvo. *Salus.*
Sanctify, sanctimony, sanction, sanctity, sanctuary. *Sanctus.*
Sanguinary, sanguine. *Sanguis.*
Sanity. *Sanus.*
Sarcasm, sarcastic. *Sarx.*
Sarcophagus. *Sarx; phago.*
Sate, satisfy. *Satis.*
Saturate. *Satis.*
Sauce. *Sal.*
Savage. *Sylva.*
Savor. *Sapio.*
Scald. *Caleo.*
Scale. *Scala.*
Scan. *Scando.*
Scarificator, scarify. *Scariphos.*
Scene, scenery. *Scena.*
Scent. *Sentio.*
Sceptic, scepticism. *Sceptomai.*
Schism, schismatic. *Schisma.*
Scholar, school. *Schola.*
Science. *Scio.*
Scientific. *Scio; facio.*
Scintillate, scintillation. *Scintilla.*
Sciomachy. *Scia; machomai.*
Scissors. *Scindo*
Scope. *Scopeo.*
Scribble, scribe, scrip, scripture. *Scribo.*
Scrutinize, scrutiny. *Scrutor.*
Sculptor, sculpture. *Sculpo.*
Scurrility, scurrilous. *Scurra.*
Scutcheon. *Scutum.*
Secede. *Se; cedo.*
Secession. *Se; cedo.*
Seclude. *Se; claudo.*
Secret, secretary, secrete. *Secretus. Se; cerno.*
Sect, sectary, section. *Seco.*
Security. *Se; cura.*
Sedan, sedate, sedentary, sediment, sedition. *Sedeo.*
Seduce, seductive. *Se; duco.*
Sedulous. *Sedeo*
Segment. *Seco.*
Seignior. *Senex.*
Selection. *Se; lego.*
Semiannual. *Semi; annus.*
Semiannular. *Semi; annulus.*
Semicircle. *Semi; circulus.*
Semicolon. *Semi; colon.*
Semidiameter. *Semi; dia; metrum.*
Semilunar. *Semi; luna*
Semimetal. *Semi; metallum.*
Seminal, seminary. *Semen.*
Seminific. *Semen; facio.*
Semipellucid. *Semi; per; luceo.*
Semiquaver. *Semi;* (*quiebro,* a musical shake).
Semivowel. *Semi; vox.*
Senary. *Sex.*
Senate. *Senex.*
Sense, sensual, sentence, sentiment, sentinel, sensation. *Sentio.*
Separable, separate. *Se; paro.*
Septangular. *Septem; angulus.*
September. *Septem.*
Septennial. *Septem; annus.*
Sequel. *Sequor.*
Serenade, serene, serenity. *Serenus.*
Sergeant. *Servio.*
Series. *Sertum.*
Sermon. *Sertum.*
Serpent, serpentine. *Serpo.*
Servant, serve, servile, servitude. *Servio.*
Session. *Sedeo.*
Seven. *Septem.*
Sever, several. *Se; paro.*
Severe, severity. *Severus.*
Sexangular. *Sex; angulus.*
Sextuple. *Sex; plico.*
Sexual. *Sexus.*
Sideral. *Sidus.*
Siege. *Sedeo.*
Sign, signal, signalize, signature. *Signum.*
Significance. *Signum; facio.*
Signification. *Signum.*
Silvan. *Silva.*
Simile, similar, similitude. *Similis.*
Simple, simpleton, simplicity. *Sine; plico*
Simplify. *Sine; plico.*
Simultaneous. *Simul.*
Sincerity. *Sine; cera.*
Sinecure. *Sine; cura.*
Sinister. *Sinister.*
Site, situation. *Situs.*
Six. *Sex.*
Sobriety. *Sine; ebrius.*
Sociable, social, society. *Socio.*
Sojourn, *Jour;* (perhaps) *sub.*
Solace. *Solor.*
Solar. *Sol.*
Solder, soldier. *Solidus.*
Sole. *Solum.*
Solecism, solecistical. *Solecos.*
Solicit, solicitation, solicitude. *Solicitus.*
Solidity. *Solidus.*
Soliloquy. *Solus; loquor.*
Solitary, solitude. *Solus.*
Solstice. *Sol; sto.*
Solve, solvency. *Solvo.*
Somnambulist. *Somnus; ambulo.*
Sonnet. *Sonus.*
Sonorous. *Sonus.*
Sophism, sophistry. *Sophia.*
Soporific. *Sopor; facio.*
Sort, sortie. *Sors.*
Source. *Surgo.*
Space, spacious. *Spatium.*
Sparse. *Spargo.*
Spasm, spasmodic. *Spasma.*
Specific. *Specio; facio.*
Specify, specimen, specious, spectacle, spectator, spectatrix, spectre, spectrum, specular, speculate, speculum, *Specio.*
Spheroid. *Sphæra; oidos.*
Spherule. *Sphæra.*
Spine. *Spina.*
Spiniferous. *Spina; fero.*
Spinous. *Spina.*

Spirit, spiritualize. *Spiro.*
Splendid, splendor. *Splendeo.*
Spoil. *Spolium.*
Spouse. *Spondeo.*
Sprite. *Spiro.*
Squadron. *Quadra.*
Square. *Quadra.*
Stamen. *Sto.*
Stand, standard. *Sto.*
State, station, statistics, statuary, statue, stay, stead. *Sto.*
Steganography. *Steganos; grapho.*
Stellate. *Stella.*
Stelliferous. *Stella; fero.*
Stenography. *Stenos; grapho.*
Stereotype. *Stereos; typus.*
Sterile, sterility. *Sterilis.*
Stigma, stigmatize. *Stigma.*
Still. *Stilla.*
Stimulate. *Stimulus.*
Stipend, stipendiary. *Stipendium.*
Strain. *Stringo.*
Strange. *Exterus.*
Stratagem. *Stratos; ago.*
Stratify. *Sterno.*
Strict. *Stringo.*
Student, studious, study. *Studeo.*
Stupefaction. *Stupeo; facio.*
Stupefy, stupendous, stupid. *Stupeo.*
Suavity. *Suavis.*
Subdivide, subdivision. *Sub; di; viduo.*
Subdue. *Sub; do* or *jugum.*
Subject. *Sub; jacio.*
Subjoin. *Sub; jungo.*
Subjugation. *Sub; jugum.*
Subjunctive. *Sub; jungo.*
Sublime, sublimity. *Sublimis.*
Sublunary. *Sub; luna.*
Submarine. *Sub; mare.*
Submerge, submersion. *Sub; mergo.*
Submissive, submit. *Sub; mitto.*
Subordinate. *Sub; ordo.*
Suborn. *Sub; orno.*
Subscribe, subscription. *Sub; scribo.*
Subsequent. *Sub; sequor.*
Subserve. *Sub; servio.*
Subside, subsidiary, subsidize, subsidy. *Sub; sedeo.*
Substance, substantial, substitute. *Sub; sto.*
Subterfuge. *Subter; fugio.*
Subtile, subtlety. *Subtilis.*
Subtract. *Sub; traho.*
Suburbs. *Sub; urbs.*
Subvert. *Sub; verto.*
Succeed, success. *Suc; cedo.*
Succinct. *Suc; cingo.*
Succor. *Suc; curro.*
Succulent. *Sugo.*
Succumb. *Suc; cubo.*
Suck, suckle, suction. *Sugo.*
Sudorific. *Sudo; facio.*
Sue. *Sequor.*
Suffer. *Suf; fero.*
Suffice, sufficient. *Suf; facio.*
Suggest. *Sug; gero.*
Suicide, suicidal. *Sui; cædo.*
Suit, suite. *Sequor.*
Sum, summary, summit. *Summa.*
Summon. *Sub; moneo.*
Sumptuary, sumptuous. *Sumo.*
Superabundant. *Super; ab; undo.*
Superannuate. *Super; annus.*
Superb. *Super.*
Supercilious. *Super; cilium.*
Superficial. *Super; facies.*
Superfine. *Super; finis.*
Superflux. *Super; fluo.*
Superintend. *Super; in; tendo.*
Superlative. *Super; latum.*
Supernatural. *Super; nascor.*
Superscribe, superscription. *Super; scribo.*
Supersede. *Super; sedeo.*
Superstition. *Super; sto.*
Superstructure. *Super; struo.*
Supervene. *Super; venio.*
Supervise. *Super; video.*
Supplant. *Sup; planta.*
Supplement. *Sup; pleo.*
Suppliant, supplicate, supply. *Sup; plico*
Support. *Sup; porto.*
Suppose. *Sup; pono.*
Suppress. *Sup; premo.*
Supreme. *Super.*
Surface. *Sur; facies.*
Surmise. *Sur; mitto.*
Surmount. *Sur; mons.*
Surpass. *Sur; passus.*
Surplus. *Sur; plus.*
Surprise. *Sur; prehendo.*
Surrender. *Sur; re; do.*
Surtout. *Sur; totus.*
Survey. *Sur; video.*
Survive. *Sur; vivo.*
Suspect. *Sub; specto.*
Suspend, suspense, suspension. *Sus; pendeo.*
Suspicion. *Sub; specio.*
Sustain, sustenance. *Sus; teneo.*
Sweat. *Sudo.*
Sweet. *Suavis.*
Sycophant. *Sycos; phano.*
Syllogism. *Syl; logos.*
Symmetrical, symmetry. *Sym; metrum.*
Sympathetic. *Sym; pathos.*
Symphony. *Sym; phone.*
Symphysis. *Sym; physis.*
Syncope. *Syn; cope.*
Synod. *Syn; odos.*
Synonyme. *Syn; onoma.*
Synopsis. *Syn; opto.*
Syntax. *Syn; tactos.*
Synthesis, synthetical. *Syn; thesis.*
System. *Syn; stasis.*
Systole. *Syn; stello.*

T.

Tabernacle. *Taberna.*
Table, tablet, tabular. *Tabula.*
Tacit, taciturnity. *Taceo.*
Tactics. *Tactos.*
Tailor. *Tailler.*
Taint. *Tingo.*
Talion, tally. *Talis.*
Tangible. *Tango.*
Tardy. *Tardus.*
Tautological, tautology. *Tautos; logos.*
Technical. *Techne.*
Technology. *Techne; logos.*
Telegraph. *Telos; grapho.*
Telescope. *Telos; scopeo.*
Temper, temperance, temperate, temperature. *Tempero.*
Temporal, temporary, temporize. *Tempus*
Tempt. *Tento.*
Tenacious, tenant. *Teneo.*
Tend, tendency, tendon, tendril. *Tendo*
Tenement. *Teneo.*
Tenet. *Teneo.*
Tense, tension, tent. *Tendo.*
Tentative. *Tento.*

Tenuity. *Tenuis.*
Tenure. *Teneo.*
Tepefy, tepid. *Tepeo.*
Term, terminate. *Terminus.*
Ternary. *Ternus.*
Terrace. *Terra.*
Terraqueous. *Terra; aqua.*
Terrestrial. *Terra.*
Terrier. *Terra.*
Terrific. *Terreo; facio.*
Terrify. *Terreo.*
Territory. *Terra.*
Terror. *Terreo.*
Tertian. *Ternus.*
Testament, testator. *Testis.*
Testify, testimonial, testimony. *Testis.*
Text, texture. *Textus.*
Theatre. *Theatrum.*
Theme. *Thesis.*
Theocracy. *Theos; cratos.*
Theological, theology. *Theos; logos.*
Theomachy. *Theos; machomai.*
Theorem, theoretic, theorize, theory. *Theoros.*
Thermometer. *Thermos; metrum.*
Thesis. *Thesis.*
Third. *Ternus.*
Throne. *Thronus.*
Time. *Tempus.*
Timid. *Timeo.*
Timorous. *Timeo.*
Tincture, tinge, tint. *Tingo.*
Title, titular. *Titulus.*
Toleration. *Tolero.*
Toll. *Tollo.*
Tomb. *Tumeo.*
Tone, tonic. *Tonos.*
Topic. *Topos.*
Topography. *Topos; grapho.*
Torment. *Tortum.*
Torpedo, torpid, torpitude, torpor. *Torpeo.*
Torrefaction. *Torreo; facio.*
Torrefy, torrent, torrid. *Torreo.*
Tortious, torture. *Tortum.*
Total. *Totus.*
Tract, traction. *Traho.*
Tradition, traditive. *Trado.*
Tragedy, tragic. *Tragœdia.*
Trait. *Traho.*
Transact. *Trans; ago.*
Transcend. *Trans; scando.*
Transcribe, transcript. *Trans; scribo.*
Transfer. *Trans; fero.*
Transfix. *Trans; fixus.*
Transform. *Trans; forma.*
Transgress. *Trans; gradior.*
Transient. *Trans; eo.*
Transit. *Trans; eo.*
Translation. *Trans; latum.*
Translucent. *Trans; luceo.*
Transmission, transmit. *Trans; mitto.*
Transmute. *Trans; muto.*
Transparent. *Trans; pareo.*
Transpire. *Trans; spiro.*
Transplant. *Trans; planta.*
Transplendent. *Trans; splendeo.*
Transportation. *Trans; porto.*
Transpose. *Trans; pono.*
Transude. *Trans; sudo.*
Transverse. *Trans; verto.*
Traverse. *Tra; verto.*
Treat. *Traho.*
Tremble, tremendous, tremor, tremulous. *Tremo.*
Trepidation. *Trepidus.*
Trespass. *Tres; passus.*
Triad. *Tres.*
Triangle. *Tres; angulus.*
Tribe. *Tribus.*
Tribunal, tribune, tribunitial. *Tribus.*
Tributary, tribute. *Tribuo.*
Trident. *Tres; dens.*
Triennial. *Tres; annus*
Trifle. *Tres; via.*
Trigonometry. *Tres; gonia; metrum.*
Trinity. *Tres; unus.*
Trinomial. *Tres; nomen.*
Trio. *Tres.*
Triphthong. *Tres; phthegma.*
Triple, triplicate, triplicity. *Tres; plico.*
Tripod. *Tres; pous.*
Trireme. *Tres; remus.*
Trisect. *Tres; seco.*
Trisyllable. *Tres; syl; labo.*
Trite. *Tero.*
Triturate. *Tero.*
Triumvirate. *Tres; vir.*
Triune. *Tres; unus.*
Trivial. *Tres; via.*
Trope. *Tropos.*
Trophy, tropic. *Tropos.*
Trouble. *Turba.*
Truncate, trunk. *Trunco.*
Tuber, tubercle. *Tuber.*
Tuition. *Tueor.*
Tumble. *Tumeo.*
Tumid, tumor, tumult, tumultuary. *Tumeo*
Tune. *Tonos.*
Turbid. *Turba.*
Turbulent. *Turba.*
Turgid. *Turgeo.*
Tutelage, tutor. *Tueor.*
Type. *Typus.*
Typical. *Typus.*
Typography. *Typus; grapho.*
Tyrannic, tyrant. *Tyrannus.*

U.

Uberty. *Uber.*
Ulterior, ultimate, ultimatum. *Ultimus.*
Umbrage, umbrella. *Umbra.*
Unalterable. *Un; alter.*
Unanimity, unanimous. *Unus; animus.*
Unartful. *Un; ars.*
Uncertain. *Un; certus.*
Uncivil. *Un; civis.*
Unconnected. *Un; con; necto.*
Unconstrained. *Un; con; stringo.*
Uncrown. *Un; corona.*
Unction, unctuous. *Unguo.*
Undesigned. *Un; de; signum.*
Undistorted. *Un; dis; tortum.*
Undulate, undulatory. *Undo.*
Unequivocal. *Un; equus; voco.*
Unessential. *Un; ens.*
Unexpert. *Un; ex; perior.*
Unfortunate. *Un; fors.*
Unguent. *Unguo.*
Unicorn. *Unus; cornu.*
Uniform. *Unus; forma.*
Uninstructed. *Un; in; struo.*
Union. *Unus.*
Unique. *Unus.*
Unison. *Unus; sonus.*
Unit, unite. *Unus.*
Universalism, universe, university. *Unus; verto.*
Unnecessary. *Un; necesse.*
Unremitted. *Un; re; mitto.*
Unsophisticated. *Un; sophia.*

Unsystematic. *Un; syn; stasis.*
Untitled. *Un; titulus.*
Urbanity. *Urbs.*
Usage, use. *Utor.*
Usury utensil. *Utor.*

V.

Vacant, vacation. *Vaco.*
Vacuity, vacuum. *Vaco.*
Vagabond, vagary. *Vagus.*
Vagrant, vague. *Vagus.*
Vain. *Vanus.*
Valediction. *Valeo; dico.*
Validity. *Valeo.*
Valor, value. *Valeo.*
Van. *Avant.*
Vancourier. *Avant; curro.*
Vanish, vanity. *Vanus.*
Vanquish. *Vinco.*
Variance, variegate, variety, vary. *Varius.*
Vascular. *Vas.*
Vasculiferous. *Vas; fero.*
Vase. *Vas.*
Vast. *Vastus.*
Vehement, vehicle. *Veho.*
Veil. *Velo.*
Vein. *Vena.*
Velocity. *Velox.*
Veneficial. *Venenum; facio.*
Venesection. *Vena; seco.*
Vengeance. *Vindex.*
Venom, venomous. *Venenum.*
Vent. *Venio.*
Ventiduct. *Ventus; duco.*
Ventilate. *Ventus; latum.*
Ventriloquism. *Venter; loquor.*
Venturous. *Venio.*
Veracity. *Verus.*
Verbiage, verbose. *Verbum.*
Verdant. *Verdis.*
Verdict. *Verus; dico.*
Verdigris. *Verdis*; (*gris*, gray).
Verdure. *Verdis.*
Verge. *Vergo.*
Verify, verily. *Verus.*
Verisimilitude. *Verus; similis.*
Verity. *Verus.*
Vermicelli. *Vermis.*
Vermiform. *Vermis; forma.*
Vermifuge. *Vermis; fugio.*
Vermilion, vermin. *Vermis.*
Vermiparous. *Vermis; pario.*
Versatile, verse. *Verto.*
Versification. *Verto; facio.*
Versify, version. *Verto.*
Vertex, vertical. *Verto.*
Vessel. *Vas.*
Vest. *Vestis.*
Vesture. *Vestis.*
Veteran. *Vetus.*
Vex, vexatious. *Veho.*
Viaduct. *Via; duco.*
Viand. *Via.*
Vicar. *Vicis.*
Vicegerent. *Vicis; gero.*
Viceroy. *Vicis; roy.*
Vicious. *Vitium.*
Vicissitude. *Vicis.*
Victim, victory. *Vinco.*
Victual. *Vivo.*
View. *Video.*
Vigil, vigilance. *Vigil.*
Vigorous. *Vigor.*
Vindicate, vindictive. *Vindex.*
Vine, vinous. *Vinum.*
Vinegar. *Vinum*; (*aigre*, sour).
Vintage. *Vinum.*
Virago. *Vir.*
Virile. *Vir.*
Virulence, virulent. *Virus.*
Visage. *Video.*
Visceral. *Viscus.*
Viscount. *Vicis; comes.*
Visible, vision, visit, visor, vista. *Video.*
Vital. *Vivo.*
Vitiate. *Vitium.*
Vitreous. *Vitrum.*
Vitrify, vitriol. *Vitrum.*
Vivacity. *Vivo.*
Vivid. *Vivo.*
Vivify. *Vivo.*
Vocabulary, vocal. *Voco.*
Vociferate. *Voco; fero.*
Voice. *Voco.*
Void. *Viduo.*
Volatile. *Volo.*
Volcanic, volcano. *Vulcanus.*
Volition. *Volo.*
Volley. *Volo.*
Voluble, volume, voluminous. *Volvo*
Voluntary, volunteer. *Volo.*
Voluptuary, voluptuous. *Voluptas*
Voracity. *Voro.*
Vortex. *Verto.*
Votary, vote, votive *Votum.*
Vow. *Votum.*
Vowel. *Voco.*
Vulgar, vulgate. *Vulgus.*

W.

Wall. *Vallum.*
Ward. *Guarder.*
Warrant. *Guarantir.*
Waste. *Vastus.*
Way. *Via.*
Whistle. *Fistula.*
Widow. *Viduo.*

Z.

Zodiac. *Zoon.*
Zoology. *Zoon; logos.*
Zoophyte. *Zoon; phyt*

THE END.

www.ingramcontent.com/pod-product-compliance
Lightning Source LLC
LaVergne TN
LVHW011208110826
845150LV00006B/1364